OrangeBooks Publication

Smriti Nagar, Bhilai, Chhattisgarh - 490020

Website: **www.orangebooks.in**

First Edition, 2021

ISBN: 978-93-92878-72-5

Printed in India

The Second Alexander

An Account of the Most Successful and Least Understood Sultan of Delhi

Neelesh Chatterjee

OrangeBooks Publication
www.orangebooks.in

Author's Note

The last year turned out to be an extraordinarily difficult one. I was laid up by an illness more severe than anything I had ever experienced before. And if my physical ordeals weren't bad enough, then fate had even more in store for me. The pandemic came down heavily on me: it took away two relatives in quick succession, and made sure that my mental health didn't remain undisturbed either.

Amidst such trials and tribulations, if there was one source of solace for my bruised soul, then it was definitely in the perusal of history. Indian History, or Medieval Indian History to be precise, which is hands down the strongest pull in my life, saw me through this singularly tough phase. Even as one misfortune followed another, I continued to scour for comfort in the pages of Medieval Indian History.

It was Sultan Alauddin Khilji — a personality as fascinating as they come — who absorbed my attention in this particular period. I wouldn't lie, writing a book on him had very much been there on my mind, ever since I watched that controversial film based on his character way back in 2018. Time, however, was the only constraint. And when I finally did get time, even though other factors remained far from propitious, I decided to go ahead and make the best of it.

Thereon, the process began. One moment I would writhe in pain, the next moment I would scribble with my pen. But, I didn't give up. As a result, in a little more than twelve months, came up this book, and no, even though most of it was composed lying down on the bed, no stone was still left unturned to present as accurate a picture as possible of the man in question.

But for all my love for Medieval Indian History, the task would still not have been possible if not for the support and assistance that I received from some very wonderful people. First and foremost among them is my mother, Nivedita Chatterjee. She is the bulwark of my life, my pillar of strength, and it was she who made it possible for me to hang in there when the going got extremely tough. No amount of praise, absolutely no amount of praise, could do justice to the colossal effort that she put in to make sure that her son could once again return to a life of normalcy.

As to friends, I must admit that I'm blessed with a special lot. Sabyasachi Sadhu has been super supportive — from lending me a helping hand anytime I needed one, to spurring me on every time I was low on motivation — writing this book would have been a far more arduous task if not for his assistance. Friends like Subham Bhagat, Sabitabrata Mondal and Sayantanie Sarkar came in when the chips were down, regularly checked on me and made sure that I remained in good spirits. Kind people like Daud Khan, Anas Khan, Hassan Ahmed, Saiyem Iftekhar and Proteeti Bhattacharya spotted the spark in me: they said I was a good storyteller, and the urge to vindicate their faith in my potential never left me.

Personally, this book shall always remain very close to my heart, not merely because it marks my debut as an author, not even because it was born out of ordeals, but because the journey itself has been a redemption of sorts for me, for reasons that are too personal to particularise here. Finally, I confess that it's the Almighty Himself who has taken me this far, and I trust that He, in His infinite mercy, would definitely endear this book to my readers.

Know Your Sources

While information gleaned from very many sources has gone into the making of this book, there however are three authors whose works have been most frequently referred to in the text. It is therefore only reasonable that the readers are introduced beforehand to the aforementioned three authors, so that the readability of the text doesn't get hampered even a bit.

1. Ziauddin Barani (d. 1358):

Easily the greatest political thinker and the finest historian of the entire period of the Delhi Sultanate rule, Ziauddin Barani is also the greatest authority on the reign of Sultan Alauddin Khilji. Born in an aristocratic household, Barani enjoyed access to the high-ups of his day, and consequently developed a limpid understanding of the ins and outs of contemporary politics. However, near the fag end of his life, he fell on hard times. And it was precisely at that stage in his life, with one foot in the grave, that he set about writing down his magnum opus, the **Tarikh-i Firoz Shahi**. Though named after the reigning sovereign, Firoz Shah Tughlaq, it contains detailed accounts of all the Sultans of Delhi from Ghiyasuddin Balban onwards. And far from being a simple narration of events, Barani's work of history was written within a cause-and-effect framework, and unlike most of his peers, he actually endeavoured to dig deep and find out why kings and princes acted and behaved the way they did. Apart from his **Tarikh**, he also composed the **Fatwa-i Jahandari**, a text that deals in detail with the nuances of statecraft and exhorts the ruler to act in a certain way that Barani thought was in the best interests for the maintenance of an ideal social order. All in all, it is safe to say that no other contemporary went to such great lengths as Barani did in writing down the history of the Sultans of Delhi, and little wonder therefore that it is Ziauddin Barani who has been quoted the most extensively in this particular book.

2. Muhammad Qasim Ferishta (d.1620):

A soldier, a statesman and a scholar, Ferishta was an unique individual, and to say that he led an extraordinary life would hardly be an overstatement. Born at Gorgan in Iran, Ferishta had to leave his home when he was hardly twelve, and make for a place that was almost two thousand miles away, where his father had been summoned to teach Persian to a Muslim prince of Maharashtra. At his new destination he lived for about seven years, whereupon a violent palace revolution forced him to pack his bags and move southward to a thriving city where ruled a line of kings that thirsted for books and hankered after scholars. Here, apart from carrying out such duties as was demanded of a royal officer — from taking very many blows on his body in the field of battle, to escorting his master's daughter to the territory of one of the most powerful potentates the East had ever seen – Ferishta also took time out to engage in other, more scholastic activities. And in this endeavour, he found a more than enthusiastic patron in his royal master, Ibrahim Adil Shah, the second in his line to bear that name. The result was the creation of a most ambitious work of history: one that covered the events of more than six hundred years, and comprised the annals of a vast region that extended from Hamadan in the west to Chittagong in the east, and from Samarkand in the north to Vijayanagara in the south. A work of epic proportions, no doubt, and its size was only matched by the delectable details it holds. About Sultan Alauddin Khilji's reign too, Ferishta's account isn't short of interesting information, and therefore it is not without good reasons that we have quoted him so frequently in this particular book.

3. Amir Khusrau (d.1325):

Amir Khusrau was a poet, mystic, musician, soldier, courtier and statesman, all rolled into one. Safe to surmise then, that geniuses of Amir Khusrau's stature come but once in a blue moon. Attending the courts of several Sultans of Delhi, Amir Khusrau had a fairly intimate knowledge of how things actually played out at the highest echelon of the society. In his long career that spanned no less than four decades, he frequently put pen to paper to record the deeds of his patrons. And these works, their eulogistic nature notwithstanding, are replete with materials significant from a historical point of view. Of the feats of Sultan Alauddin Khilji, at whose court he served for the longest stretch of time, Amir Khusrau wrote in one of his many works, the **Khazain ul Futuh**, a text that we shall have to return to again and again for it contains such invaluable information as makes it possible for us to paint a comprehensive picture of the royal character in question.

Synopsis

Delhi, at the turn of the thirteenth century, was poised for some major changes. A veteran warrior, Jalaluddin Firoz by name, brought about the so-called 'Khilji Revolution' and ended the century-long, exclusive domination of a certain section of Muslim population over North Indian polity.

Jalaluddin's achievements, though by no means insignificant, still didn't ensure him a long reign. Thus, only six years after ascending the throne of the Delhi Sultanate, Jalaluddin Khilji was done away with by his nephew and son-in-law, Alauddin.

Alauddin Khilji waded through blood to the throne, but made good his act of regicide through a string of stunning successes. For one, only in a matter of few years, he transformed the Delhi Sultanate from a small kingdom to the most dominant political force in the entire Indian subcontinent. Second, he freed the people of North India from the fear of the Mongols, by beating them back with such gruesome slaughter as sent shock waves across Asia. Indeed, such had been his military prowess that of all people, the grandiloquent title of 'Second Alexander' suited him the best. Third, he instituted a series of such administrative regulations as made life much easier for the common man.

Spurred by a sense of gratitude, he came to be looked upon by the masses as a saint, and after his death, his tomb turned into some sort of a shrine, where the people would come with their prayers and seek the dead Sultan's intermediation with the Almighty. Thus, Sujan Rai Bhandari, a Hindu author writing about four centuries after Alauddin's death, assigned angelic attributes to the Sultan. Alauddin, however, didn't have to wait for his death to gain all the laurels: even in his lifetime, a Muslim divine from Egypt claimed that because of his deeds, Alauddin would be granted a place among the Prophets in the hereafter.

But, that is only one side of the story. Even in that sanguinary age, we are told, Sultan Alauddin Khilji's reign stood out for its excesses. He shed so much blood and in so cavalier a fashion that it moved even his contemporaries with horror. In spite of the colossal political achievements to his credit, only four years after his death, Alauddin's family was wiped out from the face of the earth, and the rule of his dynasty came to a violent end at the hands of a rank upstart, a Hindu convert from Gujarat. This dramatic reversal of fortune was explained by a contemporary mystic, Sheikh Bashir Diwana, as an act of Divine Justice: arguing that nothing ever goes unpaid in God's world, he claimed that the misfortunes that befell the Khiljis was only due to the excesses committed by Alauddin.

That, at any rate, was how Sultan Alauddin Khilji stood: appreciated by many, reviled by few, and understood by hardly any. In his lifetime he was an enigma, and his legacy still continues to be enigmatic, with a fresh layer of rancour being undoubtedly added to it of late.

Our job in this book, then, is to sift through the sources — which are often at odds with each other — and extricate the man from the myth, and discover the person behind the persona.

Index

The Backdrop

Thou givest sovereignty unto whom Thou wilt, and Thou withdrawest sovereignty from whom Thou wilt.

— The Holy Quran, 3:26

1290. Delhi.

The successor of the awesome Balban, Sultan Muizzuddin, was struck by a paralytic attack that rendered him bed-ridden. Consequently, the Delhi Sultanate came to be run in the name of his three-year-old son, Sultan Shamsuddin.

While the de-jure sovereignty was vested with the child, the de-facto authority remained with the triumvirate of Aitamar Surkha, Aitamar Kachhan, and Jalaluddin Khilji. The first two were considered as pure Turks; the third wasn't.

While Islam didn't discriminate on the basis of birth, Muslims often did. As a result, there existed a fierce rivalry between Jalaluddin Khilji and his Turk colleagues.

The aforementioned Turkish duo decided to do away with Jalaluddin Khilji by a strategem, but unluckily for them, their target got wind of the trap beforehand. So when Aitamar Kachchan arrived at the Khilji camp, he was greeted with several slashes of steel, and killed on the spot.

Next, the three sons of Jalaluddin, all of them daredevils of the first order, dashed into the royal palace, seized the infant Sultan, and then set off for their own camp.

Aitamar Surkha tried to intercept them, but he fared no better than his Turkish brother-in-arms had — a volley of arrows took him down in no time.

A great tumult arose in Delhi, and men rushed in from all sides to rescue their sovereign. Jalaluddin had guessed as much, and didn't fail to take pre-emptive measures to that end: he had as hostage the sons of the kotwal of Delhi in his camp. And now the elderly kotwal, fearing lest any harm should befall his children, pleaded with the crowd to return, which it reluctantly did. The Khiljis had won the day!

Two days after, a short work was done of the incapacitated Sultan Muizzuddin: a servant wrapped his paralysed body in a bed-sheet, and tossed it into the Yamuna.

Jalaluddin Khilji then proceeded to the palace of the late Sultan Muizzuddin in Kilokheri, and there took the crown for himself.

The dynasty of Sultan Balban came to an end. Delhi now had a Khilji king: Sultan Jalaluddin Khilji.

Oh, and the child Shamsuddin, who had hitherto been kept in the Khilji camp, was heard no more of.

The Calm Before The Storm

> *'Tis easy, evil with evil to reward;*
> *If man thou art, do good for evil done.*
> *— Tabaqat-i Akbari, by Nizamuddin Ahmad Bakshi.*

Jalaluddin Khilji ascended the throne in June 1290. His coronation took place at Kilokheri, then a suburb of Delhi, not in the city proper, because of the hostility of the dominant Turkish population of Delhi, who considered him to be of a race different from them.

This prejudice, however, was misplaced. The Khiljis were essentially Turks, not Afghans, as they were mistaken to be. As early as in the tenth century, Ibn Hawqal, an Arab scholar, had asribed Turkish origins to the Khiljis.[1] And then, few centuries after, Fakhruddin in his work **Tarikh-i Fakhruddin Mubarak Shahi** emphatically declared Khiljis to be one among the sixty-four Turkish tribes.[2] Modern scholars like C.E. Bosworth too echo the same view. Nonetheless, the people of Delhi could hardly be

[1] History of the Khaljis, by K.S. Lal. Indian Press Limited, Allahabad, 1950. Page 15.

[2] ibid

blamed for their misgivings: their long stay in Afghanistan had so thoroughly Afghanised the Khiljis that even they came to regard themselves as Afghans, not Turks.[3]

The snobbish aversion of the Turks of Delhi, however, didn't last long: their racial prejudice gave way to their material interests, and most of them soon started attending Sultan Jalaluddin's court at Kilokheri. Also was responsible, at least to some extent, in their change of heart was their new Sultan's character: "his sense of equity, justice and religiosity", according to Ziyauddin Barani, made it very difficult for anybody to hold him in contempt.[4]

Sultan Jalaluddin Khilji was a septuagenarian when he came to the throne, and he soon made it clear that he valued his afterlife more than the kingdom he was called upon to head. To him kingship was nothing but a fraud — he even cursed his enemies, not so much for plotting against him as for compelling him to take the crown for himself. "Calamity may afflict the house of Aitamar Kachchan and Aitamar Surkha because of whose fear that they would kill me," he would say, "[that] I fell into this misfortune."[5]

Typically, when after many entreaties the Sultan first entered Delhi, and went to the Red Palace of Balban,

---

[3] Tarikh-i Firoz Shahi. By Ziauddin Barani. Translated by Ishtiyaq Ahmad Zilli. Primus Books, 2015. Page 110

[4] ibid. Page 109

[5] ibid

instead of riding into the courtyard, he respectfully dismounted at the gate and entered the palace on foot. When Malik Ahmad Chap, a straightforward chap, reminded him that such a behaviour didn't behove his position as the sovereign, Jalaluddin remonstrated with him: "O Ahmad, ... Seizing the kingship due to the fear of life is another thing, but if I begin to consider it legitimate, I would [then] be committing infidelity ... Just now it seemed to me that Sultan Balban is holding his court inside the palace and I am going to present myself before him. I have served that king many times in this palace and my heart begins to beat on the thought. His awe and fear has not yet left my heart."[6]

And the Sultan would behave likewise many a time more. In his second regnal year, Malik Chajju, the nephew of the late Balban, rebelled against the new dispensation. After snuffing his rebellion out, instead of punishing him, Sultan Jalaluddin Khilji sat down to drink wine with him and his other accomplices, to bridge all the differences that had lately arisen between them. Likewise, when a band of thugs was apprehended in his capital, the only punishment that the Sultan could come up with was to despatch them, presumably on his own expenses, to far-away Bengal, after exacting from them a promise to the effect that they would not commit such acts again.[7]

But Jalaluddin Khilji was not timid. Not by any means. A hero of a hundred battles, he had grown old fighting the formidable Mongols. Early in his reign, he successfully

---

[6] Tarikh-i Firoz Shahi. Translated by Ishtiyaq Ahmad Zilli. Page 111

[7] ibid. Page 117

warded off a Mongol attack, which was led by a grandson of Halagu Khan himself. Likewise, when it was reported to him that a party of Turkish nobles in their cups were repeatedly blabbering about overthrowing and killing him, he straightaway threw down the gauntlet to them, daring them to measure swords with him if they were men enough. Predictably, the nobles backed off.

But even when the Sultan tried to be belligerent, his innate gentleness more often than not got in the way. Thus, after he was done censuring the aforementioned Turkish nobles, he patched things up with them over a cup of wine. Likewise, he abandoned the siege of Ranthambore halfway because, he thought, it would cost many Muslim lives to bring the Chauhan Rajputs to heel: "I do not consider even ten such forts equal to a hair of a Muslim," he gave out.[8]

Also, there were times when Sultan Jalaluddin Khilji behaved childlike. Once, he was tempted to add to his name the title of **al Mujahid fi Sabil Allah** (the fighter in the way of God).[9] Any other Sultan would have done it without even thinking twice. Jalaluddin, however, was too modest to go about it in a straightforward way — instead, he told his wife to instruct the clerics to request him to do so in the open court. And when the request was actually made, the Sultan was overwhelmed with a sense of shame: sobbing, he confessed before everybody that he

---

[8] Tarikh-i Firoz Shahi. Translated by Ishtiyaq Ahmad Zilli. Page 132

[9] ibid. Page 121

himself was responsible for the request, and then refused outright to take up that title.

Clearly, such candour would have suited a fakir more than it did a Sultan. The robe of royalty, it seems, wasn't really sewn keeping Jalaluddin Khilji in mind.

But for all his tenderness, the embers of his fiery old spirit still smouldered in Sultan Jalaluddin, and there were occasions, even if few and far between, when they did flare up, as it happened, most strangely, in the trial of a dervish, Siddi Maula by name.

The Dervish And The Sultan

None but the excellent are slaughtered in the kitchen of love;
The lean, the old and the ugly they kill not.
Flee not, Oh! Sincere lover! From Slaughter,
He whom they slay not is no better than a corpse.

— Tarikh-i Mubarak Shahi, by Yahya bin Ahmad Sirhindi.

Siddi Maula was a Persian divine who had come to Delhi in the reign of Sultan Balban. Contemporary chroniclers consider him to be a disciple of the celebrated Chishti mystic of Ajodhan, Sheikh Fariduddin Ganj Shakar.[10] Before moving to the capital, we are told, he was warned by his spiritual preceptor to steer clear of politics. Siddi Maula, however, paid no heed to that advice.

[10] There is a considerable controversy as to which Sufi order Siddi Maula actually belonged to. Some regard him to be a member of the Chishti silsilah, but this contention has been opposed by scholars like Riazul Islam and Simon Digby.

In Delhi, Siddi Maula established his khanqah, to which he added a magnificent langar khana, where food would be served for free twice a day to all and sundry.

It was however the quality of the meal, not its free character, that was the main attraction of his langar khana. The repast served there was so sumptuous, we are told, that it could have put a royal platter to shame. No less than 500 animals, every single day, had to be slaughtered to meet the culinary requirements of Siddi Maula's establishment.[11] No wonder therefore, people from far and wide — Hindus and Muslims, nobles as well as plebeians — thronged his langar khana in their hundreds and thousands.

Humongous expenditure was involved, no doubt, but as to Siddi Maula's source of income our sources are sketchy to say the least. Ziyauddin Barani, a contemporary, attributes the dervish's munificence to his magical powers. "There were consistent reports," he says, "that for the payment of the cost of anything that was brought, or if he (Siddi Maula) wanted to give something to anybody, he would invariably ask his men to look for a particular stone or brick, under which there were so many tankas of gold and silver that they were asked to take. They did what they were asked to do, and found the same amount of tankas of gold or silver under the arch, stone or brick,

[11] Tarikh-i Firoz Shahi. Translated by Ishtiyaq Ahmad Zilli. Page 129

as if it was freshly minted and was just brought [out] from the mint."[12]

As the years rolled by, Siddi Maula's popularity only increased, and we have it from the testimony of a contemporary, that men from far-off lands would come by seaway just to meet him.[13] Indeed, many Khilji nobles frequented his khanqah as did the newly dispossessed Turkish aristocrats. Siddi Maula also counted among his many followers the crown prince, the Khan-i Khanan himself, whom he used to affectionately regard as his own son.

But for all his popularity, Siddi Maula had his detractors too. It was the orthodox clerics who were ill-disposed towards him, partly out of jealousy, and partly because he was unorthodox in his habits. He was scrupulous in his devotions, and led a life of extreme austerity — he practised celibacy, wore coarse clothes, and subsisted on the simplest of diets — but he hardly ever bothered to attend the congregational prayers.

Be that as it may, it wasn't because of his unconventional ways that Siddi Maula came at the receiving end of the Sultan's heavy hand. It was a conspiracy, a political conspiracy, that made them cross paths with each other.

A certain Qazi from Kashan (in Iran), Jalaluddin by name, whom Barani describes as "extremely seditious by nature", developed intimacy with Siddi Maula.[14] He

---

[12] Tarikh-i Firoz Shahi. Translated by Ishtiyaq Ahmad Zillii. Page 129

[13] ibid

[14] ibid. Page 130

harboured in his heart a deep hostility towards the Khilji regime for some reason, racial or otherwise, and his hatred rubbed off on Siddi Maula.

Together, they hatched a grand conspiracy: the plan was to do away with Sultan Jalaluddin Khilji, abolish the institution of Delhi Sultanate altogether, and then install Siddi Maula as the Caliph, an office that still held a lot of sway over the Muslim minds and to which Siddi Maula was the best fitted given the faith of the masses in him as a repository of spiritual power. To garner greater popular support, the Qazi even included notable Hindus in his design: two renowned Hindu soldiers, Brinjtan and Hathia by name, were made a party to the plot.

But for all the lofty planning, a rude shock was lurking just around the corner: one of the conspirators soon lost nerve, and to save his own back, divulged every single detail of the conspiracy to the Sultan.

All the accused were immediately apprehended, and then produced before Sultan Jalaluddin Khilji.

All of them, however, put up an united front: in spite of repeated interrogations, none of them budged. Islamic law requires the confession of the convict, before he could be brought to the book. Sultan Jalaluddin Khilji, in spite of being such a scrupulously religious man otherwise, cast the sanctions of the Shariat aside this time: he was evidently smelling blood, when others couldn't.

The Sultan had Qazi Jalaluddin Kashani banished from his capital. The two Hindu conspirators, he had them executed before his eyes. Then came Siddi Maula's turn. He was brought tied and fettered before the Sultan, and a heated argument immediately ensued between the two.

In no time, the Sultan flew into a rage, and he cried out: "... take my revenge from this Maula."[15] At once a zealot, Bahri by name, pounced upon Siddi Maula with a sharp dagger.[16] Meanwhile, the Sultan's second son Arkali Khan, who was inimical towards Siddi Maula for the latter's association with his late elder brother, seized this opportunity to settle scores: he signalled a mahout, who drove his elephant over Siddi Maula and instantly crushed him to death.

"A forbearing king like him (Sultan Jalaluddin) could not bring himself to bear this conspiracy and issued an order, which was not in keeping with the dignity of one who maintained himself and appeared as a dervish," laments Barani.[17]

This sacrilegious act, we are told, brought to Delhi a bunch of calamities. Minutes after Siddi Maula's

---

[15] Tarikh-i Firoz Shahi. Translated by Ishtiyaq Ahmad Zilli. Page 131

[16] Interestingly, the assassin, Bahri, wasn't one among the clerics. He actually belonged to a different Sufi order, a fact that clearly demonstrates that all was not well always between the different Sufi silsilahs. Bahri belonged to a sect called Hyderi, which reached India very early, and counted among its patrons Mughisuddin, the rebel Sultan of Bengal. The order demanded of its followers the observance of certain rules, that included among others the wearing of iron necklaces and bracelets. The *Siyar ul Arifin*, a work composed in the sixteenth century, talks about one of their bizzare practises, that involved mutilation of the male genitalia in a bid to curb sexual passions.

[17] Tarikh-i Firoz Shahi. Translated by Ishtiyaq Ahmad Zilli. Page 131

execution, "a dark storm rose and the skies were darkened."[18] The rains failed, and soon a terrible famine was raging across the capital. Food grew so scarce that the poor would assemble in batches of twenty or thirty, and then fling themselves into the Yamuna. The Sultan and his nobles tried their best to alleviate their suffering, but to little avail.

"The elders have said that the killing of dervishes is inauspicious, and it had never augured well for any ruler," Barani draws the curtain on this episode with a piece of wisdom.[19]

[18] Tarikh-i Firoz Shahi. Translated by Ishtiyaq Ahmad Zilli. Page 131

[19] ibid

An Extraordinary Raid

> *Sultan Alauddin was a nephew of Sultan Jalaluddin and was brought up by him.*
>
> *— Tarikh-i Firoz Shahi, by Ziauddin Barani.*

Jalaluddin Khilji had a brother, Shihabuddin Masud Khilji, who fathered four sons: Alauddin (Ali Gurshasp), Almas Beg, Qutlugh Taghin and Muhammad. Of the first two we know a good deal, but of the rest we know virtually nothing. It appears that Shihabuddin had died quite young, and Alauddin and his brothers were brought up under the affectionate care of their uncle, Jalaluddin Khilji.

Immediately after coming to power, Jalaluddin granted the important office of **amir-i Tuzuk** (keeper of the royal insignia) to Alauddin. In the second year of his reign, after Malik Chajju's rebellion had been stamped out, the Sultan granted the iqta of Kara to Alauddin, evidently as a reward for his exploits in the late campaign.[20]

[20] The iqtas were defined units of land whose revenues were collected by the assignee, or iqtadar. From these revenues, the iqtadar was supposed to recruit, train, equip and coomand a stipulated number of troops who would be available to the Sultan on demand. (Source: Richard Eaton, India in the Persianate Age)

This appointment turned out to be the turning point in Alauddin's life.

As the governor of Kara, Alauddin Khilji, with the explicit permission of the central government, dashed into Central India and plundered the rich town of Bhilsa. "In this expedition," says Barani, "he secured much booty."[21] Alauddin then dutifully despatched to Delhi all the spoils he had gained, which included among others "an idol made of ball metal, which was worshipped by the Hindus of those regions."[22]

The Sultan was highly pleased, and promoted Alauddin to the office of **arz-i mamalik** (minister of war), besides adding Awadh to his iqta of Kara.

Be that as it may, it was at Bhilsa that Alauddin's head turned and his imagination got fired: "When Alauddin had gone to Bhilsa, he had heard there about the enormous treasures and elephants of Deogir, and had made enquiries about its route," records Barani.[23]

Once back in his own iqta, Alauddin straight away set about making elaborate plans to lay hold of the fabled treasures of Deogir. But for any expedition in the far-off Deccan, what was crucially necessary was a strong army. To that end, he felt that he needed succour from his uncle, the Sultan. Alauddin, however, for some reason, was not willing to disclose his real design. So he went to Delhi,

---

[21] Tarikh-i Firoz Shahi. Translated by Ishtiyaq Ahmad Zilli. Page 135

[22] ibid

[23] ibid. Page 136

but instead of Deogir, he sought permission to raid another town in Central India, Chanderi. He pleaded therefore that the surplus of his iqtas be remitted, "so that he could use the income ... to raise new contingents of infantry and cavalry."[24]

"Due to the purity of his heart and good faith," Sultan Jalaluddin readily granted all that was asked of him, and having achieved his objective, Alauddin returned from Delhi.[25]

After making adequate preparations, Alauddin Khilji finally left Kara for Deogir with 8,000 crack cavalry on Saturday, the 26th of February, 1296.[26] The success of his arms depended on his rapidity, Alauddin knew fully well. Crossing irregular hills and swift-flowing rivers with an incredible speed, he soon arrived near the frontiers of Deogir, and took both its Yadava King and his men completely by surprise. To add to the King of Deogir, Ram Deo's woes, his capital at that point was denuded of his best troops, who had gone elsewhere on an expedition under the crown prince Singhana. Ram Deo still somehow managed to collect three to four thousand men, and with them, "he opposed the Mahomedans at a distance of four

---

[24] Tarikh-i Firoz Shahi. Translated by Ishtiyaq Ahmad Zilli. Page 136

[25] ibid

[26] The numerical strength of Alauddin's army has been taken from Ferishta's work, while the date has been taken from Amir Khusrau's.

miles from the city, but being defeated, retired into the fort."[27]

Alauddin at once procceded to besiege the fort, and so vigorously did he press the siege, that the garrison soon found itself in dire straits. To further demoralise the besieged, the young Khilji even gave out that his force constituted but the advance guard of the Sultan of Delhi, who was supposed to reach Deogir anytime with the entire imperial army.

Negotiations then started between Raja Ram Deo and Alauddin Khilji. After much wrangling, the terms were settled: "Alauddin, according to these proposals, accepted of 50 maunds[28] of gold, and a large quantity of pearls and jewels, and retained the elephants which he had taken in the Raja's stables," writes Ferishta.[29]

Peace having been made, Alauddin proclaimed that he would break camp and release all the prisoners immediately after receiving the stipulated ransom. But, fate had more trouble in store for the Yadavas. The whole affair could have very well ended there — but it didn't.

Just when Raja Ram Deo was about to heave a sigh of relief, his eldest son , the crown prince Singhana returned to the capital, and immediately dared the invader to measure swords with him.

---

[27] Tarikh-i Ferishta. Translated by John Briggs. Oriental Booksellers and Publishers, 1908. Volume I. Page 306

[28] The maund/mann of Alauddin Khilji's time was around 29 lbs. Avoirdupois or 13 kilograms.

[29] Tarikh-i Ferishta. Translated by John Briggs. Pages 307-308

"If you have any love for life, and desire safety, restore what you have plundered, and proceed quietly homeward, rejoicing at your happy escape" — Singhana threatened Alauddin Khilji.[30]

The King of Deogir tried a hundred tricks to temporise with his son, but the gutsy prince would have none of it.

This was an open challenge from the Maratha prince, and of all men, Alauddin wasn't the one to back down. The Khilji's killer instincts were aroused — Ferishta says he ordered "the messengers (who had brought Singhana's warning) should have their faces blackened with soot, and be hooted out of his camp."[31]

Leaving Malik Nusrat Khan with only one thousand men to guard the fort, Alauddin set off with the rest of his army to take the belligerent Singhana on. A fierce fight followed: "The Hindus by no means declined the contest," admits Ferishta.[32] Ultimately, the numerical superiority of their opponents began to tell on the Khiljis: Alauddin's men, reports the same author, were finding it difficult to hold their ground against the Marathas.

A general rout of the Khiljis seemed imminent, just when something very extraordinary happened. Nusrat Khan, not waiting for permission from Alauddin, rushed to the

---

[30] Tarikh-i Ferishta. Translated by John Briggs. Page 308

[31] ibid

[32] ibid

battlefield with his small contingent to relieve his colleagues.

This unexpected move totally changed the game.

The dust obscuring their sight, the Yadava army mistook Nusrat Khan for Sultan Jalaluddin Khilji himself. Alauddin had talked of an impending invasion from Delhi, Singhana's men remembered, and in utter trepidation fled from the battlefield. Fortune had sided with him, and Alauddin Khilji had won the day!

Alauddin Khilji then straight away renewed the sige of the fort of Deogir, this time with even greater rigour. Raja Ram Deo was now completely helpless: he submitted immediately, and pleaded with the Khiljis to open negotiations once again. "If my son, owing to the folly and petulance of youth, has broken the conditions between us," Ram Deo pleaded with Alauddin, "[then] that event ought not to render me responsible for his rashness."[33]

This time, however, Alauddin was in no mood for clemency. But only because he had no desire for annexation, did he ultimately agree on peace, albeit on much harsher terms.

Finally what Alauddin Khilji managed to wring from Ram Deo was virtually the entire treasury of Deogir, accumulated assiduously by generations of Yadava Kings —the figures recorded by Ferishta beggars belief, and is hard to even imagine. Alauddin received, according to

[33] Tarikh-i Ferishta. Translated by John Briggs. Page 309

that author, 600 maunds[34] of pearls, two maunds of diamonds, rubies, emeralds and sapphires, 1000 maunds of silver, besides a long list of other precious commodities.[35]

“Alauddin brought so much gold, silver, gems, pearls, precious things ... that two generations have passed since then ... yet still much of the elpehants, treasures, gems and pearls that Sultan Alauddin had brought from Deogir are found in the treasuries of Delhi,” claims Barani, a man who penned his account several decades after Alauddin Khilji was gone.[36]

It had taken Alauddin Khilji only 25 days to achieve so much in the distant land of Deccan. His campaign agianst Deogir had been a blitzkrieg, and an immensely successful one. Laden with booty, he was now returning to North India in triumph, but even in his hour of triumph he didn’t let his guard down: he was aware that his route northward would be through the territories of several hostile rajas and chiefs, and therefore he undertook every precaution possible to ensure that his hard-earned riches didn’t get squandered.

It is perhaps Ferishta who sums up this campaign most accurately:

“We may here justly remark, that, in the long volumes of history, there is scarcely anything to be compared with

---

[34] The reader shall remember that one maund was roughly equal to 29 pounds avoirdupois or 13 kilograms.

[35] Tarikh-i Ferishta. Translated by John Briggs. Page 310

[36] Tarikh-i Firoz Shahi. Translated by Ishtiiyaq Ahmad Zilli. Page 137

this exploit, whether we regard the resolution in forming the plan, the boldness of its execution, or the great good fortune which attended its accomplishment."[37]

The Deogir episode, though immensely significant in itself, pales into insignificance when contrasted with what was to follow it.

[37] Tarikh-I Ferishta. Translated by John Briggs. Page 311

The Great Conspiracy

When misfortune strikes a man
Nothing is of any avail to him.

— Tarikh-i Firoz Shahi, by Ziauddin Barani.

For all his splendid success in his public life, Alauddin Khilji's private life was utterly miserable. He had married his first cousin, Sultan Jalaluddin's daughter, but she turned out to be a veritable shrew, who spared no occasion to use her royal pedigree to browbeat her husband. Of the curious caricature that went on in Alauddin's household, we get a clear picture from the pen of the seventeenth century chronicler, Haji Dabir.[38]

Alauddin Khilji, Haji Dabir says, had two wives: first, the daughter of Sultan Jalaluddin Khilji; and second, the sister of his friend Alp Khan, a lady named Mahru. One day Alauddin was engaged in making love to Mahru in a garden, when Sultan Jalaluddin's daughter arrived on the scene, and then and there struck Mahru with her slippers. Alauddin could hardly bear this affront, and even at the risk of incurring royal wrath, raised his hand against the

---

[38] Zafarul Vali. By Haji Dabir. Quoted in History of the Khaljis by K.S. Lal.

princess. Luckily for him, nothing much came of it and the whole affair fizzled out before long.

Equally dominating was Sultan Jalaluddin's wife, the Malika-i Jahan, who, instead of trying to bring about a reconciliation between her daughter and son-in-law, brazenly supported the former and made life utterly difficult for Alauddin.

"Alauddin had suffered much at the hands of Malika-i Jahan, who was the wife of Sultan Jalaluddin and his mother-in-law. And due to the hostility of his wife he had come to the end of his tether," Barani admits frankly.[39]

Being a man acutely aware of his prestige, Alauddin couldn't even share with others his terrible agony, which kept gnawing at him — "fearing his own humiliation and disgrace, he could not say anything regarding his helplessness before anybody else," bemoans Barani.[40]

Perhaps, Sultan Jalaluddin Khilji had some inkling about the terrible tripartite equation that existed among his wife, daughter and son-in-law. And possibly therefore, he deputed Alauddin to Kara, far away from the queen's intrigues in the royal palace.

Before Alauddin Khilji, Kara had however been governed by Malik Chajju, that rebellious nephew of Sultan Balban — and discontent, in not insignificant a measure, still continued to simmer in that province. When Alauddin reached Kara, Barani informs us, "many of the officials

[39] Tarikh-i Firoz Shahi. Translated by Ishtiyaq Ahmad Zilli. Page 136

[40] ibid

and those who were close to Malik Chajju and were the source of his sedition ... took employment with him (Alauddin) ... [and] these seditious and flattering people [then] put it in the mind of Alauddin that a big and well-equipped army could be raised at Kara and it was possible to capture Delhi from Kara. The only requirement was treasures."[41]

But the throne of Delhi wasn't on his radar at that point — all he wanted was permanent freedom from his scheming mother-in-law and her diabolical machinations. "In Kara, he consulted his confidants and wanted to go away to some other region," writes Barani.[42] The only requirement was riches, Alauddin agreed with his counsellors, and then the independence he so much desired would be his.

The deficiency of wealth, at any rate, was overcome in a short time. Alauddin's daring raid of Deogir made him the master of a fabulous treasure.. Even then, at that point, Alauddin wasn't contemplating to murder his old uncle and seize the throne of Delhi for himself. His intention was to move towards Bengal, overthrow the successors of Balban who were ruling that province, and then set up there an independent kingdom of his own. To that end, "he sent Zafar Khan to Awadh to collect boats for crossing the river Sarayu."[43]

---

[41] Tarikh-i Firoz Shahi. Translated by Ishtiyaq Ahmad Zilli. Page 116

[42] ibid. Page 136

[43] ibid. Page 140

It is therefore clear that even if Alauddin wasn't harbouring in his heart so malicious a design as the murder of his own uncle, he still had absolutely no desire whatsoever to part with his hard-earned wealth.

Sultan Jalaluddin meanwhile continued to believe, rather credulously, that his nephew Alauddin was away in Chanderi. It was some time after and the Sultan was then in Gwalior, when "private intelligence arrived, that Alauddin, having conquered Deogir, had acquired such a wealth as was never before possessed, not even by a king of Delhi, with which he was now on his return towards Kara."[44]

And far from getting angry on Alauddin for lying to him and keeping him in the dark for so long, no sooner had the Sultan heard the news than he erupted in unrestrained joy. "The Sultan, delighted with this news (of Alauddin's success), reckoned upon the spoil as if already in his own treasury," reports Ferishta.[45] Revealing his innate innocence, Sultan Jalaluddin ordered convivial parties to be hold, and totally gave himself up to wine and merriment.

But the Sultan's nobles and intimates didn't share his gullibility: unlike their sovereign, they "justly concluded, that it was not to fill the royal coffers, that Alauddin, without the King's authority, had undertaken so bold and hazardous an expedition."[46]

---

[44] Tarikh-i Ferishta. Translated by John Briggs. Page 311

[45] ibid. Pages 311-312

[46] ibid. Page 312

The apprehensions of his companions reached the Sultan, and one day he summoned two of them, Malik Ahmad Chap and Malik Fakhruddin Kochi. Forever the outspoken man, Malik Ahmad Chap at once made clear his uncertainty about Alauddin's intentions, and warned the Sultan that "elephants and treasures ... are a source of great temptation and one who gets hold of these is most likely to turn out to be so thoroughly intoxicated and arrogant that it becomes difficult for him to distinguish hands from feet."[47]

To offset any possible perfidy from Alauddin's side, Malik Ahmad Chap advised the Sultan to intercept Alauddin before he could reach Kara. He reasonably argued that as the soldiers of Alauddin were returning laden with booty, they wouldn't risk losing it by engaging in any conflict with the imperial army. After the Sultan had satisfied himself about Alauddin's intentions, Malik Ahmad Chap continued, he could then allow his nephew to retain some portion of the wealth and take away the rest.

Such a fine suggestion, however, fell upon deaf ears: "Since the Sultan's doom had drawn near and bad times had overtaken him, he did not appreciate the counsel of Ahmad Chap," regrets Barani, with a good deal of justification.[48]

"What ill have I done to Alauddin that he would turn away from me and would not hand over the elephants and

---

[47] Tarikh-i Firoz Shahi. Translated by Ishtiyaq Ahmad Zilli. Page 138

[48] ibid. Page 139

treasures?" Sultan Jalaluddin tried to reason with himself.[49] Power politics didn't work that way, the poor old man hardly ever understood.

Like a moth rushing into fire, Sultan Jalaluddin Khilji plunged headlong into the chasm of his own destruction.

Fully realising the grave repercussions of the Sultan's naivety, Malik Ahmad Chap excused himself from the assembly, "and striking one hand upon the other, walked out, repeating the following verse: 'When the sun of prosperity is eclipsed, advice ceases to enlighten the mind.'"[50]

The Sultan, at any rate, left Gwalior for his capital shortly after. There, he received news of his nephew's safe return to Kara, but he chose to remain equally unmoved : "Only a few days after the return of the Sultan (to Delhi)," reports Barani, "successive news poured in that Alauddin had reached Kara with all the gold, gems, pearls, precious things, elephants and horses."[51]

On the flip side, after coming to know about his uncle's witless ways, Alauddin Khilji jumped for joy, and he decided to make the most of this oppurtunity that had quite unexpectedly come his way. A letter soon reached the Sultan from him "in which he (Alauddin) styled himself the Sultan's slave and stated, that all his wealth was at the Sultan's disposal; but that, being wearied with

---

[49] Tarikh-i Firoz Shahi. Translated by Ishtiyaq Ahmad Zilli. Page 139

[50] Tarikh-i Ferishta. Translated by John Briggs. Page 314

[51] Tarikh-i Firoz Shahi. Translated by Ishtiyaq Ahmad Zilli. Page 140

the tedious march, he begged for some repose at Kara."52 As because he had undertaken an expedition without the Sultan's permission, Alauddin added, he was apprehensive about his enemies at the court who could use this opportunity to turn the Sultan against him. Therefore, "If a farman in the imperial handwriting were to be despatched to him, then he would take the men who had shown such exemplary courage along with all the treasures and elephants and come to court."[53]

And if these dubious entreaties weren't enough, then in Delhi Alauddin's brother Almas Beg worked even more on the old Sultan's sentiments by telling him that Alauddin was distraught with anxiety about the possibility of the Sultan's wrath, and was even contemplating suicide to escape from it.

So blinded was Sultan Jalaluddin Khilji in his affection for his nephew, that if any well-wisher ventured to speak otherwise about Alauddin, "he (the Sultan) would get angry with him and say: 'People desire that I should harm my child (Alauddin). They make a lion out of me and show to him as such.'"[54]

As had been desired by Alauddin, the Sultan at once forwarded to him a gracious farman in his own handwriting. But the reports of Alauddin intending on suicide weighed heavily on the Sultan, and throwing caution to the wind, he decided to set out for Kara,

---

[52] Tarikh-i Ferishta. Translated by John Briggs. Page 314

[53] Tarikh-i Firoz Shahi. Translated by Ishtiyaq Ahmad Zilli. Page 140

[54] ibid. Page 141

although the month of Ramzan had commenced and the monsoon was then at its height.

"He (Alauddin) is my son and the light of my eyes. I will hold his hands and bring him along," Sultan Jalaluddin Khilji gave out and post-haste made for Kara with only a small party of troops.[55]

Before this, Alauddin Khilji had only planned to "hasten with elephants, treasures, armies, women and children ... for Lakhnauti (Bengal) and capture it."56 But when he heard that the Sultan himself was coming down to Kara largely unguarded, he could scarcely believe his luck: "Alauddin asked for the drums of joy to be beaten," tells Barani.[57] Alauddin's imagination was fired up: he would now settle for nothing less than the throne of Delhi, he decided. Murder had made its way into the young Khilji's mind!

Sultan Jalaluddin Khilji meanwhile was already on his way to Kara: travelling by a boat on the Ganges, and escorted by a small cavalry force moving along the river bank under the command of Malik Ahmad Chap.

It was Friday, the 20th of July 1296, when the royal barge was sighted from Kara.[58] "Alauddin's army became ready, wore the arms and put the elephants and horses in

---

[55] Tarikh-i Firoz Shahi. Translated by Ishtiyaq Ahmad Zilli. Page 141

[56] ibid. Page 140

[57] ibid. Page 141

[58] History of the Khaljis. By K.S. Lal. Page 64

order."[59] When the royal entourage reached Kara, they found Alauddin's forces drawn up in battle array on the opposite bank, but this too was explained away by Almas Beg as a part of the elaborate preparations undertaken to offer a grand reception to the Sultan, and he talked his sovereign into coming to the place where Alauddin was waiting.

"The Sultan, whose martyrdom was already decreed, could not discern reality even at this deceit," regrets Barani.[60]

The few nobles of Jalaluddin, who had accompanied him on that fateful journey, could comprehend clearly what fate had in store for them. According to the **Tarikh-i Mubarak Shahi**, they were seven in number, and all of them started reading such verses from the **Holy Quran** as are usually recited when the time of death draws near.61 Sultan Jalaluddin Khilji, however, remained as unperturbed as before: "he was approaching with a complete sense of security as fathers come to the houses of their sons," notes Barani.[62]

Jalaluddin finally reached his destination at the time of **Asr** prayer. What followed was a series of events that were in equal measure, both dramatic and heart-rending.

---

[59] Tarikh-i Firoz Shahi. Translated by Ishtiyaq Ahmad Zilli. Page 142

[60] ibid

[61] Tarikh-i Mubarak Shahi. By Yahya Bin Ahmad Bin Abdullah Sirhindi. Translated by K.K. Basu. Baroda, Oriental Institute. 1932. Page 66

[62] Tarikh-i Firoz Shahi. Translated by Ishtiyaq Ahmad Zilli. Page 143

To all appearances Alauddin was happy to receive his uncle. "He advanced alone, met his uncle, and fell prostrate at his feet."[63]

Sultan Jalaluddin's fatherly instincts were immediately kindled. "Like a loving father," he kissed Alauddin's cheeks, stroked his beard, and assured him in the kindest manner imaginable: "Ali **(Alauddin's birth name, Ali Gurshasp),** during your infancy you had urinated in my lap and its odour had not yet gone from my clothes ... You have been and you still are dearer to me than my [own] sons. What is this fear that you have dragged me here while I have been keeping a fast? Between you and me there is no room for anyone else ... [and] even if the entire world turns against you, my love and affection for you would not diminish in the least and I would not turn my back on you."[64]

Having addressed his nephew thus, Sultan Jalaluddin took Alauddin's hand in his own, and started walking towards his boat. Just then Alauddin made a signal to his henchmen, who were hidden nearby.[65] "Mahmud Salim, who was a despicable soldier from Samana, struck the Sultan with a sword but it missed. That wicked and mean fellow struck again."[66] Completely baffled at this sudden

---

[63] Tarikh-i Ferishta. Translated by John Briggs. Page 317

[64] Tarikh-i Firoz Shahi. Translated by Ishtiyaq Ahmad Zilli. Pages 143-144

[65] Tarikh-i Ferishta. Translated by John Briggs. Page 317

[66] Tarikh-i Firoz Shahi. Translated by Ishtiyaq Ahmad Zilli. Page 144

turn of events, the Sultan cried out: "Wicked Ali, what did you do, what did you do?"[67]

Sultan Jalaluddin tried to reach his boat, but before he could make it, a certain Ikhtiyaruddin caught up with him, knocked him down, and beheaded him at one stroke. "He (Ikhtiyaruddin) brought it (the Sultan's severed head) before the impious Alauddin while the blood was still dripping from it."[68]

"I have heard that while his head was being severed, Sultan Jalaluddin twice recited the **Kalimah-i Shahdat** and achieved martyrdom at the time of breaking fast while he was keeping fast," claims Ziauddin Barani.[69]

"The rebels then fixed the venerable head of their sovereign on the point of a spear, and carried it throughout the camp and the city."[70]

The conspirators lost no time in proclaiming Alauddin Khilji as the new Sultan of the Delhi Sultanate. "While the blood was still dripping from the severed head of Sultan Jalaluddin, these God-forsaken cowards brought the **chatr** (canopy) of Sultan Jalaluddin and raised it over the head of Alauddin," narrates Barani.[71]

Thus, on the 20th of July 1296, Sultan Jalaluddin Khilji, blinded by the innate innocence of his disposition, met his violent end at the hands of his nephew, son-in-law, and

---

[67] Tarikh-i Firoz Shahi. Translated by Ishtiyaq Ahmad Zilli. Page 144

[68] ibid

[69] ibid

[70] Tarikh-i Ferishta. Translated by John Briggs. Page 318

[71] Tarikh-i Firoz Shahi. Translated by Ishtiyaq Ahmad Zilli. Page 145

successor, Alauddin Khilji — while reciting the Muslim confession of faith and all the while maintaining the obligatory Ramzan fast.[72]

One dispensation ended, another began — Jalaluddin Khilji had died, and the reign of Abul Muzaffar Sultan Ala ud Duniya wa Din Muhammad Shah Khilji had commenced.[73]

---

[72] There is a most interesting story that Ferishta mentions in connection to Sultan Jalaluddin's death. Alauddin, the narrative goes, was told by Khwaja Gurg, a mystic of the Suhrawardi order, that his opponent "*shall lose his head in the boat, and his body shall be thrown into the Ganges*." The prophecy, Ferishta continues, came true when Ikhtiyaruddin struck Jalaluddin with his sabre and the Sultan's severed head indeed fell inside the royal barge. This anecdote, at any rate, also serves to highlight the problems involved in reducing history to a simple black-and-white narrative. Jalaluddin Khilji, being a pious, old man, should have had a far more cordial relationship with the mystics of his day than his brash and young nephew, Alauddin Khilji — historical evidence, however, shows that such an assumption was nowhere near the truth.

[73] Barani gloatingly writes about the grim fate that befell all the conspirators involved in the murder of the elderly sovereign. Thus, Mahmud Salim, who had struck the first blow, was infected with leprosy. His limbs underwent putrefaction, and he died a horrible death. Ikhtiyaruddin, who had beheaded Sultan Jalaluddin Khilji, soon lost his mental balance. He breathed his last not long after, and in his final moments, he was reported to have exclaimed to the effect that the spirit of the dead Khilji king had come with a naked sword in hand to settle scores with him.

The Road To Delhi

The gold spilled the blood of all and it still continues to enjoy its position.
There is absolutely none who could demand the blood of all these people
from it.

— Tarikh-i Firoz Shahi, by Ziauddin Barani.

Sultan Jalaluddin Khilji having been done away with, the road to Delhi was still anything but smooth, and this realisation was not lost on Alauddin either.

After the bloody catastrophe at Kara, Malik Ahmad Chap hurried back to Delhi to convey the ghastly news to the royal family. The late Sultan's widow, Malika-i Jahan, post-haste put on the throne of Delhi her youngest son, Qadr Khan who, according to Barani, "was still in the beginning of his youth and had no experience of the world."[74] Qadr Khan was rechristened as Sultan Ruknuddin Ibrahim Shah, and the Malika-i Jahan herself became the regent of the new dispensation.

Presumably, the queen mother acted with such urgency because her eldest surviving son, Arkali Khan, was then

[74] Tarikh-i Firoz Shahi. Translated by Ishtiyaq Ahmad Zilli. Page 146

in Multan, and with such a vicious nemesis as Alauddin hovering around, the throne of Delhi couldn't be kept vacant even for a moment. Or so she thought.

This, nonetheless, actually turned out to be a fatal mistake. Arkali Khan was a great warrior, and could have made an equally great Sultan. He therefore deserved his father's throne much more than his unproved younger brother did. When Arakali learnt what his mother had done, he "was deeply upset and therefore remained in Multan and did not come to Delhi."[75]

Alauddin Khilji, apprehensive of Arkali Khan's martial prowess, was at that point in two minds about his next move, but the news of this division in his uncle's household encouraged him to proceed to Delhi right away.

"In such pouring rain, the likes of which no one remembered," Alauddin set out to Delhi to claim his destiny.[76]

On the way to Delhi, in his characteristically careful manner, Alauddin spared absolutely no expense to win over the public opinion to his side. He literally went about showering gold and silver on the masses — at every stage, portable catapults were used to scatter immense quantities of gold and silver coins among the assembled people.

---

[75] Tarikh-i Firoz Shahi. Translated by Ishtiyaq Ahmad Zilli. Page 146

[76] ibid

"Recruiting troops and collecting strength," Alauddin continued steadily towards Delhi.[77] Thrown into complete desperation, the Malika-i Jahan now made frantic efforts to retrieve the situation, but to little avail. She pleaded with her son Arkali Khan to come to Delhi and grant them succour, putting the blame for her past conduct on her gender: "I am but a woman and women are deficient in judgement," she tried to reason with him.[78]

Arkali Khan, however, refused outright: it was all too late now, he observed correctly. "A stream may be diverted at its source, but when it, becomes a river, dams cannot oppose its current" — he thus confessed in no uncertain terms his inability, or unwillingness, to come to the relief of his mother and younger brother.[79]

When Alauddin Khilji learnt that Arkali Khan was not coming to Delhi even on the summons of his mother, "he ordered that drums of victory be sounded in the army."[80]

Alauddin had already won over most of the nobles of his late uncle's establishment with his largesse: "... and those ignoble persons in their greed for the dirty gold did not think twice about ingratitude and loyalty," harangues Barani.[81] In public perception, the future clearly belonged to Alauddin, and Alauddin alone, so there was a general scramble to flock to his standards: "he (Alauddin) gave

---

[77] Tarikh-i Firoz Shahi. Translated by Ishtiyaq Ahmad Zilli. Page 146

[78] ibid. Page 150

[79] Tarikh-i Ferishta. Translated by John Briggs. Page 323

[80] Tarikh-i Firoz Shahi. Translated by Ishtiyaq Ahmad Zilli. Page 151

[81] ibid

away so much gold that the killing of Sultan Jalaluddin did not seem so bad after all to the people any more and they became inclined towards his kingship."[82]

By the time Alauddin appeared near Delhi, his army had swollen into a formidable legion — according to Barani, it was composed of no less than 55,000 cavalry and 60,000 infantry. This enormous expansion was due to a deliberate policy on Alauddin's part: he told his men to recruit, on the way to Delhi, as many soldiers as they could without caring a fig about the expenses involved. His lieutenant Nusrat Khan was heard bragging to the effect that once the throne of Delhi became Alauddin's, he would "collect a hundred times more than what he was spending now and bring it to the treasury in the very first year."[83]

Finally in October, when "the star Suhail appeared and the water receded", Alauddin crossed the river Yamuna and encamped opposite the north-east gate of Delhi.[84] "Sultan Ruknuddin Ibrahim (formerly Qadr Khan) came out of the city with the troops he had ... and encamped in front of the army of Alauddin and wanted to give him a fight."[85] But right out the block, the endeavour was all show and no go. The hastily assembled troops of Ruknuddin Ibrahim had absolutely no heart for the contest, and like many others, they too wanted to hitch their wagons to the rising star that

[82] Tarikh-i Firoz Shahi. Translated by Ishtiyaq Ahmad Zilli. Page 147

[83] ibid. Page 150

[84] ibid. Page 151

[85] ibid

was Alauddin Khilji. So, even as the two armies stood facing each other, a substantial number of Ruknuddin Ibrahim's men crossed over to Alauddin's side under the cover of the darkness.

This desertion in his ranks turned out to be the straw that broke the camel's back: Ruknuddin Ibrahim's courage failed him, and he at once turned back from the field. "Towards the latter part of the night, he got Badaun Gate (of Delhi) to be opened, took a few bags full of tankas, some selected horses from the royal stables, put his mother and harem in front and while it was still night, came out of the Ghaznin Gate and headed for Multan."[86]

The fight fizzled out even before it could start — Alauddin Khilji had won the contest without even having had to nock an arrow. That Alauddin was now the Sultan of the Delhi Sultanate was a fact, and the people realised that refusing to accept the reality would do them no good. Therefore, "The citizens ... crowded to pay their respects to Alauddin, who [then] causing new coin to be struck in his name, made a pompous and triumphant entry into Delhi."[87] Totally unlike his predecessor and uncle Sultan Jalaluddin Khilji, who had shed tears of humility on his first royal visit to the celebrated Red Palace, Alauddin straight away dashed into that palace and brazenly took his seat on the throne of Sultan Balban.

---

[86]Tarikh-i Firoz Shahi. Translated by Ishtiyaq Ahmad Zilli. Page 141

[86] ibid

[87] Tarikh-i Ferishta. Translated by John Briggs. Page 324

Destiny

> *He who ought to have been viewed with detestation, became the object of admiration to those who could not see the blackness of his deeds through the splendour of his munificence.*
>
> *— Tarikh-i Ferishta, by Muhammad Qasim Ferishta.*

Once enthroned, Sultan Alauddin Khilji's immediate concern was to win the prominent people of Delhi over to his side, and this he did with consummate success, liberally scattering riches and honours among them. "He commenced his reign by splendid shows, and grand festivals, and encouraged every description of gaiety," says Ferishta, "which so pleased the unthinking rabble, that they soon lost all memory of their former King (Sultan Jalaluddin Khilji), and of the horrid scene which had placed the present one on the throne."[88]

The city of Delhi plunged into merriment like never before — "At many places in the city beautiful pavilions were installed where sherbet, betel leaf and wine were served free ... and wine drinking, beautiful women, musicians and jesters became very popular."[89] The Sultan himself followed suit, and in no time "he who ought to

[88] Tarikh-i Ferishta. Translated by John Briggs. Page 324

[89] Tarikh-i Firoz Shahi. Translated by Ishtiyaq Ahmad Zilli. Page 151

have been viewed with detestation, became the object of admiration to those who could not see the blackness of his deeds through the splendour of his munificence."[90]

Now that he was ensconced in Delhi, the next task before Alauddin was to liquidate his late uncle's family: he sent two of his most trusted men, Ulugh Khan and Zafar Khan, with a formidable force of 30,000 cavalry, to tackle the two surviving sons of Sultan Jalaluddin Khilji who had taken refuge in Multan. Immediately upon arriving in Multan, the duo of Ulugh Khan and Zafar Khan swung into action. The fort of Multan was besieged, and the siege continued for two months, by which time most of the leading citizens of the city, including the kotwal, went over to Alauddin's side. In utter distress, the two sons of Jalaluddin Khilji pleaded with the venerated Suhrawardy saint, Sheikh Ruknuddin, to try and negotiate a settlement with Alauddin's men. The holy man did as he was told, and for a time being it appeared as if he had succeeded: Ulugh Khan promised them security, and the family of the late Sultan Jalaluddin gave themselves up to him.

Ulugh Khan, we are told by Barani, treated them respectfully. "He sent a **fathnama** (letter of victory) from Multan to Delhi. In Delhi pavilions were erected, drums of rejoicing were beaten and **fathnama-i Multan** read from the pulpits and sent to the various provinces."[91] Sultan Alauddin was happy, of course, but not

---

[90] Tarikh-i Ferishta. Translated by John Briggs. Page 324

[91] Tarikh-i Firoz Shahi. Translated by Ishtiyaq Ahmad Zilli. Page 153. I have slightly modified the original translation, which reads as follows: "*In Delhi pavilions were erected, drums of* rejoicing were *beaten and fathnama-i Multan was read over the pulpits and sent to the various regions.*"

completely: the victory at Multan pleased him, but the grant of pardon to his cousins didn't.

While Ulugh Khan and Zafar Khan were on their way back to Delhi, Nusrat Khan was despatched to intercept and pass on to them a new command from their king. So was done. And in pursuance of that order, "both the sons of Sultan Jalaluddin, Alghu, the [Mongol] son-in-law of the (late) Sultan, and Ahmad Chap ... were blinded and their women were seperated from them. All their possesions , wealth, gold vessels, slaves, maids and all that they had were taken over ... The sons of Sultan Jalaluddin were kept at the fort of Hansi and all the sons of Arkali Khan (all of them being mere children) were put to death. Malika-i Jahan and the women of the harem, along with Malik Ahmad Chap, were brought to Delhi and kept at their own house."[92]

Sultan Alauddin Khilji thus became the undisputed master of the whole of Delhi Sultanate. He had clipped the wings of his formidable mother-in-law, the Malika-i Jahan, and had eliminated all possible rivals to his authority. Alauddin felt secure on the throne. He could now make his writ run without any apprehension whatsoever.

In the second year of his reign, Sultan Alauddin Khilji turned on his nobles. Their help had been invaluable in his rise to power, but after he had ascended the summit, he felt he needed to do away with the ladder — that is, he

---

[92]Tarikh-i Firozshahi. Translated by Ishtiyaq Ahmad Zilli. Page 153.

wanted to ensure that none could emulate his own example, and to that end it was necessary to make it clear that it were his nobles who were dependant on him, and not the other way round.

Alauddin was especially severe with the renegade nobles of Sultan Jalaluddin Khilji who had come over to his side in the hope of making quick gains. Sure, he himself had lavished huge wealth on them only recently, but for all his ostensible magnanimity, Alauddin was prudent enough to know that turncoats could never be trusted. He was only waiting for an opportune moment to serve them their just deserts, and now that he was comfortably ensconced in Delhi, he felt that such a time had arrived.

At one stroke, Alauddin dismissed from his service all such nobles who had betrayed his late uncle. Next, the new wazir of the Sultanate, Nusrat Khan, set about fleecing them of their ill-gotten gains. Barani tells us that to force them into compliance, these nobles were thrown into prisons and detained there as long as they didn't disgorge their wealth. The more intransigent ones among them were mercilessly blinded. This way, all that they had received from Sultan Alauddin Khilji in the period of turmoil the year before was extracted from them and returned to the imperial treasury. "Nothing whatsoever was left for their sons," observes Barani.[93]

Only three nobles of Jalaluddin Khilji's establishment remained safe from Alauddin's wrath: Malik Qutbuddin, Malik Nasiruddin, and Malik Jamal Khilji. "These three

---

[93] Tarikh-i Firoz Shahi. Translated by Ishtiyaq Ahmad Zilli. Page 154

people had not betrayed Sultan Jalaluddin and his sons, and had not received any money from Sultan Alauddin — all three [therefore] remained safe."[94]

All in all, the sum that was added to the royal treasury through these harsh methods came to around one crore silver coins (with each coin weighing a little more than 10 grams).

[94] ibid

Revelry And Religion

When the help of Heaven to the fortunate comes,
He gains his object ev'n before his wish;
While still his wish is in his heart,
The treasure to his hand doth come;
If the tilth of his purpose is in the east,
From the west to him comes rain and wind.

—Tabaqat-i Akbari, by Nizamuddin Ahmad Bakshi.

The combination of unlimited wealth, unrestrained power, and unceasing success intoxicated Alauddin Khilji. Fate smiled on him, and his affairs prospered beyond prospect. He now had everything he had once longed for — his days of struggle were behind him, and a long, singular spell of great glee appeared ahead of him.

Alauddin now plunged headlong into a hedonistic life — one that involved alcoholic inebriation and indiscriminate licentiousness in equal measure. The Sultan would spend every night either in carousing with his intimates, or in caressing one of the beautiful inmates of his harem. His want of wine was prodigal — he used to "quaff copious draughts of wine," reports one source – and he had in his collection goblets made in places as far as Ma'bar and

China, besides drinking cups that were inlaid with gold.[95] And, his desire to dally with demoiselles was no less intense. Gone were the days when he had to chafe at the restrictions imposed by the domineering daughter of Sultan Jalaluddin Khilji. He now had in his harem numerous lasses of his liking, who slaked his thirst for sensual gratification, as a result of which children were born to him every year.[96]

But for all his debauchery, there was still no room for any complaint. Not merely because Alauddin had a harsh temper, but also because success invariably attended everything he undertook. All the important affairs of the state, writes Barani, were flawlessly carried out.

The Sultan's military strength was formidable: besides countless elephants in his stables, he had at least 70,000 horses in and around his capital, with sufficient manpower, of course, to man those animals. Military ventures, as and when his army undertook them, were invariably attended by success. Erection of pavilions and public gaiety at the successful completion of military expeditions became virtually a part and parcel of the urban life in Delhi.

His wealth was prodigal, and his riches granted him great satisfaction. Contemporaries talked about "boxes and drums", filled to the brim with gems and pearls, that

---

[95] Tarikh-i Mubarak Shahi. By Yahya bin Ahmad bin Abdullah Sirhindi. Translated by K.K. Basu. Baroda, Oriental Institute. 1932. Page 73

[96] Tarikh-i Firoz Shahi. Translated by Ishtiyaq Ahmad Zilli. Page 160

Alauddin Khilji had in his possession.[97] Every single day, we are told, the Sultan would take time out to go to his treasury, and there gaze intently at the caskets and coffers that held within them his wondrous wealth.

"In this situation," says Ziauddin Barani, "it was only natural to think that there was nobody who could oppose his authority or share his power."[98] An inordinate pride took over Alauddin's mind, and he "started to entertain great ambitions and big ideas which were not only beyond his capacity but beyond that of a thousand kings like him. Given his extreme intoxication, ignorance, excessive haughtiness and imprudence ... he lost all sense of proportion and impractible ideas came to his mind."[99]

As fortune continued favouring him, Alauddin, driven by sheer megalomania, formed a series of unfeasible schemes, the first of which pertained to the sphere of religion.

Sultan Alauddin Khilji planned to publicly denounce Islam! And if that was shocking, more was yet to come.

He wanted to set up a new creed of his own, and rival none other than the Prophet of Islam himself. Evidently, what spurred Alauddin to form this fantastic scheme was a desire to make his legacy as enduring as Prophet Muhammad's. Alauddin thought that he and the Prophet

---

[97] Tarikh-i Firoz Shahi. Translated by Ishtiyaq Ahmad Zilli. Page 160

[98] ibid. I have modified the translation slightly. The original translation reads as follows: "*In this situation it was only natural to think that there was none who was opposed to his authority and wanted to share his power.*"

[99] ibid

were on an equal footing: like the latter, he too had four friends, through whose efforts, he believed, he could invent a new religion and thus ensure the survival of his name till eternity. "If I wish I could invent a new religion on the strength of these four friends of mine," Alauddin would say, "and [then] under the force of my sword and the swords of my friends, people would accept the regulations I would invent. This religion would ensure the survival of my name and the names of my friends till the end of time, as the name of the Prophet and his friends has survived among the people."[100]

The aforementioned four friends — Ulugh Khan, Zafar Khan, Nusrat Khan, and Alp Khan — didn't like this idea at all, but they were too afraid of the Sultan, who was "ill-tempered, ill-natured and hard-hearted", to voice their dislike openly. [101]

The wild aim of the Sultan didn't stay confined for long within the walls of his palace. The people of Delhi soon got wind of it: while some laughed it away as the whim of an autocrat, other, more sensible ones didn't take it as lightly. They started "likening him to a Pharaoh", and grew apprehensive of the possibly disastrous ramifications of the Sultan's schemes.[102] The whole affair was no joke — the Sultan's eagerness to equal the Prophet was real, and discussions were afoot to translate the royal dream into a tangible reality. "In his drinking parties and private conferences," we are told, "he (the Sultan) talked

[100] Tarikh-i Firoz Shahi. Translated by Ishtiyaq Ahmad Zilli. Page 160

[101] ibid

[102] ibid. Page 161

on this subject with the Amirs and Maliks, and asked them in what way, and by what means, he should discover the new religion, which should, even after his death, be current, and be held in honour among the nations of the world."[103]

There was every possibility of a general rebellion breaking out against the Delhi Sultanate, if the Sultan's blasphemous ideas had spread far and wide. Thankfully for Alauddin, such a dire situation didn't arise, because a prudent man, even at the risk of his own life, checked the catastrophe just in the nick of time. But more of that later, now it's about time we turn to the Sultan's second ambition.

"His other design was equally absurd," says Ferishta, and he couldn't have been more accurate in his assessment.[104] The second of Alauddin's ambitions was aimed at global domination: he wished to conquer the whole of the inhabited world, and bring the entire earth under his singular sway. Like how he had sought to emulate the Prophet of Islam in the realm of religion, he now wanted to outdo Alexander in the canvas of conquest. He was wont to boast before his nobles: "Treasures, elephants, horses and troops beyond computation have come into my possession. I [therefore] wish to leave Delhi to somebody and myself take to the conquest of the world like

---

[103] The Tabaqat-i Akbari. By Khwaja Nizamuddin Ahmad. Translated by B. De. Published by the Asiatic Society of Bengal. Calcutta, 1927. Page 160

[104] Tarikh-i Ferishta. Translated by John Briggs. Page 333

Alexander, and bring the inhabited world under my control."[105]

The idea of leading his men from one corner of the globe to another, marching across foreign terrains and subjugating alien people, completely consumed Alauddin. He assumed the title of "Alexander the Second", which was inscribed on the coins of the Delhi Sultanate as also recited in the khutba prayers in the mosques across that Sultanate. "No one would dare to stand up before him," Alauddin was dead sure, and the consummation of his second scheme appeared even more likely than his first one.[106]

Whether or not anybody in foreign land could stand up to him, it is crystal clear that at least nobody in his court could do that. No minister, no general, no warrior could muster enough courage to simply walk up to Alauddin and acquaint him with the utter absurdity of his plans, because all of them were mortally afraid of his "ill temper and ill manners".[107] This Khilji king did indeed inspire some dread!

It took an exceptionally upright man to bring Alauddin back to his senses. And that man happened to be the Kotwal of Delhi, Ala ul Mulk, who also was an uncle to the greatest historian of the Sultanate period, Ziauddin Barani.

---

[105] Tarikh-i Firoz Shahi. Translated by Ishtiyaq Ahmad Zilli. Page 161

[106] ibid

[107] ibid

This man, Ala ul Mulk, because of his extremely corpulent frame, found it difficult to attend the royal court more than once a month. One day when he was present at the court, the Sultan, then deep in his cups, asked his opinion on his grand projects. Realising that his own life was hitched to the Sultanate's stability, the fat kotwal mustered courage and boldly set about to present the real picture before his king.

"**Din and Shariat** are dependent on divine revelationa and could not be invented by human advise and management," the Kotwal said. "[And therefore] it is the humble request of this servant of the court that after this there should be no talk in the wine parties or outside it regarding the invention of **Din and Shariat** and all that is concerned with the prophets and has been sealed with our Prophet (Prophet Muhammad)." If the Sultan however decided to act otherwise, it would then surely bring disastrous consequences. "If the word goes out that the king wants to invent a new religion and [the news] comes to the notice of the masses and the elite, everybody would turn away from the king and no Muslim would ever come near the king. It would lead to widespread rebellions, and this kind of statements would create great confusion in the kingdom."[108]

Hearing these words, the Sultan grew pensive, and his appearance turned sombre. The four friends of Alauddin stood in utter trepidation, and so did Ala ul Mulk. After some time, the Sultan broke his silence, and to the relief

[108] Tarikh-i Firoz Shahi. Translated by Ishtiyaq Ahmad Zilli. Page 161

[108] ibid. Page 162

of all, pronounced his consent to the kotwal's suggestion, and promised that "after this nobody will ever hear any such thing in any of the assemblies."[109]

But what about his second plan, the plan for world domination, Alauddin inquired of his kotwal.

"Regarding the second project, which relates to the conquest of the world, it is fully in keeping with the traditions of the great and ambitious rulers," Ala ul Mulk admitted. However, in this project too, there was a drawback — because what had been possible in Alexander's time, would hardly be feasible now. "I know fully well that in the elephants' stables numerous elephants, in the royal stables a very large number of horses have been collected, and in the treasuries enormous riches have been accumulated," the Kotwal continued. "But the king should also consider as to whom he would entrust Delhi ... [because] the age of Alexander and their customs and traditions were completely different from this age." Alexander was fortunate to have Aristotle as his deputy, but where would Sultan Alauddin find such a man? "Now the case with the people of this age is entirely different ... If they don't find a successful and mighty ruler over their heads ..., they would not remain obedient ... and would resort to disobedience and rebellion."[110] Hence, the kotwal suggested the Sultan to abandon his grandiose goal of world domination, and instead keep his attention

[109] Tarikh-i Firoz Shahi. Translated by Ishtiyaq Ahmad Zilli. Page 162

[110] ibid. Page 163

restricted to India, the geographical entity of which his kingdom was a part.

This time, however, the Sultan was not satisfied, not entirely at least. “If I don’t resort to the conquest of other regions and remain content with the kingdom of Delhi, then what would be the use of the treasures, elephants and horses that I have acquired?” Alauddin pressed. “How [then] would I be known as a conqueror?”[111]

Even in the face of this fierce Sultan’s protestation, the wise kotwal didn’t lose his nerve. He held his ground, and calmly represented that the fame the Sultan sought could be achieved even without resorting to something as far-fetched as world-conquest. All that the Sultan needed to do was to undertake two important tasks. The first task was to bring about the submission of the hitherto unconquered parts of Hindustan. The second was to stop the Mongol depredations, and drive them out of the Indian frontiers. “Whenever these two tasks ... are accomplished, then the king should [then] remain peacefully established in his capital and busy himself in the task of governance.” But even these two practicable goals, the kotwal cautioned, would be hard to achieve “until the king does not desist from excessive drinking of wine, continuously holding parties and festivities and hunting.” That was because the “excessive consumption of wine by the king causes the affairs of state to be neglected” and “an excessive involvement in hunting involves the possibility of betrayal ... and the person of the king remains exposed to danger.”[112]

---

[111] Tarikh-i Firoz Shahi. Translated by Ishtiyaq Ahmad Zilli. Pages 163-164

[112] Tarikh-i Firoz Shahi. Translated by Ishtiyaq Ahmad Zilli. Page 164

"Our objective from all these is the life of the king because our own lives and those of our dependants are contingent on the life of the king," Kotwal Ala ul Mulk's verbose oration finally came to an end.[113]

Sultan Alauddin Khilji heeded his kotwal's counsel in its entirety. He was also extremely pleased with Ala ul Mulk's frankness: himself a strong man, Alauddin knew how to appreciate strength in others. As a reward for his brilliant counsel, "the Sultan bestowed upon Ala ul Mulk a robe embroidered in the shape of a lion, a golden waistband ..., 10,000 tankas, two fine horses and two villages as **inam**."[114] The four friends of Alauddin — Nusrat Khan, Ulugh Khan, Zafar Khan, and Alp Khan — who had hitherto unwillingly acquiesced to the Sultan's megalomaniacal schemes, also gifted Ala ul Mulk sumptous presents separately.[115]

[113] Tarikh-i Firoz Shahi. Translated by Ishtiyaq Ahmad Zilli. Page 165

[114] ibid

[115] A work of questionable historicity, *Nizami Bansari*, actually attributes the Sultan's change of mind to Sheikh Nizamuddin Auliya's inspiration. It was due to the exhortations of the Sheikh, the *Nizami Bansari* says, that kotwal Ala ul Mulk could muster enough courage to confront his sovereign, and dissaude the latter from his fanciful designs. (Reference: Nizami Bansari, by Raj Kumar Hardev. Translated into Urdu by Khwaja Hasan Nizami; abridged by Mahmudur Rahman. Dost Publications, Islamabad. 2000. Pages 111-113.)

The Temple With Arabian Connection

> *Gujarat contains 70,000 villages and towns, all populous, and the people abound in wealth and luxuries. Its air is pure, its water is clear, and the circumjacent country beautiful and charming both in scenery and buildings.*
>
> *— Tarikh-i Wassaf, by Abdullah Wassaf.*

The first of Sultan Alauddin Khilji's expansionist campaigns was directed against the rich province of Gujarat. In the thirteenth century, Gujarat gave out an unblemished picture of peace and prosperity: its agriculture was thriving, its commerce was flourishing, and its proximity to the coastline ensured that vast sums of gold and silver regularly reached the royal treasury through trade routes.

The political affairs of Gujarat, however, were nowhere near that rosy. The ruling Baghela dynasty was fast losing its hold over the province, and embers of discontent were simmering all round. Much of that had to with the ruling prince, Raja Karan Baghela who, if tradition is to be trusted, was becoming unpopular because of his lecherous ways. He is alleged to have forcibly bedded the beautiful wife of his prime minister Madhava, when the latter was away on a campaign.

Alauddin, of course, had wind of all that was brewing in Gujarat. Its wonderful wealth lured him, and its dilapidated defence encouraged him. Thus, a campaign against Gujarat was decided on: and while other Turkish Sultans of Delhi had only raided and plundered the province previously, the intention this time was to conquer and annex it permanently to the fledgling Delhi Sultanate. Accordingly, two of Alauddin's finest generals — Ulugh Khan and Nusrat Khan — were despatched to Gujarat with a formidable force in February 1299.

On their arrival in Gujarat, Ulugh Khan and Nusrat Khan set out on their usual course of loot and plunder. At Anhilwara, the capital of Gujarat, they met some resistance, which however was overcome without much trouble. Anhilwara was then given up completely to ravage and pillage, in the course of which, according to Amir Khusrau, "much blood was shed."[116] Unable to stand the Sultanate onslaught, Raja Karan Baghela fled pell-mell to Deogir, managing to take only his younger daughter with him. Rest, his women, treasures and his elephants — all of that fell into the hands of the marauding Khiljis. Among the captives was Rani Kamala Devi, the chief queen of the Baghela king of Gujarat, "who, for beauty, wit and accomplishments, was the flower of India."[117] In spite of having already mothered

---

[116] Khazain ul Futuh. By Amir Khusrau. Translated by Muhammad Habib. D.B. Taraporewala, Sons & Co. Madras, 1931. Page 35

[117] Tarikh-i Ferishta. Translated by John Briggs. Page 329

two children, Rani Kamala Devi was still so beautiful that, we are told, only a single sight of her was enough to sweep off his feet Sultan Alauddin, who then lost no time in taking her to his burgeoning harem.

After the fall of its capital and the flight of its king, the whole of Gujarat lay prostrate at the feet of the Delhi army. The victorious generals, on their part, agreed that the inland had been satisfactorily subdued, and therefore it was now time to carry the Khilji banner to the shores of the Arabian Sea. The Sultanate army now advanced to Somnath, that fabled temple-town on India's western coastline.

The stunning Shiva temple of Somnath had already been sacked once by Mahmud Ghazni: but like other temples destroyed by that raider, the temple of Somnath too had been grandly rebuilt once Mahmud's threat disappeared.

The grandeur of the Somnath temple was striking in the time of Mahmud Ghazni, and there is no reason to believe that the grandeur had diminished much when the Khilji troopers trotted into that town almost three hundred years later. In fact, grandiose additions had been made to the temple in the intervening period by one of the Solanki rulers of Gujarat, Kumarapala, who ruled the province from 1143 to 1174. In this context, it wouldn't be out of place to furnish some details about the sheer scale of ostentation that was associated with the shrine of Somnath. The thirteenth-century Arab historian, Ibn al-Athir, furnished graphic details of all that went into the worship of Lord Somnath:

"This idol (of Somnath) was the greatest of all the idols of Hind. Every night that there was an eclipse the Hindus went on pilgrimage to the temple (of Somnath), and there congregated to the number of a hundred thousand persons. They believed that the souls of men after separation from the body used to meet there, according to their doctrine of transmigration, and that the ebb and flow of the tide was the worship paid to the idol by the sea, to the best of its power.

"Everything of the most precious was brought there; its attendants received the most valuable presents, and the temple was endowed with more than 10,000 villages (for its upkeep). In the temple was amassed jewels of the most exquisite quality and incalculable value. The people of India have a great river called Gang (the river Ganges) ... Between this river and Somnat (sic) there is a [great] distance ... but water was brought daily from it with which the idol was washed. One thousand Brahmins attended every day to perform the worship of the idol, and to introduce the visitors. Three hundred persons were employed in shaving the heads and beards of the pilgrims. Three hundred and fifty persons sang and danced at the gate of the temple. Every one of these received a settled allowance daily."[118]

But for all its wealth, the temple of Somnath assumes significance in our account for a very different reason —

[118] Kamilut Tawarikh. By Ali ibn al-Athir. Quoted in Sir H.M. Elliot's work, The History of India as told by its own historians (Muhammadan Period, Vol iI). Page 468-69.

its connection to the holiest city of the Muslims, situated some 1800 miles westward.

Gujarat had had trading ties with the Arabian world since antiquity. Port-towns of that province, Somnath for example, saw brisk trade with the ports along the Arabian Peninsula and the Persian Gulf. The trade was geared towards importing war horses from the lands to the west, in exchange for products that were manufactured in Gujarat. Not surprisingly therefore, much before the hooves of the Khilji horses trotted on the turf of Gujarat, Somnath already had a sizeable Muslim population, most of them of course being traders. The dargah of Mangroli Shah, holding within its precincts several Muslim tombs of the pre-Khilji era, is a telling testament to that end.

So far, so good. But it's Amir Khusrau's allusion that "the idols (of Somnath), who had fixed their abode midway to the House of Abraham (Mecca), and there waylaid stragglers" that piques interest.[119] Almost three hundred years before his patron's victory over Gujarat, Sultan Mahmud of Ghazni had also plundered the temple of Somnath, and as a spin-off of that campaign did a most fantastic anecdote take its roots in the Islamic world. But to savour the essence of that anecdote all the better, it is necessary that we digress just a little.

We know from the Quran that Lat, Uzza and Manat were the three pre-Islamic deities most widely worshipped in the Arabian world, and the destruction of their shrines and figurines, it is said, was ordained by the Prophet of Islam

---

[119] Khazain ul Futuh. Translated by Muhammad Habib. Page 36

himself. Two of them — Lat and Uzza — were indeed destroyed, but the third idol, Manat, was somehow saved from destruction. Now Farrukhi Sistani, a Persian poet attached to Sultan Mahmud's court in Ghazni, after his master's exploits at Somnath, utilised the fertility of his imagination to the hilt and came up with a most wonderful theory that connected Somnath with the idols of pre-Islamic Mecca. The idol of Manat, he said, was smuggled off by non-Muslim Arabs to Gujarat, and it ultimately ended up in Somnath. Even the name of the town, Farrukhi continued, was derived from the idol it housed: he tells us that the name **Somnat** (as it was often written in Persian) is actually **Su-Manat,** the place of Manat. To buttress his claim, he delved into iconographic nuances. He asserted that the idol of Manat had originally been aniconic and black, attributes that were remarkably similar to those of the **lingam**.

Needless to say, the narrative was out-and-out fictional, but strangest of the strange, it readily gained the acceptance of a vast audience, in spite of the best efforts of more rational minds like al-Biruni to deflate it. Mahmud, a second-generation convert to Islam, whose ancestors had been pagan tribals in the Qarakhanid Khanate of Central Asia, suddenly found that his raid for riches had been metamorphosed into the greatest service to the cause of Islam: hardly surprising therefore that he, for one, wouldn't have wanted the myth to explode. In fact, in his letter to the Abbasid Caliph of Baghdad, Mahmud stressed not much on his raids of other Hindu temples, or on his exploits against Ismailis and other Shias, who were dubbed heretics by the Sunni orthodoxy, but dwelled the most on his attack on the temple of Somnath. And the Caliph, on his part, also bought into this tale: he praised Mahmud for having carried out the injunction of the Prophet himself, and bestowed on him titles that were grandiose to say the least.

The myth stuck, and more than 200 years later, it stirred a Persian litterateur, Sheikh Saadi of Shiraz, who was otherwise essentially a man of pen **(ahl-i qalam)**, to concoct in his work, Bustan, his fictional visit to Somnath where he got involved in acts that smacked of iconoclasm.

So when Alauddin's men set out to pillage Somnath, the Sultan's panegyricists were quick to place their patron on the same page with Sultan Mahmud of Ghazni, and they regurgitated the same myths that were fabricated at the court of Ghazni, and used them to play up Alauddin's persona and highlight his stature in the wider Islamic world. Thus, both Ziauddin Barani and Amir Khusrau, the two chief sources on Alauddin's reign, echoed virtually the same narrative in different ways. "The idol (of Somnath)," says Barani, "which subsequently to Sultan Mahmud's victory and the destruction of the Manat, had been named Somnat by the Brahmins, and had become a popular object of worship among the Hindus, was also dragged from thence and forwarded to Delhi, where it was trampled under foot by the populace."[120] Amir Khusrau, likewise, alludes to the "House of Abraham (Mecca)" in his exposition of the Somnath campaign.

---

[120] The Reign of Alauddin Khilji. Translated from Ziauddin Barani's Tarikh-i Firoz Shahi. By A.R. Fuller and A. Khallaque. Pilgrim Publishers, Calcutta. 1960. Page 23

Khursau, however, wasn't merely drawing a comparison between Mecca and Somnath. His words, according to Professor Muhammad Habib, hide in them a deeper purport. Somnath, as we know, was a port-town, and Muslim pilgrims would come here to embark on ships that would take them to Mecca. Khusrau's allusion to the effect that the temple of Somnath waylaid Muslim stragglers, could be, Professor Habib feels, referring to the custom of Muslim pilgrims praying at the shrine of Somnath for safety on the turbulent waters before boarding their ships.[121] Not that such an act was unthinkable in medieval India anyway. Numerous instances of such sort could be gleaned from the annals of that period, though it must be admitted that the Muslim historians, writing in Persian, most of the time tried to gloss over such eclectic episodes. Even in the town of Somnath itself, we have irrefutable inscriptional evidence that testifies the death of a certain Muslim resident of Somnath, who perished at the hands of his co-religionists while defending the town he belonged to.[122]

Be that as it may, Somnath was sacked thoroughly, its shrine was smashed, and its deity sent off to Delhi as a trophy of war. Although already laden with booty seized from the shrine, the Sultanate generals' lust for loot still

---

[121] Khazain ul Futuh. Translated by Muhammad Habib. Page 36

[122] New Indian Antiquary. Volume II. September 1939. Page 598. The inscription itself is a most telling one. Although composed in Sanskrit, it beigns with the customary Islamic invocation, *Bismillah Rahman Rahim*, and then proceeds to narrate the tale of a certain Farid, who died fighting for protecting his city and its Hindu sovereign against his co-religionists, the Turks.

hadn't satiated however, and they now turned to Cambay, another port-town on the coastline of Gujarat.

The same show was repeated here: the residents of Cambay fared no better than their counterparts in Anhilwara and Somnath had. The merchants of this town, Barani says, were extremely rich, presumably because of the great seaborne trade that happened regularly between Gujarat and the lands to its west. "A prodigious booty," we are told, fell into the hands of the Khiljis.[123]

In Cambay, besides the regular rapine, another event took place that deserves some discussion. There was a certain wealthy merchant in the town, presumably Muslim by faith, who had in his possession a slave that he had purchased for a thousand **dinars**. Nusrat Khan, that reputed general of Alauddin Khilji, seized the slave from his owner, and carried him off to Delhi.

This was the famous Malik Kafur, who would rise through the ranks to become the most powerful man in the Delhi Sultanate, holding in his hands the sinews of the Sultanate for quite some time. Also, lest we forget, also in the same train with Malik Kafur was Rani Kamala Devi, the ex-queen of Gujarat, who too was slated to wield extraordinary influence in the place of her destination. Gujarat, at any rate, would continue to hang over the fortunes of the Khilji dynasty, even after Alauddin was long gone, and we shall have the occasion to dilate on that aspect later in this book.

---

[123] Tarikh-i Ferishta. Translated by John Briggs. Page 327

The campaign in Gujarat had been a great success: resistance the Khiljis hardly faced any, wealth they seized of temples many. Now, it was time to go home, that is, to return to Delhi. Trouble, however, erupted on the way. At Jalore in Rajasthan, the two generals — Ulugh Khan and Nusrat Khan — "made a demand of the fifth of the spoil from the troops, besides what they had already realised for themselves."[124]

And to force the troops into compliance, they employed harsh methods. "By dint of persecution," reports Barani, "they endeavoured to exact the gold, silver, jewels, and all other valuables, and used to put the troops to all kinds of torture, till at last the soldiery were unable to bear such tyranny and ill-usage any longer."[125] A general insurrection now broke out in the army, and spearheading it were the Mongol soldiers, new-converts to Islam who managed to gather at least 3,000 troopers on their side.

In the actions that ensued, a brother of Nusrat Khan was killed, and Ulugh Khan barely managed to escape with his life. In his stead was killed a nephew of the Sultan himself, who for some reason was found sleeping in Ulugh Khan's tent when the Mongols barged in. The situation was serious indeed, and all the wealth gathered from Gujarat could have been lost — but Nusrat Khan proved equal to the task he was up against, and by an extraordinary ruse succeeded in saving the day.

---

[124] Tarikh-i Ferishta. Translated by John Briggs. Page 328

[125] The Reign of Alauddin Khilji. Translated from Ziauddin Barani's Tarikh-i Firoz Shahi. By A.R. Fuller AND A. Khallaque. Pilgrim Publishers, Calcutta. 1960. Page 24

Nusrat Khan ordered the drums to be beaten and the trumpets to be blown. Those of his soldiers who had nothing to do with the rebellion, "conceiving that the enemy was at hand, quickly fell into their stations, and the mutineers separating, dispersed, and escaping in the confusion, fled by different routes to a place of rendezvous."[126] They were pursued, we are told, and while some of them were taken down, the bulk of them made good their escape to the Chauhana citadel of Ranthambore.

"As Alauddin's power was on the ascent," remarks Barani, "such a tumult subsided soon ... and Ulugh Khan and Nusrat Khan returned to Delhi with all treasures, elephants, slaves and booty seized from the pillage of Gujarat."[127]

Alauddin's men returned to his capital, and placed all the spoils they had seized at his feet. The Sultan, on his part, took only those that were the finest: like, the ex-queen of Gujarat and the slave from Cambay. While the lady roused his passion, the lad attracted his attention, and both were at once taken into the royal establishment.

This done, the Sultan next turned to the rebels in his ranks. Alaudddin's vengeance, at any rate, was considered terrifying, even by medieval standards. And this time it was his army, the mainstay of his power, that was affected: it provided him with a reason, if he needed one,

---

[126] Tarikh-i Ferishta. Translated by John Briggs. Page 328

[127] Tarikh-i Firoz Shahi. Translated by Ishtiyaq Ahmad Zilli. Page 155

to be all the more savage in meting out punishments. "Sultan Alauddin," says Barani, "because of the arrogance that had taken root in his head, ordered that the wives and children of all the mutineers, both high and low, be apprehended and imprisoned. The seizing of women and children for the crimes of the men begins from this date. Earlier in Delhi, women and children were never seized and imprisoned for the crimes of men."[128]

And that's not all. Nusrat Khan, whose brother had been killed by the mutineers, received a free hand from his sovereign to exact his revenge in any way he liked. All those men whose complicity in the death of his brother the Khan was certain of, he had their wives, daughters and other female relatives publicly violated on the streets of Delhi. Their children, he had them butchered in cold blood before their helpless mothers. "In no religion has this kind of cruelty ever been committed as was perpetrated by him," Barani notes with horror. "The people of Delhi expressed their astonishment and surprise and trembled among themselves."[129]

The conquest of Gujarat was now over and done with, but it was from this extinguished fire that a singular spark

---

[128] Tarikh-i Firoz Shahi. Translated by Ishtaiyaq Ahmad Zilli. Page 155. I have altered the translation only slightly. The original text reads as follows: "*Sultan Alauddin, because of the arrogance that had taken root in his head, ordered that the wives and children of the main and common mutineers be apprehended and imprisoned .*"

[129] ibid

flew which, in turn, gave rise to such a conflagration as would threaten to set aflame the very throne of Delhi.

Regicide Repeated?

While the head of the claimant on his shoulder stands,
The kingdom wears rebellion as a garb.
— Tabaqat-i Akbari, by Nizamuddin Ahmad Bakshi.

After Gujarat, Sultan Alauddin Khilji's next military target was the redoubtable fortress of Ranthambore in Rajputana. The conquest of Ranthambore was crucial from the Sultan's point of view. It was dangerous to let the truculent Rajputs remain in power in the very backyard of Delhi. Moreover, Ranthambore was a colossal citadel — Amir Khusrau calls it a towering fort that talked to the stars through its lofty pinnacles — and therefore could be converted into an excellent outpost for the Delhi army. To these strategic considerations were added certain personal factors. Alauddin's uncle, Sultan Jalaluddin, had failed to reduce Ranthambore — as a usurper, Alauddin felt himself called upon to achieve what his predecessor couldn't, and thus legitimise his position on the throne of Delhi. Besides, the ring leaders of the late rebellion in the Delhi army, Muhammad Shah and his men, had been granted asylum by the Chauhana Raja of Ranthambore, Hamir Deva, reportedly a descendant of the legendary Prithiviraj Chauhan himself.

Settling scores with the Chauhanas, therefore, had a special appeal to Alauddin.

The victors of Gujarat, Ulugh Khan and Nusrat Khan, were once again called on to take the field. They did as they were told, and at once set out for Ranthambore. "Ulugh Khan and Nusrat Khan captured Jhain," says Barani, "and [then] besieged the fort of Ranthambore."[130] But Hamir Deva was not Rai Karan — and Ranthambore turned out to be a much tougher nut to crack than Gujarat had been. The Rajputs were resolute, and the Turks found that defeating them was no easy task. Some sources even say that Ulugh Khan, to save face, made conciliatory overtures to the Chauhana Raja, promising him to end the siege if he simply gave up his Mongol refugees. But the proud descendant of Prithviraj wouldn't give an inch: he gave out that he wouldn't betray his guests no matter what, and if that meant incurring the Sultan's wrath, then he wasn't afraid of it either.[131]

It was clear that war was the only option left. The Khiljis pressed on the siege with renewed vigour, while the Rajputs didn't fail to rise up to the challenge. One day, in the heat of action, Nusrat Khan was knocked down: a stone hurled by the besieged struck him on his forehead,

---

[130] Tarikh-i Firoz Shahi. Translated by Ishtiyaq Ahmad Zilli. Page 165

[131] "*O Khan, I have enough money and enough soldiers, and I have no desire to quarrel with anyone. But I am not afraid of fight, and I will not give up those who have fled to me from fear of their lives,*" ran the Chauhana Raja of Ranthambore's reply to Ulugh Khan's overtures. (Reference: A Comprehensive History of India, Volume Five. People's Publishing House, 1970. Page 342)

and injured him grievously. Treatments were tried, but to no avail, and he passed away three days after.

Hearing the news of this veteran general's death, Raja Hamir Deva sallied forth from the fort with his men, and fell vigorously on the Khiljis. So desperate was the attack that Ulugh Khan simply couldn't stand it: he barely managed to save his life, and fled pell-mell from the scene of action. A great loss, as per Ferishta, befell the imperialists, and particulars of this reversal were forwarded post-haste to the Sultan.[132]

Alauddin deemed this defeat to be a serious affair, and decided to take the field in person and accomplish this task that had proved too onerous for his generals. The Sultan thus set out from his capital, with a firm resolve to capture Ranthambore by hook or by crook.

It was in the course of his march to Ranthambore, that history came perilously close to repeating himself, and the regicide was almost paid back in his own coin — all of a sudden, such an incident played out as very nearly claimed Sultan Alauddin Khiljis's life.

It so happened that after leaving Delhi, the Sultan felt the need to drill his army. And what better way to reinvigorate his men than to indulge in an elaborate hunting exercise, he thought. Accordingly, a halt was ordered for a few days at a place not far from Delhi. One night, we are told, the Sultan forayed a bit too far, and couldn't make it back to

---

[132] Tarikh-i Ferishta. Translated by John Briggs. Page 337

his camp. Although only ten troopers were with him, the night passed safely for Alauddin.

The next morning, instead of returning at once to his tent, the Sultan unwisely decided to shoot some more games. Alauddin took his sit on a low stool **(murha)** in a clearing in the woods, and waited for his hunt to be driven to him by his men. "It was at this time that Akkat Khan, the brother's son of the Sultan, who held the office of **wakil-i dar** rebelled against the Sultan, hoping that as Sultan Alauddin [had] killed his uncle and ascended his throne, he would also kill Sultan Alauddin and take his throne."[133]

Perceiving Sultan Alauddin to be virtually defenceless, Akkat Khan, with a contingent of newly converted Mongols, "rode up to the King, and discharged a flight of arrows, two of which entered his (Alauddin's) body."[134]

Alauddin fainted then and there on account of the loss of blood, but fortunately for him the wound wasn't fatal. The Sultan had been wearing his winter garments, and had also tried to use his stool as a shield, as a result of which, says Barani, "though he was injured, he didn't suffer any fatal injury."[135]

Meanwhile the Sultan's guards, few in number, covered his fallen body with their spears, and as the assailants drew near, they cried out that Alauddin was dead. One of them, Manak by name and presumably Hindu by faith, placed his own body over the Sultan's, in a bid to save his

[133] Tarikh-i Firoz Shahi. Translated by Ishtiyaq Ahamd Zilli. Page 166

[134] Tarikh-i Ferishta. Translated by John Briggs. Page 338

[135] Tarikh-i Firoz Shahi. Translated by Ishtiyaq Ahamd Zilli. Page 166

sovereign from any further harm, and in the process took three-four arrows on himself.

"Akkat Khan was young, foolish and without any discernment ... In spite of the fact that he had reached the Sultan with so many riders who were excellent archers, he could not bring his rebellion to its culmination."[136] Seeing the royal guards stand with naked swords around the Sultan's fallen frame, Akkat Khan couldn't muster enough courage to dismount and behead Alauddin. Instead, he made a dash towards the royal camp, and "sat on the throne of Alauddin. He told the attendants of the court that he had killed the Sultan. People thought that had he not killed the Sultan, he could not have come to the court riding his horse and could not have dared to sit on the throne of Alauddin."[137]

"Meanwhile, the army was thrown into the utmost confusion; the great men assembled to pay their court, and present their offerings on the occassion; the customary prayers were read out from the Quran, [and] the Khutba was formally pronounced in the name of [Akkat Khan]; and the public criers were ordered to proclaim his accession."[138]

Akkat Khan then straightaway made for the imperial harem, evidently to satiate his secret — and forbidden — desires. But "Malik Dinar (Malik Kafur), in charge of the

---

[136] Tarikh-i Firoz Shahi. Translated by Ishtiyaq Ahamd Zilli. Page 166

[136] ibid

[137] ibid

[138] Tarikh-i Ferishta. Translated by John Briggs. Page 338

harem, did not let him do so. He took up arms along with his men and sat at the door (of the harem) and secured it. He asked the wicked Akkat Khan to show the head of Sultan Alauddin, and only then would he let him enter his harem."[139]

On the flip side, Sultan Alauddin Khilji regained his consciousness after a short while. He then reflected on what had happened, and came to the conclusion that Akkat Khan would not have dared to do what he did, had he not enjoyed the support of powerful elements in the empire. He therefore felt that it would be dangerous for him to return to the camp, and that his personal safety was in retreating somewhere and then regrouping his forces.

However, a certain Malik Hamiduddin, who happened to be with the Sultan in this hour of distress, talked him out of this plan. He "recommended him (Sultan Alauddin) immediately to go to his own camp, and there show himself to the army; observing, that the usurper (Akkat Khan) had not yet had the time to establish himself, and that upon seeing the Emperor's canopy, he doubted not but the whole army would return to its duty; adding, at the same time, that the least delay might render his (Alauddin's) affairs irrecoverable."[140]

Sultan Alauddin Khilji heeded Hamiduddin's advise. He immediately mounted his horse — not without great difficulty though, given his extreme physical weakness at that point — and straightaway set off for his own camp.

---

[139] Tarikh-i Firoz Shahi. Translated by Ishtiyaq Ahmad Zilli. Page 167

[140] Tarikh-i Ferishta. Translated by John Briggs. Page 339

He would either die or kill Akkat, but he wouldn't flee — the Sultan had made up his mind. On his way he was joined by many of his men, so that by the time he reached his camp he had at least 500 soldiers with him. "When the Sultan reached the camp, he went to an elevation and showed himself. Many among the army saw the chatr (canopy) of Sultan Alauddin; the people assembled at the royal camp and the servants of the court came along with all the elephants to his presence."[141]

At this sudden development, Akkat Khan completely lost his nerve. He rushed out of his camp, mounted his horse, and hurriedly fled. Sultan Alauddin immediately sent his men to go after him, and "they got hold of him in the village of Afghanpur and severed his head and brought it to the court. The Sultan ordered the head of that luckless person (Akkat Khan) to be tied with a lance, raised and paraded in the entire army and also in the city of Delhi."[142]

Akkat Khan being finished, Sultan Alauddin now turned towards his accomplices. "After much investigation, [the Sultan] got all those officers, cavalrymen and others who had anything to do with the rebellion apprehended, and put to death by beating them with iron scourge. Their establishments were taken over as imperial property, and [their] women and children were imprisoned and sent to different forts."[143]

---

[141] Tarikh-I Firoz Shahi. Translated by Ishtiyaq Ahmad Zilli. Page 167

[142] ibid. Pages 167-168

[143] ibid. Page 168

The danger to his life having been averted, it was now possible for Alauddin to pay undivided attention to the reduction of Ranthambore. And with the Sultan himself now in their ranks, the Khilji army devoted themselves wholeheartedly to the task. From all parts of the country, we are told, workmen were called in to weave leather bags in huge numbers. Once weaved, the bags were distributed among the soldiers, who were told to fill them up with sand and then throw it into the ditch that separated the fort from the besiegers. The ditch being thus filled, a mound was raised on it that was so high that it reached the western tower of the fort. Next, siege engines were dragged up the mound, and an incessant shower of projectiles was maintained.

But the garrison still showed no sign of relenting. Instead, they kept raining down arrows — fire-emitting ones, according to Amir Khusrau — on the imperialists.[144] Besides, state-of-the-art weaponry was not wanting inside the citadel either, and the Chauhans and their Mongol friends made good use of them: such catapults as were lighter were brought to the roof of the fort, and from there made to hurl projectiles at the besiegers, wreaking havoc in the enemies' ranks. "Many people were killed from both sides," Barani's observation is hardly surprising.[145]

The contest now boiled down to a test of patience. The Khilji army was clearly out of their element in Ranthambore — the sweltering heat of the desert coupled with the risk to their life proved very difficult for them to

---

[144] Khazain ul Futuh. Translated by Muhammad Habib. Page 39-40

[145] Tarikh-i Firoz Shahi. Translated by Ishtiyaq Ahamd Zilli. Page 168

put up with. But, such was the dread that Alauddin inspired that not even a single soldier in his camp could voice their discontent. "Such a big army that was pressed in the siege of the fort was driven to desperation and was reduced to great distress," writes Barani, "but due to the fear of the punishment of Sultan Alauddin, not a single cavalryman or footman dared to head for Delhi or go elsewhere."146. Even as the Khiljis bore great privations, the garrison fared hardly any better. Provisions were fast running out in the fort. Amir Khusrau, in his characteristics manner, says that the lack of food reduced the defenders to such dire straits that they were forced to eat stones. "Famine prevailed to such an extent within the fort, that they would have purchased a grain of rice for two grains of gold but could not get it."[147]

For all their chivalry, it appeared that the conclusion of the Chauhanas' resistance had drawn near. Exactly at that point, fate turned once again on Sultan Alauddin Khilji. Several rebellions suddenly broke out almost at the same time, and for once it seemed as if the Sultan was losing his Sultanate.

Once again it was the Sultan's nephews who were raising the tumult: history was repeating before Alauddin's eyes, and repeating with a vengeance. Last time, it had been Alauddin's brother's son — Akkat Khan — who had raised the banner of rebellion. This time, it was

[146] Tarikh-i Firoz Shahi. Translated by Ishtiyaq Ahmad Zilli. Page 171

[147] Khazain ul Futuh. Translated by Muhammad Habib. Page 40

Alauddin's sister's sons — Malik Umar and Mangu Khan — who were stoking the fire of sedition.

Finding the Sultan entangled in the siege of Ranthambore, Malik Umar, the governor of Badaun, and Mangu Khan, the governor of Awadh, joined forces and broke out in open rebellion against the Sultanate. Senior generals, we are told by Barani, were appointed by Alauddin to deal with the insurrection.

Luckily for Alauddin, his nephews were not made of the same stuff as he was. Akkat Khan had failed ignominiously to topple his uncle, and now the duo of Malik Umar-Mangu Khan couldn't fare any better either. Soon, they fell into the hands of the imperialists, who brought them shackled before their uncle, the Sultan, at Ranthambore.

"Sultan Alauddin was bad-tempered, hard-hearted, and of a very harsh nature. He got both his sister's sons killed in his presence and their eyes gorged out of their sockets using knives, and overthrew their families and establishments. Those cavalrymen and footmen, who had sided with them, either fled and dispersed or fell into the hands of the **amirs** of Hindustan and were [then] imprisoned."[148]

But, it wasn't only his blood that was bothering him: the Sultan's stars were not at all favouring him, and now another rebellion, far more serious than his nephews', came to threaten his capital.

---

[148] Tarikh-i Firoz Shahi. Translated by Ishtiyaq Ahmad Zilli. Page 168

There was a certain man in the capital, Haji Maula by name, who had formerly been a slave to the celebrated kotwal of Delhi, Fakhruddin, and had known palmy days when his master was alive. But after his master's death — which happened to coincide with the commencement of Alauddin's reign — he lost much of what he had previously enjoyed. A deep dissatisfaction against the new regime therefore took root in the man's mind, and he remained forever on the lookout to foment trouble any time he could.

The Sultan had been away in Ranthambore for long, and the people of Delhi were finding it increasingly difficult to put up with the oppressive ways of the man who had been left behind in the charge of the capital. This was the new kotwal of Delhi, who had come from Tirmiz in Uzbekistan, and against whom public discontent was fast building up.

The news of this simmering discontent didn't fail to reach the ears of the disgruntled Haji Maula. He realised this was the opportunity he had been waiting for, and then plunged into action immediately.

It was the month of Ramazan, and Muslim households generally preferred to spend the afternoon indoors. One such afternoon, Haji Maula procured a forged royal farman and gathered a band of ruffians to his side. "With these he hastened to the house of Tirmizy Khan," reports Ferishta, "and sent word to tell him that a messenger had arrived with an order from the King."[149]

---

[149] Tarikh-i Ferishta. Translated by John Briggs. Page 341

Having completed his **zuhur** prayers, Kotwal Tirmizi was fast asleep in his house. Haji Maula's call broke his siesta: hearing that a message had come from the Sultan, he rushed out of his house even before he could gather his wits. And as soon as he came out, "[Haji Maula] asked the **payaks** to strike his neck and severe his neck from his body."[150]

After thus doing away with the unpopular kotwal, "Haji Maula sent parties to secure the city gates, and despatched a person to Alauddin Ayaz, kotwal of the new city (Shahr-i Nau or Siri), to come and examine the King's order."[151]

Alauddin Ayaz, however, had already got wind of the mischief — "One of the rebels informed him about the situation and narrated the details of his (Haji Maula's) rebellion before him," informs Barani — and he therefore wisely refused to walk into the trap set up for him. Instead, Kotwal Alauddin "gathered his forces, fortified himself and closed the doors of the new fort (Hisar-i Nau)."[152]

Finding Siri well protected, Haji Maula then turned towards the fabled Red Palace of Balban (Kaushak-i Lal). There, after overpowering whatever little resistance he encountered, he freed all the state prisoners. Needless to say, all of them at once became his partisans. Next, he laid

---

150 Tarikh-i Firoz Shahi. Translated by Ishtiyaq Ahmad Zilli. Page 169

151 Tarikh-i Ferishta. Translated by John Briggs. Page 341

152 Tarikh-I Firoz Shahi. Translated by Ishtiyaq Ahmad Zilli. Pages 169-170

hold of the treasury and the armoury, distributing gold, silver and weapons of all sorts among his followers.

But for all his daring, Haji Maula was but an ex-slave, and that too of a mere kotwal. He therefore felt that he needed some sort of legitimacy to crown his insurrection with success. To that end, he laid his hands on a certain Shah Nuni Alavi, who happened to be a distant descendant of Sultan Iltutmish: "There was an Alavi ... [who] from his mother's family was a grandson of Sultan Iltutmish," writes Barani.[153]

Shah Nuni Alavi (Alavi means descended from Imam Ali) had spent virtually his entire lifetime in prison — Haji Maula now forcibly made him ascend the throne in the Red Palace of Balban. Thereafter, all the elites and notables of the capital were coerced to come and personally pay their homage to the new king.

Haji Maula squandered a profuse amount of wealth, and day by day the number of his followers increased. Sultan Alauddin received all the tidings in Ranthambore — but so resolute was the man's resolve, that not for once did the thought of returning to Delhi cross his mind. The Sultan instead made sure that not even an inkling of all that was happening in Delhi could reach any of his soldiers, who remained as invested as before in the siege of the Chauhana citadel.

The capital city of Delhi, however, needed to be saved, and saved urgently. The Sultan therefore forwarded a confidential message to Malik Hamiduddin, that man who

---

[153] Tarikh-i Firoz Shahi. Translated by Ishtiyaq Ahmad Zilli. Page 170

had so sagaciously saved his life only a little ago, and urged him to rush to the rescue of Delhi.

"On the third or fourth day of the sedition of Haji Maula, Malik Hamiduddin ... opened the Ghaznin gate and entered the city (of Delhi)," reports Barani.[154] Thereon, for two days the rebels grappled with the royalists. Then, a contingent belonging to the late Zafar Khan forced its way into the capital, and decisively turned the scale of the contest in favour of the royalists.

With his strength having been augmented by the troops of Zafar Khan, Malik Hamiduddin decided that the time for the final showdown had arrived. In the locality of shoemakers, he personally took on Haji Maula. "Malik Hamiduddin, being dismounted, ran up to Haji Maula (who was leading on his party with great bravery), and dragging him from his horse, threw him down in the street and slew him, having himself, in the mean time, received several wounds," reports Ferishta. "The faction of Haji Maula, dispirited by the death of their chief, gave ground, and dispersed throughout the city."[155]

The final act of the play, however, was not yet over: and in this concluding chapter, the central character would be Shah Nuni Alavi, that helpless Alavi who had been used throughout as a mere pawn in this chessboard of conspiracy. After doing away with Haji Maula, Malik Hamiduddin, notwithstanding his very many wounds, straightaway made a dash for the Red Palace of Balban,

---

[154] Tarikh-i Firoz Shahi. Translated by Ishtiyaq Ahmad Zilli. Page 170

[155] Tarikh-i Ferishta. Translated by John Briggs. Page 342

and there, "deposed and slew Shah Nuni Alavi, causing his head to be exhibited on the point of a spear, and thus put an end to the rebellion."[156]

At Ranthambore, the Sultan soon received the glad tidings. He was relieved: Malik Hamiduddin's impetuous bravery had saved his capital, and his reputation for good measure. Next, the Sultan sent his brother Ulugh Khan to Delhi, "in order to punish all who were supposed to have had any share in the late insurrection."[157]

Once in Delhi, "the rebels were brought before him (Ulugh Khan). He massacred all of them and caused a rivulet of blood to flow."[158]

Even the family of Haji Maula's former master, Kotwal Fakhruddin, was not spared, even though they had no stakes whatsoever in Haji Maula's insurrection: "The sons and the survivors of the family of the late Fakhruddin, kotwal," writes Ferishta, "were put to death, merely on suspicion, for no other cause than that the rebel had been one of their dependants."[159]

Ulugh Khan, after spilling as much blood as he could, then set about recovering the vast amount of money that Haji Maula had squandered to win public support. "All those who had sided with Haji Maula and [had] received money from him ... were apprehended in the city and imprisoned. The money that he had given to the people

---

156 Tarikh-i Ferishta. Translated by John Briggs. Page 342

157 ibid

158 Tarikh-i Firoz Shahi. Translated by Ishtiyaq Ahmad Zilli. Page 171

159 Tarikh-i Ferishta. Translated by John Briggs. Page 342

was recovered in its entirety and returned to the [royal] treasury," reports Barani.[160]

All this while, even as political affairs turned topsy-turvy in the Doab, and the capital of the Sultanate came within a whisker of getting lost, the siege of the Ranthamore fortress continued unabated. Not only did the Sultan make sure that no unpropitious tidings could reach his soldiery, but he himself also remained thoroughly focused throughout on the task at hand: he had placed a "kingly resolution" on the conquest of Ranthambore, says Barani, and had made up his mind not to move without conquering the Chauhanas, come what may.[161]

At this point however, the garrison didn't have much fight left in them. They had been under siege for almost a year, and now the want of provision made it virtually impossible for them to hold on. "Man can bear all afflictions except that of a starving stomach," Amir Khusrau remarks poignantly.[162]

On the flip side, Alauddin's camp presented as contrasting a picture as could be imagined: sure, having had three serious rebellions snuffed out, the Sultan was happy, but the display of his gaiety was as much a genuine reflection of his emotions as it was a cunning move to dispirit his enemy. On the occassion of Nauroz, we are told, the Sultan put up a great show of ostentation: "tankas

[160] Tarikh-i Firoz Shahi. Translated by Ishtiyaq Ahmad Zilli. Page 171

[161] Tarikh-i Firoz Shahi. Translated by Ishtiyaq Ahmad Zilli. Page 170

[162] Khazain ul Futuh. Translated by Muhammad Habib. Page 40

of gold were showered on the earth like falling leaves," notes Amir Khusrau.[163]

This display of wealth demoralised the besieged all the more, and such among them as valued gold more than they did their honour promptly went over to the Khilji side, leaving the Chauhana king and his adherents utterly consternated. The situation was hopeless, and the garrison realised it. There were now only two options before them: to surrender before the Sultan and accept whatever terms he dictated, or to face a certain death, either at the hands of hunger or the Khiljis. Hamir Deva, in quintessentially Rajput fashion, chose death over dishonour, and decided to stake his life on the point of sword, rather than give his life up to the pangs of hunger. His men, Rajput and Mongol, consented to him with one voice.

Self-sacrifice having been decided upon, it was now time for the gruesome rite of **jauhar**: one night, says Khusrau, the Rai of Ranthambore lit up a massive fire, "which rose like a mountain-tulip on the hill,"[164] into which entered the ladies in the fort, led by Ranga Devi,[165] the chief queen of Hamir Deva Chauhana. Then, in the terrible embrace of that devouring flame, perished in the twinkle of an eye countless "rosy-coloured young maidens."[166]

---

163 Khazain ul Futuh. Translated by Muhammad Habib. Page 40

164 ibid

165 Mentioned in the History of the Khaljis. By K.S. Lal. Page 112

166 Khazain ul Futuh. Translated by Muhammad Habib. Page 40

Their womenfolk having been annihilated in the inferno of **jauhar**, it was now time for the men to sacrifice their lives. This, they did soon: before the next dawn, we are told, Hamir Deva Chauhana and his men sallied out of the fort and fell upon the Khiljis. Their fury notwithstanding, it was easy work for the imperialists to finish off this final flourish of resistance.

Thus, on the 3rd of July, 1301, the fort of Ranthambore finally fell into the hands of Sultan Alauddin Khilji after a siege that had extended for almost a year and had claimed lives on both sides by the thousands.

Alauddin then set about finishing things up in his own style, displaying in this process such flairs as set him apart as a leader of men. Those of Hamir Dev's men, who had come over to his side in the lure of gold, were summarily put to death: "Those who have betrayed their natural sovereign will never be true to another," the Sultan opined.[167] Alauddin himself had made his way to the top through treachery, and he therefore always remained on guard against treachery — he had zero tolerance for those that betrayed their masters, even in the instances when he benefitted from such defections.

Next, the Sultan turned to those Mongol soldiers who had taken refugee in Ranthambore after mutinying against the imperialists. Most had already perished in the defence of the fort, and only a certain Mir Muhammad Shah, a Mongol captain of note, was found alive: though much wounded, he still had a few breaths left to him. Impressed

---

[167] Tarikh-i Ferishta. Translated by John Briggs. Page 344

by the Mongol's loyalty to the Chauhana cause, Alauddin offered to spare him his life, and even went to the extent of ordering his royal physicians to dress his wounds. But the gallant Mongol at once spurned the Sultan's generosity: "If I recover from my wounds," Muhammad Shah threatened Alauddin Khilji, "I would have thee slain, and raise the son of Hamir Deo on the throne [of Ranthambore]."[168]

No matter how impressed he was by the fallen Mongol's gallantry, conventions had to be taken care of him: which meant passing the death sentence on the enemy, for having insulted the Sultan himself in public. This was accordingly done: raging elephants were set upon Muhammad Shah, who was then trampled to death in an instant.

The plucky Mongol having died, Alauddin next made sure that he was consigned to the grave with all the honours that he deserved — himself a strong man, the Sultan for sure knew how to respect strength in others. "He (Sultan Alauddin) directed his body to be put in a coffin," tells Ferishta, "and [then] interred with decent solemnity."[169]

At long last, the affairs of Ranthamore came to a close. The Sultan was finally free from the sweltering heat and the stifling sandstorms of Rajputana, and could now enjoy some well-deserved comfort that the opulent palaces in his capital provided. Placing Ranthambore and the

---

[168] Tabaqat-i Akbari. By Nizamuddin Ahmad Bakshi. Translated by B. DE. Calcutta, 1927. Page 168

[169] Tarikh-i Ferishta. Translated by John Briggs. Page 343

surrounding tracts under the charge of his brother Ulugh Khan, the Sultan hurried homeward. But return to Rajputana he would, and that too sooner than later, for another fortress as mighty as Ranthambore would beckon him, with such an allure as the Sultan would find irresistible. And it is to that story that we turn now.

Of Chivalry And Mystery

The fort of Chittor was the paradise of the Hindus, with springs and lawns on every side. It had a Rai with an organised army, heavily armoured but light-footed; compared with the thrones of other Hindus, his throne was higher than the seventh heaven (haft kursi).

— Dewal Rani, by Amir Khsurau.

"Wonderful was the fort, which even hailstones were unable to strike!" remarks Amir Khusrau on Chittorgarh. "For if the flood itself rushes from the summit, it will take a full day to reach the foot of the hill."[170]

Perched over a rocky hill and spread majestically across hundreds of yards, to a soul stepped in history, there is scarcely any place in the whole inhabited world that evokes more awe, romance and wonder than the fort of Chittor does.[171] One can't help but sympathise with the

---

[170] Khazain ul Futuh. Translated by Muhammad Habib. Page 47

[171] Of the fort's dimensions, the best description comes from the pen of V.A. Smith: *"The fortified hill of Chittor is an isolated mass of rock rising steeply from the plain, three miles and a quarter long and some twelve hundred yards wide in the centre. The circumference at the base is more than eight miles, and the height nowhere exceeds four or five hundred feet."* (Source: Akbar the Great Mogul. Oxford, 1917. Page 82)

nineteenth-century English officer, Colonel Tod who, in his stint in India, got so enamoured with Chittor that he literally set about rhapsodizing about it — "My heart beat high as I approached the ancient capital of the Sesodias, teeming with reminiscences of glory, which every stone in her giant-like **kunguras** (batllements) attested ..." reads the Colonel's paean.[172]

A stronghold of Suryavanshi Rajputs, Chittor, and the territory of Mewar of which it was the capital, had already attracted the malevolent attention of the Khilji Sultan when its ruling Rana, Ratan Singh, had ruffled the feathers of Ulugh Khan and Nusrat Khan while the duo were on their way to Gujarat. Besides, much like Ranthambore, such a majestic fort as Chittor couldn't be allowed to remain in the hands of a man as truculent as the Rana of Mewar. A campaign against Chittorgarh was therefore definitely on the cards, and the idea was put into action in the year 1303 — that is, less than two years after the successful subjugation of Ranthambore.

On Monday, the 28th of Januray, 1303, the boom of loud drums announced the Sultan's march at the head of a large army to conquer Chittor.[173] On his arrival in Chittor, the Sultan pitched his tents between the two rivers, Gambhiri and Berach, while his troops quickly fanned out over the entire town: the two wings of the imperial army, informs

---

[172] Annals and Antiquities of Rajasthan. By Colonel Tod. Volume III. Page 1812

[173] The date has been taken from the Khazain ul Futuh by Amir Khusrau, who puts it at the 8th of Jumada al-Thani, 702 A.H.

Amir Khusrau, were ordered to encamp on either sides of the fort. The siege of Chittor thus began in all earnest.

Every day, we are told, the Sultan would ascend a nearby hillock, and use that vantage point to personally oversee the siege operations. But for all that, at least for two months, the imperialists' progress remained slow and tortuous. At any rate, such was only to be expected, for it wasn't easy to reduce a stronghold as impregnable as Chittorgarh, which was dubbed "a celestial fort" by Amir Khusrau with good reason. [174]

Brute strength having failed to make any substantial headway, advanced technology was taken recourse to. Powerful siege engines were brought in to reduce Chittor, and wrestlers were called in to man those huge machines. Heavy stones were put in the catapults, and then hurled with full force at the fort walls. The new manoeuvre immediately started showing results, and the struggle between the two sides intensified greatly. The army of the Sultan, Khusrau says, was unrelenting in assaulting the fortress. And Rana Ratan Singh too must have matched blows with blows, or else the siege couldn't have been protracted in the first place. Though Khusrau doesn't speak much about the Rana's resistance, yet elsewhere he remarks on the Rana's exalted stature in the Hindu cosmos: the King of Mewar, he says, was the most exalted of all Hindu rulers, and his capital, Chittor, was like the

---

[174] Khazain ul Futuh. Translated by Muhammad Habib. Page 48

paradise of the Hindus.[175] A King with such a substantial standing, and an army to match his standards, would have definitely put up a brave fight in the face of Khilji onslaught.

But for all their bravery, it was Alauddin who was fated to carry the day: after the siege had dragged on for eight months, the fortress of Chittor finally capitulated to the Sultan of Delhi. On Monday, the 26th of August, 1303, Sultan Alauddin Khilji, with all pomp and show, entered the historic citadel of Chittor on his sedan.

The details accompanying the fall of this fort, however, are shrouded in mystery. Apart from Amir Khusrau, who was an eyewitness, other contemporary and near-contemporary writers are remarkably vague in their elucidation of this event: Ziauddin Barani merely says that the Sultan conquered Chittor without much fuss, and Yahya bin Sirhindi likewise avoids delving into details. It is thus only Amir Khusrau with whom we are left: his account, however, is so extraordinary that it borders on incredibility. Finding his position irredeemable, the King of Mewar threw himself on the Sultan's mercy: he was forgiven, and the Sultan's wrath fell on the rest of the defendants, some 30,000 in number, who were all slaughtered on the Sultan's order. Or so goes Amir Khusrau's narrative.

---

[175] Khazain ul Futuh. Translated by Muhammad Habib. Page 50. Khusrau's remarks on the Rana of Mewar are to be found in another of his work, Dewal Rani, but Professor Habib has included this extract in his translation of Khazain ul Futuh..

Some say that the Rajput polity, at least in the period in question, was largely decentralised: the King had to share his authority with his kinsmen, who more often than not weighed in on important matters of the state. Their opinions had to be respected — there was no way they could be sidelined, not least because most of them were also the headmen of villages, from where came the surplus that fueled the state machinery. Seen in this light, Amir Khusrau's allusion to the wind of imperial wrath uprooting all **muqaddams** suddenly starts making sense. Perhaps, of all the men that had a stake in the defence of the fort, only Rana Ratan Singh had the prudence to come to terms with the Sultan, at a point when defending Chittor was no longer feasible. Others, co-sharers in his authority, didn't concur with them, and therefore had to meet a terrible end at the hands of the Sultan.

Still, there are detractors to this theory, and quite rightly so. No matter what, that a King who held such an exalted status among his co-religionists should have merely stood by and watched his people getting slaughtered by the thousands at the hands of an invader is definitely hard to imagine. Besides, even if we agree that Rana Ratan Singh did save his neck from Alauddin's sword, the question still remains as to what happened to him after the military operations got over? On this, Amir Khusrau and all other chroniclers are completely silent. In fact, there is absolutely no mention of Ratan Singh any more after the Sultan left Chittor — it seems as if he suddenly vanished into the whirlpool of time. Such incongruity leads us to surmise that Ratan Singh, like his Chauhana counterpart in Ranthambore, also died fighting the imperialists — he too was one of those 30,000 men that fell victim to the Delhi Sultan's sharp scimitar.

Be that as it may, in the month of August, the mighty fortress of Chittor did fall into the hands of the Delhi Sultan who, after being done with the bloodshed, bestowed the newly conquered citadel on his son Khizr Khan, then a mere lad.[176] The town was rechristened as Khizrabad and a red canopy, usually reserved for the heir apparent, was granted to him. "The red canopy was placed over Khizr Khan's head," records Khusrau in detail, "like the red heaven over the blue sky. He (Khizr Khan) wore a robe of honour ornamented with jewels, as the sky is inlaid with stars. Two banners, black and green, were raised so high above his threshold that the Saturn and Sun were struck with melancholy and bile. Further, his court was adorned by a baton **(durbash)** of two colours, each of which seemed a tongue from the solar lamp."[177] Thus, after settling his son down in Chittor with princely trappings and leaving behind a strong army to guard his life and property, the Sultan set out to return to Delhi.

So far, so good: sure, the fate of Rana Ratan Singh is swathed in some mystery, but this opacity fades into oblivion when put against the legendary narrative that sprung up from the pen of a sixteenth-century mystic of Awadh, Malik Muhammad Jayasi. According to this colourful tale, it wasn't political or military considerations that drove Alauddin Khilji to take

---

[176] Abdul Malik Isami says that a slave of Sultan Alauddin Khilji, Shahin by name, was entrusted with the duty of looking after Khizr Khan in Chittor.

[177] Khazain ul Futuh. Translated by Muhammad Habib. Page 49

possession of the Chittor citadel, but the enchanting beauty of the alluring queen of Ratan Singh, Padmini, that spurred the Sultan to action. Padmini, as the story goes, spurned the Sultan's amorous advances outright. But realising that countless lives were at stake, the queen agreed to concede a little: she would allow Alauddin to catch a fleeting glimpse of her in a mirror, she gave out, provided the Sultan pledged to strike camp immediately after this promised rendezvous. Alauddin Khilji agreed, and the meeting came off. The sight of Padmini, however, inflated the Sultan's lust all the more, and he made up his mind to acquire Padmini by any means necessary, even if that meant going back on his word.

This inevitably led to a war between the two parties, in which the defending Rajputs, though not wanting in valour, failed to match up to the vastly superior forces that the Sultan fielded. In the face of certain defeat, the queens of Chittor, led by the fair Padmini, voluntarily immolated themselves in the blazing flames of **jauhar**. Then, the Rajput men, with nothing left to live for, sallied out of the fort and charged headlong at the Khiljis, with all of them perishing in the ensuing fight.

Needless to say, this fantastic tale — which has romance, adventure and romance in just the right proportions — is, after all, only a work of fiction. There isn't any element of history in it, and the author himself clarified it before concluding his work: "In this narrative Chittor stands for the body, the Raja (Ratan Singh) for the mind ... Padmini for wisdom ... and Sultan Alauddin for lust."'[178]

---

[178] Quoted in K.S. Lal's History of the Khaljis. Page 127

Still, if the reader wishes for a critical analysis before concurring with Jayasi's own statement, then details to that end are not lacking either. First, Padmini has been called as the princess of Ceylon, and as per the text, the King of Mewar, Ratan Singh, spent no less than twelve long years to woo her in Ceylon, before the maiden finally gave in to his advances. If this is not incredible enough, then we have a major discrepancy regarding the name of Padmini's father, the King of Ceylon. Jayasi says he was one Govardhana. However, the King of Ceylon who was actually contemporaneous with Rana Ratan Singh was Parakramabahu III: in fact, the dynasty which he belonged to didn't produce any king with the name of Govardhana. Again, Jayasi says that reducing Chittor took the Sultan of Delhi no less than eight years, while we know from unimpeachable evidences that the task took the Sultan only eight months — in fact, eight years down the line, the Sultan was busy not with Chittor but with the states south of the Vindhyas.

Be that as it may, the work of fiction that emanated from the pen of Malik Muhammad Jayasi — no matter its author's original intention to use it as a pedagogical text for Sufis — became extremely popular in no time, and managed to capture the imagination of a vast audience. Successive generations of Muslim chroniclers, writing in Persian, took Jayasi's story as a factual account, and then went on to reproduce it in their own works with such additions and subtractions as they thought fit. Thus, Abul Fazl mentioned this story in his text, and so did Ferishta. Over the years, bards and poets kept embellishing it with their own inputs so that by the time Colonel Tod was putting pen to paper in the early nineteenth century, the narrative — or at least, the core kernel of it — had assumed some sort of a gospel-like status. And then Tod, with his flowery words, did what his predecessors couldn't — "The fair Padmini closed the throng which was augmented by whatever of female beauty or youth could be tainted by Tartar lust," wrote the Colonel in his work that sounded no less than a panegyric and which, in spite of its historical inaccuracies and racial mishmash, catapulted the triangular affair of Padmini-Ratan Singh-Alauddin to the status of an epic of transcontinental fame. [179]

Still, some people even today find it difficult to do away with the habit of scouring historicity in Jayasi's work, arguing that the smoke indicates that somewhere or other there was a fire, no matter how feeble its flame.

Sultan Alauddin Khilji, at any rate, wasn't the sort of king that Jayasi's account would have us believe: an utterly unsentimental man, he wasn't the one to risk his life and empire for the sake of a femme fatale. To slake his sensual thirst, he already had a harem stocked with beauties. Sure, he did marry and take into his harem Hindu ladies, princesses to be precise, but those were more in the nature of political alliances between an overlord and his subordinate, than any telling testament to the Sultan's extraordinary lust. In fact, as far as marrying Hindu princesses and establishing matrimonial bonds with the Hindu ruling houses are concerned, it would hardly be an

---

[179] Annals and Antiquities of Rajasthan. By Colonel James Tod. Edited by William Crooke. Volume I. Oxford University Press, 1920. Page 311

exaggeration to say that Sultan Alauddin Khilji was actually the forerunner to Jalaluddin Muhammad Akbar, that great Mughal emperor who would rule India for almost half a century more than two hundred years after Sultan Alauddin's death.

But, more on the Sultan's inter-faith efforts later. It's now time we take our narrative back to the centre of the action, Chittor, where no sooner had the Sultan finished finalising the paraphernalia of his prince than he received the menacing news that his biggest enemies, indeed of the Sultanate itself, were knocking on the gates of his capital. The Sultan at once hurried homeward, and in the next section of this book we would look at what all did the Sultan do once he was back in his capital.

The Mongol Menace

They (the Mongols) came, they sapped, they burnt, they slew, they plundered and they departed.

— Tarikh-i Jahangushay, by Ata Malik Juvayni.

It was late in August and the Sultan was still in Chittor when the menacing news of the appearance of the Mongols on Indian frontiers reached him. Delhi was denuded of troops, the Mongols had heard in Transoxiana — a strip of land in Central Asia between the Syr Darya and the Amu Darya rivers — and they rushed to make the most of this opportunity. The Sultan, sure, hurried back home with all haste, but by the time he reached Delhi, his army was in no position to take the Mongols on. "The rains and the task of capturing the fort (of Chittor) had reduced the army that had accompanied him to complete disarray," reports Barani.[180] The surplus soldiery of the Sultan had been sent away to Telangana under the leadership of Malik Fakhruddin Jauna, the future Muhammad bin Tughluq who, much like how he would later fare as the Sultan, failed in his assignment and

[180] Tarikh-i Firoz Shahi. Translated by Ishtiyaq Ahmad Zilli. Page 183

returned to the capital ignominiously, with his army battered and most of its equipments lost.

Besides, there was also the numerical factor that was involved: the Sultan was vastly outnumbered by the Mongol chief Targhi who, according to Ferishta, had brought with him as many as one lakh troopers.

Realising the gravity of the situation he was caught in, Alauddin urgently summoned his military commanders who were scattered throughout the country, but to little avail: "As the Mongol army was in control of roads and had made their camps there, no cavalryman or footman from the armies of Hindustan could enter the city," informs Barani. "All the fords of the Yamuna were [also] captured by the Mongols."[181]

A desperate situation now prevailed in Delhi — the capital of Hindustan laid virtually defenceless before the Mongols, and Alauddin, the proverbial master of siege craft, was besieged in his own den by the worst enemies that he had.

The Sultan, as a last ditch effort, set out with his meagre army and pitched his camp in Siri. But this seemingly confident gesture failed to make any impression whatsoever on the Mongols, who knew that Alauddin was in no position to take them on and therefore adopted so dominating a demeanour that bands of them fearlessly rode up even to Mehrauli, where they drank wine and made merry on the banks of the Hauz-i Sultani. And Sultan Alauddin was utterly powerless to punish their

[181] Tarikh-i Firoz Shahi. Translated by Ishtiyaq Ahmad Zilli. Page 183

pride: he dared not ride out into the open and confront them because, as Ferishta writes, "the King was in no condition to face the enemy on equal terms."[182]

Still, even when faced with certain destruction, Alauddin didn't give up his characteristics caution, and spared no effort to tighten the security of his camp to the extent that he could — he got a circular ditch dug around his encampment, which was further strengthened by a bulwark composed of the doors removed from the houses in Delhi, which were then strongly fastened together and erected deep into the ground. Not for a moment would the Sultan let his guards down. On each side of his camp, as many as 50 elephants, clad in full battle armour, stood guard round the clock. Foot soldiers stayed up all night and kept watch, lest a party of Mongols intrudes into the imperial encampment.

But for all his efforts, it was clear to the Sultan, as it was to everyone else, that his cause was a losing one, and that he hardly stood any chance against this lethal horde of Mongols that had come this time with a single-minded intention, to capture Delhi at all costs. Inside the camp, sure, Alauddin and his men were safe from the marauding Mongols. But such an arrangement couldn't last an eternity: for survival, the imperialists needed provisions, and all provisions were in the hands of the Mongols. Two full months passed in the twinkling of an eye, with the Mongols showing not the least sign of relenting — and now the fragile equilibrium, it appeared, would break down any time soon.

---

[182] Tarikh-i Ferishta. Translated by John Briggs. Page 354

When everyone was about to give up, just then something very extraordinary happened. The Mongols, all of a sudden, were seized with a great panic that rendered it impossible for them to continue any longer in India. As a result of which, Targhi, "in a bewildered condition returned to his own country. The fact that the city of Delhi remained safe seemed to the wise to be one of the wonders of the age," says Barani.[183]

The sudden retreat of the Mongols, when they were on the verge of a complete victory, appears as incredible today as it did seven hundred years before. Modern writers offer varying explanations for this phenomenon: from pointing out what they consider to be the inherent faults in Mongols' siege techniques, to claiming that Targhi and his men had by then looted so much that they no longer felt any need to carry on in India.

Medieval writers, however, had completely different explanations to offer. Sultan Alauddin Khilji, according to Ferishta, took recourse to "supernatural aid". The Sultan supplicated before Sheikh Nizamuddin Auliya to be delivered out of the grave predicament he was in. The Sheikh, Ferishta says, granted the Sultan his prayer, as a result of which, "one night, without any apparent cause, the Mongol army was seized with a panic, which occasioned their precipitate retreat to their own country."[184] Ziauddin Barani, the contemporary, says nothing different: he attributes Targhi's return to the "prayers of the indigent" and "the grace of God".

---

[183] Tarikh-i Firoz Shahi. Translated by Ishtiyaq Ahmad Zilli. Page 184

[184] Tarikh-i Ferishta. Translated by John Briggs. Pages 354-355

Whatever might have been the real reason behind the retreat of the Mongols, for the people of Delhi it was no less than deliverance from the jaws of destruction, because, as Barani aptly puts it, "had Targhi stayed for another month, a cry would have risen from Delhi and it would have been lost."[185] The fact that they somehow remained safe from the Mongol menace appeared to them as a wonder, "and the citizens of Delhi ascribed this to the favour of Sheikh Nizamuddin, may his tomb be holy; and counted it as one of his miracles."[186]

Targhi's invasion, at any rate, wasn't the Sultan's first brush with the Mongols: earlier in his reign, he had to contend with another, even bigger Mongol army led personally by a prince of royal blood. That contest, however, owing to other factors staying propitious, hadn't turned out to be as much serious. A son of Duwa, Qutlugh Khwaja by name, who had the blood of Chengiz Khan himself coursing through his veins, had come to measure swords with the Sultan of Delhi in the winter of 1299. Alauddin Khilji was quite prepared to take this threat on, not least because he had with him a commander as intrepid as Zafar Khan, whom the contemporary chroniclers were wont to style as the "Rustam of the Age".

Of all the Sultanate generals that were arrayed in the field of that battle, it was Zafar Khan alone who rushed headlong at the enemy, and so ruthless was his charge that

---

185 Tarikh-i Firoz Shahi. Translated by Ishtiyaq Ahmad Zilli. Page 184

186 Tabaqat-i Akbari. By Khwaja NIzamuddin Ahmad. Translated by B. DE. Page 174

it proved enough to drive back the entire Mongol army, that numbered, as per Barani, no less than 200,000. Though Zafar Khan ultimately fell fighting the Mongols gallantly, yet before his death he had done his job for his Sultan: he had not only routed the horde, but had also succeeded in mortally wounding their commander, the Mongol prince Qutlugh Khwaja.[187]

The Sultan perhaps took for granted the easy success that had come on Zafar Khan's account. After Qutlugh Khwaja's attack, he hadn't undertaken any step that could be called as drastic. But Targhi's invasion was different: it had left in the Sultan's mouth a bad taste, a fatal taste almost, and Alauddin now felt himself called upon to take such concrete steps as would secure his fledgling Sultanate from the successive Mongol onslaughts. Steps he would take indeed, giant, revolutionary steps, that were far, far ahead of their time, but to that we would come later on. Now it's about time we digress a little and take a detour to the origin of this feud between the Delhi Sultanate and the terrifying Mongols.

From time immemorial, a race had inhabited the wild region north of the Gobi desert in China. In the twelfth century, an exceptional man sprang up from that unassuming land. He was Chengiz Khan, the scourge of God, who transformed his kinsmen into such a formidable fighting force that only in the span of some decades, one

---

[187] According to the contemporary chronicler Abdul Malik Isami, before leaving India Qutlugh Khwaja is reported to have remarked: "*No one* can *remember such an army and such a king (as Alauddin Khilji) in Hindustan.*" (Reference: A Comprehensive History of India, Volume Five. People's Publishing House, 1970. Page 340)

after another, the richest and the strongest kingdoms and empires fell before them like a house of cards.

Thus, at the turn of the twelfth century, Asia and Europe alike were thrown into a convulsion by the Mongol invasion, more terrifying and devastating than anything known in recorded history. Such strong monarchies as the Khwarizm Sultanate in Central Asia and the Abbasid Caliphate in Baghdad were violently stamped out. The last of the Khwarazm Shahs was hounded out from one corner of the world to another, till the hapless royal breathed his last in an obscure, mountaineous hideout. The Abbasid Caliph, that titular head of the entire Muslim world, fared even worse — after a gory sack of his capital, Baghdad, that was renowned as a centre of high culture, the Caliph was sealed up in a sack and then literally kicked to death. For good reason, a modern Britsih scholar opined that no invasion in history could even come close to that of the Mongols as far as the sheer scale of devastation is concerned.[188]

Even as the whole of Asia submitted before the Mongol might, by a combination of good fortune and prudent policy, the Turkish Sultanate based in Delhi somehow managed to remain out of the pale of Mongol domination. Under Iltutmish, when the Great Khan himself was alive, the policy was one of abject appeasement. The fugitive Khwarizimi prince was straightaway refused an asylum by Iltutmish, and that Sultan even preferred maintaining a

[188] A History of Persia, by Brigadier General Sir Percy Sykes. Volume II. Macmillan and Co. Limited. London, 1921. Page 70

low profile on the western marches of his Sultanate, at least as long as Chengiz Khan was alive.

History suggests it is easier to carve out a great empire than to preserve it, and the fate of Chenghiz Khan's house proved no exception to this rule. Sure, the conquests that Chengiz had initiated were definitely expanded by his sons and grandsons, but none of them were possessed of the same savage genius which Chengiz had been endowed with. Thus, at least four decades after, with the death of Mangu Khan, the great age of Mongol conquest came to its end, and the vast empire of the Great Khans came to be fractured into four warring factions: the Ikhanate in Persia, the Chaghtai Khanate in Central Asia, the Yuan Dynasty in China, and the Golden Horde in Russia.

Thus, under Sultan Balban, we find the Delhi Sultanate adopting a more belligerent stance vis-a-vis the Mongols. Still, there wasn't much of a latitude on offer: when the Khanates united, which they did at times, the Mongols proved as much formidable as they once had been under that gifted general, Chengiz. Why, Sultan Balban's eldest and favourite son himself was killed in an action against what was only a raiding detachment of the Mongols.

Therefore, when Sultan Alauddin Khilji came to the throne of Delhi, the Mongol threat was definitely around — and it was real, palpable and very much formidable. It is against this backdrop that Sultan Alauddin rose up as a hero, who attained more success against Mongol arms than any Muslim ruler — or perhaps any other ruler, for that matter — ever did.

At any rate, between the Mongols and the Sultans of Delhi, it was a life-and-death contest. Not surprisingly therefore, acrimony reached incredible heights. More so in Delhi, where a combination of racial, religious and political antagonism created such a bitterness towards the Mongols as didn't stay limited only to the military elites, but even got rubbed off on the city's literati. Thus, the poet Amir Khusrau, who attended the courts of several Sultans of Delhi, hardly had a good word to say about the Mongols.[189] The Mongols' eyes, Khusrau says, "were so narrow and piercing that they might have bored a hole in a brazen vessel. Their stink was more horrible than their colour. Their faces were set on their bodies as if they had no neck. Their cheeks resembled soft leathern bottles, full of wrinkles and knots ... Their nostrils resembled rotten graves, and from them the hair descended as far as the lips ... Their chests, of a colour half black, half white, were so covered with lice, that they looked like sesame growing on a bad soil."[190]

Still, it is a singularly interesting fact that such a king as Alauddin Khilji who paid the Mongols back in their own

---

[189] The acrimony towards Mongols was almost universal among Delhi's men of learning. Barani, thus, hardly ever talked about the Mongols without cursing them. As to Amir Khsurau, his hatred was born out of an incident that played out quite early in his life. He was held to ransom by a Mongol commander, and made to undergo great privations. About his abductor, Khusrau wrote: "*He sat on his horse like a leopard on a hill. His open mouth smelt like an armpit, and whiskers fell from his chin like pubic hair.*" (Source: *Wast al-Hayat*, quoted in Abdul Qadir Badayuni's *Muntakhab ut Tawarikh*)

[190] The History of India as told by its own historians. The Muhammadan Period. By Sir H.M. Elliot. Volume III. London, 1871. Pages 528-529

coin and managed to inspire terror in those that had terrified the whole world, had an antecedent that was steeped in the Mongol milieu. Alauddin's grandfather, according to the **Tarikh-i Mubarak Shahi**, was a certain Yughrush.[191] And Minhaj Siraj, the court chronicler of the Mamluk Sultans of Delhi, tells that the son of Yughrush — who was, in all probability, Jalaluddin Khilji himself — visited Delhi with a Mongol embassy in 1260.[192] Then again, an Ilkhanid source says that prior to his service under the Sultans of Delhi, Jalaluddin Khilji had been in charge of Mongol territories west of the river Indus.[193] Thus, when the Khilji Sultan took the Mongols on, it was a case of diamond cutting diamond — Alauddin, of all people, had had the training to fight fire with fire.

Be that as it may, after the passing of the storm that was Targhi, Alauddin at once set out to bring about a series of drastic steps which dramatically enhanced his military strength in a short time. Already, after being beset by several rebellions breaking out simultaneously in the course of his Ranthambore campaign, the Sultan had introduced a number of well-thought-out and far-reaching measures that had strengthened his hold over the economic apparatus of his empire. And now, such

---

[191] Tarikh-i Mubarak Shahi. By Yahya bin Ahmad Sirhindi. Translated by K.K. Basu. Baroda, Oriental Institute. 1932. Page 57. The text has *Baghrash*, which must be a corruption for *Yughrush*, the name found in Minhaj Siraj's work.

[192] Tabaqat-i Nasiri. By Minhaj Siraj. Quoted in "The Ignored Elites", by Sunil Kumar. Expanding Frontiers in South Asian and World History. Cambridge University Press.

[193] Quoted in The Delhi Sultanate. By Peter Jackson. Cambridge University Press. Page 80

measures were brought into effect which completely revamped his fighting force and put it on an equal footing with the strongest armies in the world.

Old forts were renovated, and new ones put up; every fort was placed under a general of note and stocked with the most advanced weapons; and most importantly, the army was enormously increased. This expansion in the size of army brought out the genius in the Sultan: he reduced the pay of his troops, and at the same time brought down the prices of essential commodities in the market, so as to ensure that his soldiers didn't have to suffer from pecuniary privations. And the enormity of his army was matched by its exceptional efficiency, and not least responsible in it was the rigorous tests that an applicant had to pass through before getting enrolled as an imperial trooper. Ibn Battuta, visiting India during the reign of Muhammad bin Tughluq, observed the strictness that was involved in the recruitment process, and there is no reason to believe that things were even one bit easier in Alauddin's time.[194] Also, lest he got cheated by his

---

[194] *"They had a number of bows there,"* writes Ibn Battuta, *"and when anyone comes desiring to be enrolled in the army as an archer he is given one of the bows to draw. They differ in stiffness and his pay is graduated according to the strength he shows in drawing them. For anyone desiring to be enrolled as a trooper there is a target set up; he puts his horse into a run and tries to hit it with a lance. There is a ring there too , suspended to a low wall; the candidate puts his horse into a run until he comes level with the ring, and if he lifts it off with a lance he is accounted among them a good horse-man. For those wishing to be enrolled as mounted archers, there is a ball placed on the ground; each man gallops towards it and shoots at it, and his pay is proportioned to his accuracy in hitting it."* (Rehla of Ibn Battuta , Translated by H.A.R. Gibb, Pages 605-606)

troopers, the Sultan introduced the system of branding their horses, one of those innovative measures of Alauddin Khilji that would outlive their inventor by many a century.

Add to all such measures the Sultan's extreme strictness. Thus, if one of his soldiers failed to turn up for the muster, his three years' salary was exacted from him, failing to pay which would take the soldier in question to prison, where he would continue to stay as long as the sum demanded of him had not been arranged. Also, dereliction of duty amounted to the termination of the concerned troop's career: there was no way he would be taken back in the army, no matter how much he pleaded or no matter who pleaded on his behalf. It was easy to get into Sultan Alauddin's bad books; it was impossible to get out of it.

And through such measures, the Sultan succeeded in a short while to amass a formidable force that was made up of almost half a million men. It was quite probably the largest and the strongest force in Asia at that point.[195]

Not that winds of these developments didn't reach the ears of the Mongols in Central Asia, but India was too rich a pasture for the Mongol mounts to keep away for too long. Thus, once again, in 1305, the Mongols entered India.

---

[195] The pride of place in Alauddin's army was occupied by the archers. Such, indeed, had always been the case under the successive Sultans of Delhi. Thus, a near-contemporary work by one *Fakhr-i Mudabbir* listed more than half-a-dozen varieties of bows and almost as many types of arrows. The bows made from the horns of mountain goats were considered the best, while the arrows made of reed were regarded the finest.

This time, the expedition was led by Ali Beg, another descendent of Chengiz Khan, who had with him his lieutenants Targhi and Tartaq, besides 50,000 troopers under his command. This time they had come not to conquer, but only to loot and plunder. Perhaps, their narrow failure to capture Delhi last time had kindled in their heart a strong desire for revenge, and they therefore swept down the Indian plains with a firm resolve to carry fire and sword everywhere they would go.

The Mongols crossed the Indus and the Jhelum quickly, took the route north of Lahore, and skirting the Himalayan foothills, made straight for the Doab — that fertile tongue of land between the Ganga and the Yamuna — all the while burning, raping and killing the inhabitants. On the way, Targhi, who was on his third campaign in India, was taken down by an arrow shot by an anonymous native defender. Both nothing daunted Ali Beg and Tartaq — they continued their forward march with the same thrust with which they had set out from their mountainous home. "They (the Mongols) had fifty thousand trained and ferocious horsemen," reports Amir Khusrau, "[and] the hills trembled at their tread."[196] A calamity came down upon the masses — "People fled from their burning houses, and with their heads and feet on fire, threw themselves into rivers and torrents."[197]

At first, the novel approach of the Mongol marauders perplexed Alauddin: why did they bypass Delhi, which he

[196] Khazain ul Futuh. Translated by Muhammad Habib. Page 26

[197] Khazain ul Futuh. Translated by Muhammad Habib. Page 26

had kept so strongly guarded this time, he wondered. But once the Sultan learnt of the Mongols' real intention, he lost no time in swinging into action. A formidable army was made ready, and then despatched to measure swords with the Mongols under a distinguished general of the Delhi Sultanate.

Now, there is a lot of ambiguity however as to who this general actually was. Abdul Qadir Badayuni, writing more than two hundred years after the actual event, claimed that it was Malik Kafur who was at the helm of the Delhi army. Many modern writers, following suit, assert that this encounter with the Mongols was in fact the first of Malik Kafur's military expeditions. But the contemporary chroniclers, who actually witnessed the unfolding of this event before their eyes, have different things to say. Both Ziauddin Barani and Amir Khusrau make it absolutely clear that it was not Malik Kafur, but another Malik who held the office of Akhur Bak **(master of horses)**, who actually took the field against the Mongols. But as to the name of that particular general, the two sources differ with each other: while Barani calls him Malik Atabak, Khusrau names him Malik Naik. Professor Muhammad Habib, basing himself on Amir Khusrau's work, goes as far as to claim that the commander who led the soldiers of the Sultanate against the Mongols was actually a Hindu by faith.

Be that as it may, the debate regarding the general's identity need not deter us any further, because no matter who he was, he received explicit orders from his master, the Sultan, "to slaughter without stint".[198]

On Thursday, the 30th of December, 1305, the rival armies met near Amroha — "[And] The Almighty granted victory to the army of Islam."[199] So vigorously were the Mongols attacked that "in the battlefield heaps and piles were formed of the slain."[200] Amir Khusrau, being the literary genius that he was, offers a picturesque description of this contest: "The field of battle, strewn with elephant-bodies Mongols, looked like a chess board ... Ali Beg and Tartaq, the two kings of the chess board, were checkmated by their large-boned enemy, the Malik Akhur Beg, who wished to send them to the Emperor, so that he may either spare their lives or else cast them under the feet of elephants."[201]

After the battle was over, "with a rope around their necks, along with many other Mongol prisoners, Ali Beg and Tartaq were brought to the presence of Sultan Alauddin."[202] Along with the prisoners, as many as 20,000 horses that had been captured from the Mongols were also brought to Delhi.

---

[198] Khazain ul Futuh. Translated by Muhammad Habib. Page 26

[199] Tarikh-i Firoz Shahi. Translated by Ishtiyaq Ahmad Zilli. Page 196

[200] ibid

[201] Khazain ul Futuh. Translated by Muhammad Habib. Pages 27-28

[202] Tarikh-i Firoz Shahi. Translated by Ishtiyaq Ahmad Zilli. Page 196

A public trial of the prisoners was decided on. And to that end, magnificent arrangements were made.

The proceedings were simply spectacular. All the way from the imperial court to the suburbs of the capital, the Sultan's soldiers, armed and in full battle gear, were drawn up on two rows. A huge crowd had assembled to witness the fate that would be meted out to the Mongol prisoners. So many people had assembled that, according to Barani, one small cup of water cost as much as half a tanka — to give an idea as to how great was this rise in price, it is worthwhile to mention that at that point a beautiful slave girl could be had in the markets of Delhi for around 20 tankas.

Sultan Alauddin Khilji had decided to make this whole affair public very deliberately: he wanted to give out a message that would not fade away before it reached Central Asia, to the effect that invading India meant death. Plain and simple.

At the fixed hour, the Sultan appeared before the public, ascended the platform and took his seat on his magnificent throne. The Mongol prisoners were then brought before him — "the two adventurers (Ali Beg and Tartaq), who had claimed equality (with the Sultan), cast their eyeballs like dice on the carpet of submission," writes Amir Khusrau.[203] Court officials then came forward and laid

[203] Khazain ul Futuh. Translated by Muhammad Habib. Page 28

out before the Sultan all the stuffs that had been captured from the enemies on the field of battle.

Now came the time for the verdict to be pronounced. First things first, Alauddin might have thought as he proceeded to punish Ali Beg and Tartaq before others. These two Mongol chiefs, according to Ferishta, were ordered to be thrown under the feet of raging elephants.[204] This was accordingly done. Next came the turn of the other prisoners, the rank and file in the Mongol army. Their number was not insignificant, but imperial decree demanded all of them to be killed at once, without allowing for any exception whatsoever.

Alauddin's men straightaway swung into action to carry out their master's command. Some were beheaded, some were impaled, while others were done away with by elephants — all of these happened together, simultaneously and really fast. The Sultan wanted to behold everything with his own eyes — and of all people, the Sultan couldn't be left waiting.

---

[204] Of this event, Amir Khusrau has a completely different version to offer. He says that both Ali Beg and Tartaq were pardoned by Sultan Alauddin Khilji, and while one of the two Mongols died soon after, the other went on to live for a fairly long period of time. Though he was a contemporary, the account furnished by Khusrau appears to be less plausible than the one provided by Ferishta. That, however, doesn't mean that Khusrau's version carries absolutely no credibility: why, didn't Alauddin Khilji have that knack of coming up with out-of-the-box ideas?

By the time the killing spree ended, some 9000 people had been killed, "and a stream of blood was made to flow from those who were punished."[205]

In spite of so awful a carnage, the wealth of India turned out to be too strong an allure for the Mongols to overcome, and they made yet another attempt to somehow make their way through the Sultan's watertight security system. Also, there was the added motive to extract revenge of the death of Ali Beg and Tartaq. Thus, a fresh Mongol army was made ready to invade India: it consisted of three separate contingents, led by Kabak, Iqbalmanda, and Taibu.

Kabak, who was commanding the bulk of the Mongol soldiers, took a northern route after crossing the Indus. On the other hand, Iqbalmanda and Taibu, with their contingents, took a southern detour and managed to reach as far as Nagore in Rajasthan. This way, the Mongol marauders succeeded in fanning themselves out. The Mongols practically poured into India like a terrible deluge — this was, at any rate, their second invasion of India in as many years, and they spared absolutely no effort to crown their attempt with success.

Kabak, in spite of the huge army he was heading, could not make any substantial headway in Punjab, not least because the province was being defended like a rock by Ghazi Malik (the future Ghiyasuddin Tughluq).

---

[205] Tarikh-i Firoz Shahi. Translated by Ishtiyaq Ahmad Zilli. Page 196

Meanwhile, "messengers as fast as the wind" brought news of the Mongol menace before the Sultan, whose response, as always, was propt and immediate.[206] Alauddin Khilji nominated Malik Kafur to lead the expedition against the Mongols, "[and] he ordered the Muslim army to proceed against them; but the news was to be kept a secret, lest in fear of the approaching sandal (the Delhi army), the horrid stench (the Mongols) should fly back to the fragrant willows of Khurasan."[207]

On the banks of the river Ravi, the Khiljis clashed with the Mongols. So violently did Malik Kafur fall on his opponents that the Mongol ranks broke up in the very first clash itself. Thousands of Mongols perished on the field of battle, and their leader, Kabak, was chained up and despatched to Delhi, where Sultan Alauddin had him promptly trampled to death under the feet of an elephant without any fanfare whatsoever.

Meanwhile, Iqabalmanda and Taibu started losing heart after Kabak's defeat. They retreated hurriedly from Rajasthan, intending to cross the Indus and return home with whatever booty they had till then managed to capture. But destiny, and Sultan Alauddin Khilji, had other plans!

Ghazi Malik, the governor of Punjab, was waiting for just such an oppurtunity. At first, the soldiers of Ghazi Malik captured the fords of the river Indus so that the fleet-footed Mongols could not escape their swords. "As was

---

206 Khazain ul Futuh. Translated by Muhammad Habib. Page 29

207 ibid

destined, the Mongols and their horses reached the riverbank, parched and worn out. The army of Islam that lay there waiting for them got complete control of them."[208]

It was now left to Ghazi Malik to mop things up in his own style — "[Ghazi Malik] in the meantime, having taken up a position in the ambuscade, on the banks of the Indus awaited the return of the Mongols to their country, and falling suddenly upon them, defeated with great slaughter," writes Ferishta.[209]

All the Mongols, along with their women and children who had accompanied their menfolk to India, fell into the hands of the Sultanate soldiers. "The army of Islam achieved a spectacular victory (over the Mongols) ... Their children and women were brought to Delhi and were sold in the slave market of Delhi like maids and slave boys of Hindustan," reports Barani.[210]

Finally, after Malik Kafur and Ghazi Malik had done playing their parts, the Mongol prisoners, who had not been killed till then, were despatched to Delhi in fetters. Straightaway an order was issued by Sultan Alauddin to have all of them trampled under the feet of elephants. But the Mongols were too many in number, and there simply wasn't available enough elephants to do away with so many people all at once. So the Sultan ordered the left out ones to be beheaded, and the Sultan's servants complied.

---

[208] Tarikh-i Firoz Shahi. Translated by Ishtiyaq Ahmad Zilli. Page 196

[209] Tarikh-i Ferishta. Translated By John Briggs. Page 364

[210] Tarikh-i Firoz Shahi. Translated by Ishtiyaq Ahmad Zilli. Page 197

"From their severed heads a tower was erected at the Badaun Gate, which the people see even today, and remember Sultan Alauddin," claimed Ziauddin Barani, almost fifty years after the event.[211]

Fifty years might come across as a big deal, but it pales into insignificance when we take into consideration the account of Ferishta, who was putting pen to paper almost three centuries after the demise of Sultan Alauddin: "... a pillar was raised before the Badaun Gate, formed of their skulls; and I am informed that a portion of it is to be seen at this day."[212]

The narrative can't be completed without mentioning Amir Khusrau, an eyewitness to the whole event, who writes — "Their (the Mongols') wrteched heads were cut off with shining swords, and a bastion, so high that it touched the head of the sky, was formed of them."[213]

This was the last major Mongol incursion into India — "Thereafter, till the end of the rule of Sultan Qutbuddin Khilji, the Mongols did not even bring the name of Hindustan on their tongues," writes Barani.[214] The Mongol race, taken as a whole, had not received anywhere in the world so rough a treatment as they received at the hands of Sultan Alauddin Khilji. "Apprehension from the Mongols was fully removed from Delhi and the

---

[211] Tarikh-i Firoz Shahi. Translated by Ishtiyaq Ahmad Zilli. Page 197

[212] Tarikh-i Ferishta. By Muhammad Qasim Ferishta. Translated by John Briggs. Page 364

[213] Khazain ul Futuh. Translated by Muhammad Habib. Page 32

[214] Tarikh-i Firoz Shahi. Translated by Ishtiyaq Ahmad Zilli. Page 197

dominions of Delhi and complete peace was established so much that the people of the territories which lay on the way of the Mongol incursions got busy in cultivating activities with absolute peace of mind."[215]

For so long, Delhi had had to remain on the backfoot against the Mongols. But now under Sultan Alauddin Khilji, the tide was reversed. Far from looting and pillaging Indian territories at will, the Mongols themselves were now hardpressed to defend themselves from the forces of the Delhi Sultanate. Ghazi Malik, that incredibly valiant warden of the marches, not only effectively guarded the north-western frontier of India but also made it a policy to launch annual raids into the territories of the Mongols. As a result, "[Ghazi Malik] came to be greatly acclaimed in Khorasan and Hindustan. Till the end of the reign of [Sultan] Qutbuddin, he remained entrenched ... in the iqtas of Depalpur and Lahore where he emerged as the main bulwark against the Mongols."[216]

Indeed, it became an established habit of Ghazi Malik to set out with his army from Depalpur every winter, and plunder the territories of "Kabul, Ghazni, Qandahar, and Garmsir" and extort a heavy contribution from the locals there.[217]

In fact, Alauddin's dominance over the Mongols had reached such a pitch that even the Mongol ambassadors didn't feel safe from his fury. Thus, when in 1311, the

---

[215] Tarikh-i Firoz Shahi. Translated by Ishtiyaq Ahmad Zilli. Page 197

[216] ibid

[217] Tarikh-i Ferishta. Translated by John Briggs. Page 364

ambassadors of the Ilkhan of Persia tried to talk the Sultan of Delhi into an alliance with their suzerain against the Chaghtay Khanate, and to that end politely asked for the hand of a Khilji princess for the Ilkhan Uljaytu, Alauddin Khilji for one was not at all amused. Not only was he strong enough to rebuff any offer of alliance, but the matrimonial request also did not go down well with him. So what if the suitor happened to be the Mongol Khan of Persia himself, Sultan Alauddin Khilji still didn't consider him an equal. The Sultan's wrath was aroused, and no prizes for guessing what happended next: the Mongol ambassadors, all eighteen of them, were thrown at the feet of murderous elephants, which then did away with them in no time.

The Mongol Khan of Persia was powerless to retaliate. His court historian merely whined about how Sultan Alauddin Khilji had tarnished his reputation by this act: at any rate, that was about as far as the Mongols could dare to go against the Sultan of Delhi.

What is even more interesting is that the contemporary chroniclers of Delhi Sultanate — Ziauddin Barani and Amir Khusrau — simply didn't bother to mention this event at all. To them, massacre of Mongols was hardly out of the ordinary: why, hadn't they seen before the severed heads of several thousand Mongols being piled up near the Badaun Gate in Delhi?[218]

---

[218] Reference: Abdullah Wassaf's Tarikh-i Wassaf. From THE HISTORY OF INDIA AS TOLD BY ITS OWN HISTORIANS, THE MUHAMMMADEN PERIOD. Volume III. By Sir H.M. ELLIOT. London, 1871. Pages 51-52.

Needless to say, Alauddin's success against the Mongols was extraordinary. No other Sultan of Delhi could even come close to achieving what he accomplished against the Mongols. Not exaggerating, but perhaps no other king in Asia had manhandled the descendents of Chengiz Khan, that terrible scourge of God, the way Alauddin did. Such a stupefying achievement, however, didn't happen all of a sudden. It was the product of a serious of extremely well thought out measures that Sultan Alauddin Khilji implemented over a period of time, and it is to those of his sagacious policies, which transformed the Delhi Sultanate into such a formidable polity, that we shall now turn to.

Radical Reformer

> *Every one, who has a brain capable of thinking, will realize that the status of the good administrator (jahandar) is higher than the conqueror (jahangir).*
>
> *— Khazain ul Futuh, by Amir Khusrau.*

Long before the gruesome slaughter of Ali Beg, Tartaq and the likes — actually even before that fateful encounter with Targhi and his men in 1303 — Sultan Alauddin had been deeply invested in devising permanent solutions to the several problems that he felt were gnawing at the very roots of his Sultanate. The campaign in Ranthambore had been an eye-opener, for it was in the course of that campaign that as many as four rebellions broke out against the Sultan, one of which very nearly claimed his very life. Although he ultimately managed to triumph over the crisis, but that critical period didn't fail to make a deep impression on his mind: quite a few things, he felt, were amiss in his Sultanate, and without correcting them his rule would never know stability.

Sultan Alauddin Khilji was ruthless, but not thoughtless. He was aware of his limitations, and in spite of being a self-willed man, never shied away from seeking help when he felt it was necessary. Thus, when he realised that the knotty task of seeking solutions to the very many problems that were plaguing him and his Sultanate required the brains of many a competent man, he at once set about holding elaborate discussions with those of his counsellors as were trusted by him the most.

After several days and nights of deliberation, the Sultan and his advisers arrived at a certain understanding. There were certain primary factors, they felt, which were at the root of the rebellions that were wont to break out in the Sultanate.

First, the Sultan's neglect of public affairs and his lack of attention towards the activities of his subjects. Second, convivial wine parties held by nobles where friendships were forged and conspiracies against the Sultan hatched. Third, the intimacy existing among the nobles of the Delhi Sultanate, "so that if any accident befalls one of them, a hundred others on account of their connection, relationship, and attachment to him, become his confederates."[219] Fourth, the abundance of wealth among the people that stoked in their minds ideas of sedition. "If people did not have money," Barani explains the Sultan's view, "everybody would be busy in some profession or work and nobody would remember rebellion and sedition."[220]

After thus gaining a clear picture of the several problems at hand, Sultan Alauddin Khilji set about devising thorough solutions to remedy the situation. And these

---

[219] The Reign of Alauddin Khilji. Translated from Ziauddin Barani's Tarikh-i Firoz Shahi. By A.R. Fuller and A. Khallaque. Page 69

[220] Tarikh-i Firoz Shahi. Translated by Ishtiyaq Ahmad Zilli. Page 171

solutions, much like everything else that the Sultan did, were daringly innovative and immensely effective.

His first measure was to apply himself heart and soul into the administrative affairs of the Delhi Sultanate. "He first applied himself to a strict enquiry into the administration of justice, to redress grievances," informs Ferishta, and so sincere were the efforts of the Sultan, "that robbery and theft, formerly so common, were not heard of in the land. The traveller slept secure on the highway, and the merchants carried his commodities in safety from the sea of Bengal to the mountains of Kabul, and from Telangana to Kashmir."[221]

To remain acquainted of all that went on in his vast empire, the Sultan set up an elaborate intelligence network. So effective was this intelligence machinery that "the Maliks in the Hazar Sutun (the palace of thousand pillars) could no longer say a single word openly, and if they had to say anything, they made use of gestures."[222] Worse, the fear of the Sultan's spies even intruded into their domestic sphere, so that even in their homes the great nobles of the Delhi Sultanate could no longer dare to utter anything that could potentially displease their Sultan.

The Sultan's second measure was aimed to prohibit the manufacture, sell and consumption of wine. "Great exertions were made to carry out the prohibition of the

[221] Tarikh-i Ferishta. Translated by John Briggs. Page 345

[222] The Reign of Alauddin Khilji. Translated from Ziauddin Barani's Tarikh-i Firoz Shahi. By A.R. Fuller and A. Khallaque. Page 72

sale of wine," tells Barani, "and special wells were constructed to serve as prisons."[223]

The Sultan himself set a precedent: he entirely gave up drinking wine and holding wine parties. All the china and glass vessels in the imperial palace were smashed, and jars and bottles of wine were taken out from the royal cellars and then emptied before the Badaun Gate. "Due to the great quantity of wine that was spilled the mud appeared like it would in the rainy season."[224] Also, Alauddin willingly let go of "very great amounts of revenue" that would otherwise have made its way to his treasury as the tax on production and selling of wine.[225]

To enforce prohibition, Alauddin ordered his officers "to mount elephants and go to the various gates of the city, localities, bazars, streets and inns located outside the city, and proclaim that nobody should consume wine, sell it or go near it."[226]

Those who loved their life more gave in to the Sultan's command, but those who loved their drink more resisted the Sultan. Stoutly. And it was precisely against them that the Second Alexander had to fight the most tiring and least successful battle of his life. Neither side was willing to give up. The Sultan, in his characteristically ruthless manner, wanted his order to be followed in letter and

---

[223] The Reign of Alauddin Khilji. Translated from Ziauddin Barani's Tarikh-i Firoz Shahi. By A.R. Fuller and A. Khallaque. Page 72

[224] Tarikh-i Firoz Shahi. Translated by Ishtiyaq Ahmad Zilli. Page 173

[225] ibid. Page 172

[226] ibid. Page 173

spirit. The drunkards, on the other hand, were also equally determined to have their drink, even if that meant grappling with death itself. And thus began a terrible tug-of-war: neither would the Sultan relent, nor would the addicts budge.

Every day the imperial officers would apprehend hundreds of men, accused of selling or consuming alcohol, and throw them into the specially constructed well-cum-prisons. "Due to the narrowness and hardship of the wells," tells Barani, "many died therein, and those who were taken out of it after some time were brought out half-dead. It took them long time to recover and regain strength."[227]

But, prohibition still couldn't be enforced in entirety. Even after such brutal punishments, the drinkers could not be brought to heel. They kept coming up with ingenious ways to remain out of harm's way — leather bags would be filled with wine, placed under piles of wood and grass, and then "with much trick, deceit and fraud brought in the city (of Delhi)."[228]

The Sultan finally grew exasperated and realised the futility of this ongoing tussle — he relented, even if not fully, but to a considerable extent nonetheless. Then, "Sultan Alauddin issued orders that if anybody were to secretly distil wine in his own house, or closes the house and drinks the wine and does not sell it or organise a party

---

[227] Tarikh-i Firoz Shahi. Translated by Ishtiyaq Ahmad Zilli. Page 173

[228] ibid

[then] the **munhis** (spies) should not harass him, nor enter his house and take him in custody."[229]

Thus took shape the second of Sultan Alauddin Khilji's measures, though not as successful as he would have liked it to be, but still quite effective to say the least.

Later in his life, when talking about the obstinacy of the drunkards, the Sultan would ruefully remark: "Nobody has had enough with God's creatures, how can I?"[230]

Third, Alauddin Khilji at one stroke virtually severed all the ties that existed among his nobles. The Sultan, says Barani, "issued orders that maliks, amirs, dignitaries, notables and the people connected with the court should not visit each others' houses, should not hold banquets and organize entertainments and parties. Moreover, they were not to enter into matrimonial alliances without bringing it to the imperial notice and obtaining necessary permission. They were also not to allow people to visit their houses."[231]

So rigorously was this order enforced that, continues the same author, "no stranger could have access to the house of the **maliks** and the **amirs**. Banquets and feasts in which many people used to assemble were totally eliminated ... They (the nobles) did not allow anyone known for rebelliousness, infamy and sedition to come near them. When they went to court, they did not dare huddle together, talk to and hear from each other, sit knee to knee

---

[229] Tarikh-i Firoz Shahi. Translated by Ishtiyaq Ahmad Zilli. Page 173

[230] ibid. Page 181

[231] ibid. Page 174

with each other and share their problems and anxieties with each other."[232]

Fourth, the Sultan employed the Morton's fork to fleece the people — not the entire population of course, but only such social groups as were suspected of contumacy.[233] Ziayuddin Barani tells us that of all the causes of rebellion, Alauddin Khilji gave the greatest consideration to the confiscation of wealth. "He ordered that wherever there was a village held by any one in **milk** (state grant), **inam** (revenue grant free from service) or **waqf** (charitable endowment) should be resumed in the khalsa (crown land) with one stroke of the pen and money should be extracted from the rich by means of coercion and those in possession of money should not be spared. With the passage of time no money was left except in the houses of **maliks, amirs, officials, Multanis** (Hindu merchants) and **sahas** (Hindu bankers) and that too in a measured way."[234]

The Sultan's aim was to deprive the people of the material means and the leisure to contemplate rebellion, and he

---

[232] Tarikh-i Firoz Shahi. Translated by Ishtiyaq Ahmad Zilli. Page 174

[233] Barani's language, according to Banarsi Prasad Saksena, should not lead us to believe that every man of wealth was stripped of his riches and reduced to destitution. Alauddin Khilji didn't head a state that was geared towards looting its own citizens. Besides, high taxation coupled with lack of money in the hands of people would have caused a phenomenal inflation, and this realisation could not have been lost on a man like Alauddin who was so particular about prices.

[234] Tarikh-i Firoz Shahi. Translated by Ishtiyaq Ahmad Zilli. Page 172

was entirely successful in attaining his objective. "The entire population got busy earning a livelihood," confirms Barani, "such that even the thought of rebellion did not arise to anyone."[235]

Along with these measures, Alauddin also introduced certain other administrative reforms, that he thought were imperative for the effective implementation of his policies and the smooth functioning of his government. He paid special attention to the lower echelons of the administrative hierarchy, particularly to those that were working at the rural level, for these men, he knew, formed the bedrock of the entire administrative framework, and any weakness in them would inevitably have an adverse impact on the efficient running of the Sultanate itself. Throughout the entire period of the rule of the Delhi Sultans, that covered a period greater than three centuries, nearly all the subordinate government officers had been Hindus, and among them the conduct of the hereditary revenue collectors irked the Sultan much, for many of them were in the habit of browbeating the humble peasants and cheating the central government of its dues.

It was reported that this class of hereditary revenue collectors (called variously as **khuts** and **muqaddams** in our sources) lived very affluently — they rode fine horses, dressed handsomely, carried weapons, went hunting and

[235]Tarikh-i Firoz Shahi. Translated by Ishtiyaq Ahmad Zilli. Page 172

organized parties — but when orders came from the central government, they would flout it nonchalantly.[236]

If his command was not obeyed right under his nose, Alauddin contemplated, then his dreams of world conquest really amounted to nothing. What was needed was strict action to bring this truculent group to heel, Alauddin realised, and he set about curbing the powers of the hereditary tax collectors by depriving them of all their privileges and withdrawing all the concessions and perquisites that they had hitherto enjoyed.

In one fell swoop the Sultan levelled the rural society: in the eyes of the central government, the humble peasant was now at the same level with the landlords, headmen and the tax collectors. It was now no longer possible for the village elites to exploit the humble peasants: the Sultan, says Barani, had made sure that "the burden of the strong should not fall on the weak."[237]

After he was done dealing with the village elites, the Sultan then fixed the land revenue demand at 50% of the

---

[236] In Arabic *muqaddam* means the principal man of the village or the first person. *Chaudhury* was a Hindi word and Barani has made it equivalent to khut and muqaddam. The word *khut* was not a Hindi word and had come perhaps from the Persian word *khat*. The collection of the revenue of the village was done by the khut. (Source: The Sultanate of Delhi (1206-1526): Polity, Economy, Society and Culture. By Aniruddha Ray. Manohar, 2019. Page 112)

[237] Tarikh-i Firoz Shahi. Translated by Ishtiyaq Ahmad Zilli. Page 174

produce of the land.[238] Village headman or an ordinary farmer, the Sultan would no longer allow any distinction, and anyone who tilled a piece of land had to pay at the same rate to the central exchequer. Concessions were granted to none — "There was to be one rule for both the weak and the strong regarding the payment of the revenue," informs Barani.[239]

Neither was it any longer possible for the rural influentials to let loose their cattle to graze on the lands of their weaker neighbours. Rich or poor, every household that domesticated cattle, now had its pasture demarcated by the government. And while the poorer lot was exempted from taxation, the moneyed elements that kept ruminants by the dozen, had to shell out a substantial sum as tax to the central exchequer.

Around the same time, the Sultan also decided to firmly weed out the problem of corruption that had indeed become endemic in the Delhi Sultanate. To that end, he adopted a two-pronged approach. On one hand, he maintained strict supervision over the officers and collectors, and didn't hesitate one bit to inflict the most severe punishment on the corrupt, no matter how high his rank was. On the other hand, the Sultan also ensured that there remained no longer any financial compulsion on his

---

[238] The land under cultivation was first measured. Then the yield was estimated per unit of area (*biswa*, or one-twentieth of a *bigha*), and finally by multiplying the area by the yield was the total produce worked out.

[239] Tarikh-i Firoz Shahi. Translated by Ishtiyaq Ahmad Zilli. Page 174

men to indulge in corruption: the salaries of his officials were increased significantly, so that they could live a decent and comfortable life.

So ruthless was the Sultan in the implementation of his policy that before long "submission reached such an extent that one foot soldier... would put a rope round the neck of twenty **khuts, muqaddams** and **chaudharis** and would beat them up with blows and sticks for the realisation of revenue ... Due to destitution, the wives of the **khuts** and **muqaddams** came and worked in the houses of the Muslims and received wages."[240]

And after taking up jobs in the aristocratic households, if by chance some of them found it extraordinarily difficult to adapt to the new setting, and wanted to leave their job, then even that provision was made scarce on the Sultan's order. "Neither were they permitted to resign their employments, till they found others as capable as themselves to execute their duties," Ferishta informs us.[241]

But for all its rigours, the policy's benefits were undeniable, and they showed up soon. "It was no more possible that anyone could misappropriate [even] a single tanka or take it as a bribe from Hindus or Muslims," Barani tells us.[242] Some imperial officers, no doubt, continued with their dishonest dealings, but the Sultan inflicted such savage punishments on them as inspired

---

240 Tarikh-i Firoz Shahi. Translated by Ishtiyaq Ahmad Zilli. Page 175

241 Tarikh-i Ferishta. Translated by John Briggs. Page 347

242 Tarikh-i Firoz Shahi. Translated by Ishtiyaq Ahmad Zilli. Page 175

awe and fear among the others. Alauddin Khilji insisted on a regular checking of the ledgers of the **patwaris** (hereditary village accountants), and if any discrepancy in the accounts came to light, then the Sultan would come down heavily on the concerned revenue officer: the offender would be apprehended, beaten black and blue, and then dumped into a dark dungeon. In the Khilji Sultan's scheme of things, it didn't matter if the sum embezzled was paltry or colossal: the rule was same for everyone, and anyone who broke it found himself in the middle of an ordeal worse than he could have ever imagined.

"Employment in the revenue department was considered worse than fever," informs Barani. "The post of a revenue clerk became a matter of disgrace and people would not give their daughters in marriage to clerks in the department of revenue. Only those accepted an employment in the department of revenue who had no regard for their life."[243]

And to supervise over both the affairs — the collection of revenue as well as the curtailment of corruption among the revenue officers — was appointed a man named Sharaf Qai. Indeed, if Barani is to be believed, then Sharaf Qai was a man of extraordinary competence, "who was unrivalled in the art of accountancy, calligraphy, discernment, competence, and ingenuity in the entire kingdom."[244] The same authority also tells us that Sharaf

---

[243] Tarikh-i Firoz Shahi. Translated by Ishtiyaq Ahmad Zilli. Page 175.

[244] ibid

Qai was trusted by the Sultan greatly, and that he worked tirelessly to justify his sovereign's faith in him.

Sharaf Qai, we are told, had a trait in common with the Sultan — the willingness to get ruthless when the situation so demanded. We have it from the testimony of the contemporaries that to realise even a single jittal (the lowest unit of currency current in the Delhi Sultanate), Sharaf Qai would go to the extent of imprisoning and physically punishing the accused officers, some of whom held high offices and came from respectable families. Of course, he couldn't have exercised such vast powers without the express approval of his sovereign whom, in any case, he served exceedingly well.

But for all that severity, at least as far as Sultan Alauddin Khilji was concerned, these policies were only the means to an end. The Sultan never lost sight of his aim, which ultimately was to create such a formidable fighting force, that would not only carry his banners across the subcontinent but also save his Sultanate from the Mongol menace. At any rate, as the Sultan himself realized, even for maintaining his hold over the state machinery, "a big army was needed, and it should be a chosen and select army which should be adept in archery, fully equipped with arms and fine cavalry." [245]

But recruiting and maintaining such an army were tasks that were easier said than done. For one thing, it involved immense expenses. "If we settle high stipends for the troops and wish to pay them according to that rate every

[245] Tarikh-i Firoz Shahi. Translated by Ishtiyaq Ahmad Zilli. Page 175

year in cash," the Sultan rightly observed, "[then] even though we have great treasures but in five-six years time nothing would be left in the treasury."[246]

To carry out such grandiose military plans as the Sultan had, he needed talented men in his army. And talent merited reward — talented men could not be had without a handsome pay. Thus, recruiting the finest martial talents available in the Asian military market, and that too in such large numbers, entailed an expense that was too high even for a man who was one of the richest kings to have ever ruled from Delhi. Sure, the Sultan had streamlined his administrative machinery and had weeded corruption out, and this way managed to augment his finances. But, that was not enough — more, much more money was still required.

Here was indeed a predicament: the very survival of the Delhi Sultanate depended upon a powerful army, while the maintenance of such an army involved the risk of bleeding the Sultanate dry.

Alauddin Khilji, however, didn't get overwhelmed with this impasse — instead, in his customary manner, he immersed himself in deep deliberation. And his counsellors followed suit.

Finally, "the counsellors who were attached to the court of Sultan Alauddin ... after much deliberation submitted their unanimous opinion before the court ... They submitted that the idea that has occurred in the mind of the Sultan regarding augmentation in the numbers of the

[246] Tarikh-i Firoz Shahi. Translated by Ishtiyaq Ahmad Zilli. Page 175

army and its durable maintenance on small stipend could only be achieved if the horses, arms and other items which are needed for the preparedness of the army and expenses for the livelihood of the troops become very cheap.

"If the King could drastically reduce the prices of the needs of livelihood, [only then] a large army could be recruited and properly maintained and would continue to be properly maintained on small stipend. This increase in the ranks of the troops would then effectively root out the Mongol menace."[247]

This suggestion hit home. The Sultan was convinced. He would bring the prices of the commodities down, and to that end he would go to any length.

Soon, as many as seven market regulations were rolled out.

First, he issued an order regulating the price of grains, and this was so rigorously enforced that "as long as Sultan Alauddin was alive it did not rise even by a single **dam** whether rains were good or there was drought."[248] And to ensure that the traders complied with his order strictly, the Sultan appointed one Malik Qabul Ulugh Khani, a wise and efficient man, as the controller of the markets.

The Sultan, however, was also aware that cheap prices could not be maintained for long through coercion alone.

---

[247] Tarikh-i Firoz Shahi. Translated by Ishtiyaq Ahmad Zilli. Page 175

[248] ibid. Page 186

The key factor was to maintain the regular supply of grain in the market, and that was only possible if there existed a judicious balance between supply and demand. Therefore, to streamline the supply of grain, the Sultan ordered, as a part of his third measure of market control, "that throughout the crown lands in the Doab, they should take the grain itself in place of money payments for revenue and send it into the royal granaries at the capital."[249] For the villages in the neighbourhood of Delhi too, it was ordered that half of the stipulated revenue should be paid in kind to the Sultan. As a result of these orders, "so much of the royal grain reached Delhi, that there was scarcely a street, which did not contain two or three of the royal storehouses filled with it."[250] Setting up such royal granaries, at any rate, had been the Sultan's second measure of market control. And when the rains failed, or there emerged a scarcity of grain in the market for some reason or the other, the Sultan would then generously allow the grains to be taken out from the royal granaries into the market, and there sold at the officially fixed prices **(nirkh-i sultani)**.

To take his endeavours a step further, Sultan Alauddin also ordered, as his fourth measure of market regulation, the grain merchants and the grain carriers to be placed under the authority of Malik Qabul, that controller of the markets we mentioned before. "Sultan Alauddin issued orders that all the grain merchants of the royal dominion

---

[249] The Reign of Alauddin Khilji. Translated from Ziauddin Barani's Tarikh-I Firoz Shahi. By A.R. Fuller and A. Khallaque. Page 106

[250] ibid. Page 107

were to be made subject to the Shahna (Malik Qabul) and their chiefs **(muqaddams)** were to be handed over to the Shahna in chains. The Shahna was directed to keep them in his presence in chains until they agreed to act in one body and give surety for each other, bring their women, children, cattle and beasts of burden along with their chattel and settle them in villages. These villages were located on the banks of the Jamuna and a superintendant was appointed by the Shahna of the mandi over them ... Due to implementation of these regulations, so much grain began to reach the mandi that there was no need to take the grain from the royal granaries."[251]

To ensure that unscrupulous people couldn't create a false scarcity in the market, the Sultan issued his fifth market regulation that aimed at prohibiting hoarding. The ban was so rigorously enforced, Barani tells us, that it became absolutely impossible for anyone to hoard even a handful of grain. "If the hoarded grain was discovered, it was taken over as royal grain and the hoarder was fined."[252] Due to the effective ban on hoarding, prices never increased in the mandi, no matter it rained or not.

And precisely to carry this prohibition a step further, the Sultan rolled out his sixth regulation, which required taking "written commitments from the officials and governors (of the outlying provinces) to the effect that they would ensure sales of grain to the grain merchants on

---

[251] Tarikh-i Firoz Shahi. Translated by Ishtiyaq Ahmad Zilli. Page 187

[252] ibid

the threshing floor itself."[253] In those villages, where the revenue was paid in cash, it was Alauddin Khilji's express command to his revenue collectors to demand the **kharaj** (revenue) with such severity so as to force the peasant to sell his produce "in the sowing field itself at a lower rate to the grain merchants."[254] This way, the Sultan, at one stroke, eliminated once and for all the possibility of farmers stockpiling grains and thereby hampering the supply in the market.

All that was left now was to properly oversee the operations of the market and ensure that the imperial orders were followed to the letter. With exactly that intent in his mind, the Sultan introduced his seventh regulation which involved receiving daily reports about the prices and other affairs of the market from different sources.

It required no less than three sources — the market superintendant (Shahna-i Mandi), official reporters (Barids), and hidden spies (Munhis) — to send to Alauddin Khilji daily reports, seperately, on everything that took place in the market. And if there ever emerged even the slightest discrepancy in the reports, the Sultan would fly into a rage and the superintendant of the market would find himself in all sorts of trouble.

Alauddin, at any rate, was no respecter of ranks — once Malik Qabul, one of the topmost nobles of the Delhi Sultanate, received as many as twenty blows with a stick from the Sultan himself, merely for suggesting a slight

---

[253] Tarikh-i Firoz Shahi. Translated by Ishtiyaq Ahmad Zilli. Page 186

[254] ibid. Page 188

increase in the price of grains on account of the failure of rains — and of this aspect of the Sultan's temperament, every man working for the Delhi Sultanate was fully cognisant. "Since the functionaries of the mandi knew fully well that reports of all the events of the mandi reached the Sultan from three different sources," informs a contemporary, "[therefore] even the slightest violation of the regulations of the mandi was not possible."[255]

Finally, to ensure that not even a single soul in Delhi had to go to sleep on an empty stomach, even when famine raged across the Sultanate and destruction stared the capital in the face, Sultan Alauddin Khilji rolled out the last and eighth of his market regulations, one that reflected more than anything else the workings of a humanitarian heart beneath a grim veneer.

"In seasons of draught," Barani informs us, "the merchants of each quarter of the town (Delhi) received daily supply of grain according to the number of inhabitants in each quarter, and they then issued grain to the common people at a rate not exceeding half a **man** per individual."[256] If perchance a poor man could not get his quota from the market, or a weak individual got injured in the crowd, and report of that reached the Sultan — which it often did anyway, courtesy the numberless spies operating in the empire — then the Shahna-i Mandi would be in for a severe chastisement at the hands of his

---

[255] Tarikh-i Firoz Shahi. Translated by Ishtiyaq Ahmad Zilli. Page 186

[255] ibid

[256] The Reign of Alauddin Khilji. Translated from Ziauddin Barani's Tarikh-i Firoz Shahi. BY A.R. Fuller and A. Khallaque. Page 111

sovereign for his purported neglect of duty. So solicitous was Sultan Alauddin Khilji for his poor subjects!

"Whenever the white clouds have had no water left and destruction has stared people in the face, he (the Sultan) has cheapened the price of grain for every section of the public by opening the royal stores," Amir Khusrau hardly exaggerates.[257]

Controlling the prices of foodgrains, however, was only the first step in Alauddin's market control measures, which in their final shape were very comprehensive and covered virtually the entire gamut of market operations. The prices of virtually everything that could be had in the market — "from cap to stockings, comb to needle, sugarcane to vegetables, pottage to broth, sweet meat to reori, dry bread to roasted bread, fish, bete leaf, colour, areca nut, and from flowers to vegetables" — were all regulated by Sultan Alauddin Khilji himself.[258]

The prices, however, were not arbitrarily fixed: the Sultan, says Barani, "spent days and nights" in determining the cost of production of even the most trifling of commodities.[259] Only after taking into account the cost of production were the prices fixed, which were then forwarded to the officials whose job it was to look after the markets. Even at the risk of sounding far-fetched, one can't help but underscore the uncanny similarity between the principles that guided Alauddin and the cost-

[257] Khazain ul Futuh. Translated by Muhammad Habib. Page 13

[258] Tarikh-i Firoz Shahi. Translated by Ishtiyaq Ahmad Zilli. Page 193

[259] ibid

of-production theory of value that was expounded by the classical economists.

"The open space inside the Badaun Gate, in the direction of the Kaushak-i Sabz (The Green Palace), which for years had not been used," was taken over by the Sultan, and he ordered a great mart to be set up there, which was to go by the name of Sara-i Adil.[260]

Alauddin Khilji ordered that all the merchandise coming to his capital were to be brought to the Sara-i Adil, and there sold at the rates fixed by him, "[and] if anybody were to take any merchandise to some house or to some other bazaar and sell even one jital over and above the officially fixed rates, his merchandise would be confiscated and he would stand for severe punishment. This regulation ensured that merchandise worth one tanka to a hundred tankas and goods worth 1,000 tankas to 10,000 tankas were brought only to the Sara-i Adil."[261]

"And if anyone (among the merchants) opened his packages elsewhere (apart from the Sara-i Adil), the joints of his body were to be 'opened' with the sword," Amir Khusrau remarks in a caustic vein.[262]

The prices of all the commodities to be sold at the Sara-i Adil, as mentioned before, were meticulously fixed by the Sultan himself. Thus one ser of sugar candy could be had for two and a half jitals, and animal fat was cheaper than

---

[260] The Reign of Alauddin Khilji. Translated from Ziauddin Barani's Tarikh-i Firoz Shahi. BY A.R. Fuller and A. Khallaque. Page 112

[261] Tarikh-i Firoz Shahi. Translated by Ishtiyaq Ahmad Zilli. Page 189

[262] Khazain ul Futuh. Translated by Muhammad Habib. Page 13

sugar candy. Of textiles, the **Khazz silk** of Delhi, with its fine, velvety texture, fetched the highest price and was used almost exclusively by the aristocracy and the royalty. As to the rest of Delhi's population, the more prosperous ones among them preferred the **Shirin Baft**, which too was of a reasonably fine quality but, most importantly, didn't cost a fortune. "The Sara-i Adil was open from early morning till the time of the last prayer," informs Barani. "People thus got what they needed, and no one returned disappointed."[263]

To ensure that goods of all varieties reached Delhi regularly, "Sultan Alauddin ordered that the names of all merchants, whether Hindus or Mussalmans, of the empire should be registered in the book of the Diwan (Diwan-i Riyasat)." The merchants were then made to sign written engagements, "whereby they were compelled to bring a certain quantity of wares to town (Delhi) and to sell them at the rates fixed by the Sultan."[264]

Failure to comply with this order, of course, implied doom for the merchants, and therefore, not surprisingly, they remained by and large obediant throughout the reign of Sultan Alauddin Khilji. "Registered merchants brought so many commodities from various cities of different countries to the Sara-i Adil that they were kept there and remained unsold for days."[265]

---

[263] The Reign of Alauddin Khilji. Translated from Ziauddin Barani's Tarikh-i Firoz Shahi. BY A.R. Fuller and A. Khallaque. Page 114

[264] ibid

[265] Tarikh-i Firoz Shahi. Translated by Ishtiyaq Ahmad Zilli. Page 190

While the Sultan dealt harshly with the defaulters, he nevertheless remained benevolent, almost indulgent, towards the other, more obediant merchants. Thus, besides reducing taxes to help the merchants to cope up with the drop in prices, the Sultan also made the Multanis, who were mostly Hindus, the officials of Sara-i Adil and a colossal sum of 20 lakh tankas was advanced to them. They were to purchase all sorts of commodities from different countries and then bring them to the Sara-i Adil. This was a preventive measure: to act as a counterfeit if in case the officially registered merchants failed to bring the required amount of merchandise at the Sara-i Adil. Such a situation, however, virtually never arose — "no need ever arose for officially procured commodities **(aqmisha-i sultani)**," Barani informs us.[266]

There was now in Delhi such a mart as was absolutely unique in its conception and working, where could be obtained all the finest stuffs from across the world. A system was put into place, whereby to purchase luxury items at the Sara-i Adil at the subsidized rate, a parwana (license) had to be procured from the government. "Sultan Alauddin had issued orders that fine clothes such as **tasbih, tabrizi, kaj** of Ma'bar, clothes of **zarbaft** and **zarnigar, khaz** of Delhi, **kamkhwab** of Tabrez, **hariri, chini, bhiram** and **deogiri** and such other cloths not needed by common people" should not be sold to anyone,

[266] Tarikh-i Firoz Shahi. Translated by Ishtiyaq Ahmad Zilli. Page 190

until and unless that concerned person produced a proper license to that effect.[267]

Yaqub Nazir, the Parwana Rais, who was asked to look after this licensing sytem, "issued parwanas for fine clothes [only] to the amirs, maliks and dignitaries keeping in view their status and circumstances."[268]

"The very reason why the pass sytem had been introduced, had in fact been this, to prevent merchants, both in and outside the town (Delhi), from obtaining costly stuffs from the Sara-i Adil at the rates fixed by the Sultan, and then taking them to the countryside where they could not be had, and selling them at high prices."[269]

This was basically a safety measure, to prevent fraudulent men from buying cheaply at the Sara-i Adil and then selling them elsewhere at a much greater price. To check corruption, the Sultan likewise came down heavily on the brokers who, according to Barani, "were a most arrogant, rebellious and audacious class of people."[270] The most notorious ones among them were exiled from the capital, and the lot that befell them served as a deterrant to the other brokers.

"However, reforming the shameless brokers is indeed a difficult task," admits Barani. "They would not have adopted a proper attitude but for the fear of the severity of

---

[267] Tarikh-i Firoz Shahi. Translated by Ishtiyaq Ahmad Zilli. Page 190

[268] ibid

[269] The Reign of Alauddin Khilji. Translated from Ziauddin Barani's Tarikh-i Firoz Shahi. BY A.R. Fuller and A. Khallaque. Page 114

[270] ibid. Page 118

Sultan Alauddin's temperament. This has not left any room for their machinations and feigning lies."[271]

Needless to say, Alauddin's measures were a grand success. The price of every single commodity in the market, from food grain to luxury products, dropped drastically, and remained at the same level so long the Sultan was alive.

"The aged and old people were amazed at the low cost of all commodities during the reign of Sultan Alauddin," Barani reports correctly.[272]

"It is difficult to conceive how so extraordinary a project should have been put in practise ... Such a plan was neither before carried into effect, or has been tried since," opines Ferishta, as much accurately.[273]

Delhi thus became the envy of the world, and its Sultan the wonder of the age.

A **man** of wheat could be had for 7.5 jittals. That is, with one silver tanka that weighed roughly 11 grams, no less than 85 kilograms of wheat could be bought! Likewise, a **man** of barley could be had for 4 jittals, and a **man** of rice for 5 jittals. The price of cattle was equally cheap. "The cow meant for meat was priced at 1-1.5 tankas and the price of milch cows was fixed at 3-4 tankas. The milch buffalo was priced at 10-12 tankas and the one meant for

---

[271] Tarikh-i Firoz Shahi. Translated by Ishtiyaq Ahmad Zilli. Page 192

[272] ibid. Page 190

[273] Tarikh-i Ferishta. Translated by John Briggs. Page 356

meat fetched a price of 5-6 tankas."[274] An entire fat sheep was available for only 10 jittals.

In those days when slavery was in vogue even in non-aristocratic families, especially in Muslim households, the Sultan's measures also brought the price of slaves down. Female slaves cut out for household chores came at anywhere between 5 to 12 tankas. Those female slaves who were beautiful in appearance and were sought for sexual services fetched anything between 20 to 40 tankas. Sodomy being widely prevalant in the contemporary society, catamites were also eagerly sought after: such "a beardless and handsome young slave" was available for 20 to 30 tankas.[275]

Sultan Alauddin Khilji's measures were so comprehensive that, if Ferishta is to be believed, he even went to the extent of fixing the rates of prostitution. According to this account, it so happened that one day a certain nobleman, "by way of a joke," proposed that since the Sultan had made everything cheap, prostitution too should not be left out. And strangely enough, the Sultan at once accepted his suggestion. "Accordingly, prostitutes were classed under the denominations of first, second, and a third, and a price fixed on them," with the most beautiful ones among them and those that were most skilled in the arts of seduction, for obvious reasons, earning the highest amount.[276]

---

[274] Tarikh-i Firoz Shahi. Translated by Ishtiyaq Ahmad Zilli. Page 192

[275] ibid

[276] Tarikh-i Ferishta. Translated by John Briggs. Page 359

The arrangements were perfect, no doubt, but they would have amounted to nothing were they not properly maintained. And here Sultan Alauddin shone bright — he was as brilliant in framing grandiose plans, as he was tenacious in supervising them continuously. "It was due to his scrutiny and precautions," says Barani, "that the prices of commodities of the bazaar and their cheapness, which is very difficult to achieve, became constant."[277]

Those that practised fraud in commercial dealings were subject to severe chastisement. Yaqub Nazir would visit the markets regularly, and make sure that things were being sold at the rates fixed by the Sultan. Any merchant who didn't, he would beat him up in public. This way, at least to a large extent, Yaqub Nazir succeeded in making sure that his Sultan's directives were followed to the letter.

But, Alauddin Khilji was almost a maniac for perfection. For all the efforts of Yakub Nazir, the Sultan still wasn't satisfied. He was particularly concerned about the issue of weights: the merchants, even if they sold stuffs at the rates fixed by him, could still resort to underweighing their merchandise, not least when the customer happened to be a gullible one. So, the Sultan would summon young boys, give them money, tell them to go to the market and fetch for him such sundry stuffs as sweatmeats and breads. The boys did as they were told, and more often than not, the Sultan's apprehensions came true: taking advantage of

---

[277] Tarikh-i Firoz Shahi. Translated by Ishtiyaq Ahmad Zilli. Page 194

their young age, the shopkeepers would sell them less than what they had been paid for.

And when such discrepancies were discovered, Alauddin felt no compunction whatsoever in meting out to the offender the harshest of retributions. That Sultan, at any rate, did have a thing with savage and innovative punishments. Thus, Barani tells us that the Sultan would have the convicted merchant apprehended, and then awarded the most sanguinary sentence imaginable — flesh would be chopped off the offender's buttocks, "twice the quantity of the weight of the deficiency."[278]

And the effects of such punishments showed: in market transactions, Barani tells us, often the weight of the merchandise bought would turn out to be greater than what had been paid for.

As per the Sultan's directive, weights to be used in the market had to be uniform: all of which were to be "made of iron and their correct weight written upon them; so that if any one (among the merchants) gave less than the correct measure, the iron turned into a chain round his neck. If he was impudent still, the chain became a sword and the extreme punishment was meted out to him."[279]

The rigours involved in it, however, should not lead us to the conclusion that the price control measure was just another act of oppression undertaken by an autocrat. The whole affair, in fact, was extremely well thought out, and involved forging a fine balance between the different

[278] Tarikh-i Firoz Shahi. Translated by Ishtiyaq Ahmad Zilli. Page 195

[279] Khazain ul Futuh. Translated by Muhammad Habib. Page 10

social groups that together ran the economy of the Delhi Sultanate. Thus, the government's strict attitude towards the merchants doesn't mean that they were allowed to make no profit. It's only that the margin of the profit came down — and if that was a problem, then to offset that the Sultan also struck off many taxes that the traders previously had to pay. Likewise, if to maintain the supply of grain in the market, the officials were stern in demanding the due from the husbandmen, then ameliorations to that end weren't wanting either: any time such a need arose, the Sultan didn't think twice before remitting the stipulated revenue.

Finally, the Sultan's desire came to fruition — necessities of livelihood having been made cheap, it was now possible to raise the army of his dreams, adept in warfare and numbering in lakhs. With that formidable force, he overawed the awesome Mongols, the details of which had been furnished in the preceding chapter. But beating the Mongols back wasn't his only aim, not by any means — the wealth of the Peninsular India allured him, and the desire to extend his sway over the states south of the Vindhyas never left him, at least not after that dashing raid to Deogiri which he had made when he was yet to become the Sultan. But, to cross the Vindhyas and bring the kingdoms beyond it effectively under Delhi's control, it was necessary to dismantle the geo-political barriers that stood in the way. And it is to that story that we turn now.

The Antimony Of Pride

When the lancers of the victorious army had put antimony into the eyes of the more distinguished Rais with their spears, many powerful Zamindars, gifted with greater keenness of vision, threw aside their boldness and impudence from fear of the stone-piercing arrows of the Turks. They came to the imperial court with open eyes and turned its threshold into antimony by rubbing their black pupils upon it; at the same time they saved their bones from becoming antimony-boxes for the dust.

— Khazain ul Futuh, by Amir Khusrau.

The fall of Ranthambore and Chittor, maintains Amir Khusrau, convinced most Rajput chiefs of the invincibility of Khilji arms and induced them to submit before Sultan Alauddin. However, the ruler of Malwa, Mahlak Deo, and his relative-cum-minister, Koka Pradhan, weren't among them, not least because they had a truly formidable army at their disposal, that was composed of 40,000 cavalry and 100,000 infantry. And with this vast legion, they lorded over a vast territory that, according to a contemporary, was composed of close to two millions towns and villages.[280]

---

[280] Tarikh-i Wassaf. By Abdullah Wassaf. Quoted in THE HISTORY OF INDIA, AS TOLD BY ITS OWN HISTORIANS. THE

"The darkness of their (minds) and the dust raised by their legions," rants amir Khursau, "had put the antimony of pride in their eyes."[281] But for all that rancour on Khusrau's part, it was clear that the Rajput ruler of Malwa wouldn't give in without a fight. On the flip side, to carry out the grandiose camapaigns that he had planned in the Deccan, for Alauddin Khilji it was indispensable to secure Malwa, even more important than keeping Rajasthan in control at least as far as the expeditions southward were concerned.

A military clash between the two powers was therefore inevitable.

It was Sultan Alauddin Khilji who dealt the first blow. He chose one of his premier nobles, Ain ul Mulk Multani, placed him at the head of 10,000 select troopers, and then despatched him to attack Malwa.

In the very first encounter with the imperialists, Koka Pradhan was killed. 'In the twinkling of an eye he was pierced by innumerable arrows," says Amir Khusrau.[282] The death of his aide-de-camp unnerved the King of Malwa, who then lost no time in shutting himself up in the hilltop fortress of Mandu.

The Sultan now instructed Ain ul Mulk to stay put in Malwa, and mop the military operations up. He was also directed to somehow wrest from Malwak Deo the fortress

---

MUHAMMADAN PERIOD. VOLUME III. By Sir H.M. Elliot. London, 1871. Page 31

[281] Khazain ul Futuh. Translated by Muhammad Habib. Page 43

[282] ibid

of Mandu which, in Khusrau's own words, was "the key to the conquest of Deccan."[283]

To beat Ain ul Mulk back, the King of Malwa sent his son off with a siezeable force. "All at once a body of Ain ul Mulk's troops fell upon them, like the dust storm that overpowers the eyes of men," Khusrau narrates the action with engaging details. "In an instant the boldest among them were rolling in blood and dust, while the Rai's son slept the sleep of death."[284]

With his minister and son gone, it was now the turn of the King of Malwa. One night, through a secret passage, the Khilji army made its way into the fort.[285] Mahlak Deo and his men were taken totally by surprise, and before they could even come to their senses, the imperialists put all of them to the sword. "This event occured on Thursday, the 5th of Jamadiul Awwal, 705 A.H. (November 23, 1305) " reports Amir Khusrau. "When this good news was brought to the Emperor, he bowed down in thankfulness and assigned the territory of Mandu also to Ain ul Mulk."[286]

With Malwa firmly annexed to the Delhi Sultanate, the road to Deccan was now clear. Soon Malik Kafur, that noted slave-general of the Sultan, was carrying fire and sword into the territories of the southern potentates. None

---

[283] Quoted in The History of the Khaljis. By K.S. LAL. Page 133

[284] Khazain ul Futuh. Translated by Muhammad Habib. Page 45

[285] The Khiljis, says Amir Khusrau, were assisted in this task by a traitor in the Rajput ranks.

[286] Khazain ul Futuh. Translated by Muhammad Habib. Page 46

could escape the Khilji fury: from Deogir to the southernmost tip of the peninsula, every power trembled and every king cracked up at the approach of the Khilji army.

The whole of North India, however, was not yet subdued. Sure, the major players were all gone, but their still remained a few minor ones who, although didn't pose any substantial military threat to the Sultanate, still managed to irk the Sultan by virtue of their autonomous existence. So, while his trusted general carried out his grand imperialist designs in the southern lands, the Sultan personally turned to the vestiges of resistance that still remained to be uprooted in the lands near his capital.

Thus, sometime in 1310, Sultan Alauddin Khilji decided once again to take the field in person, this time to take Raja Shital Deva on and seize from him the stronghold of Siwana which, according to Ferishta, had not fallen in the hands of the imperial generals in spite of several attempts made to that end.

Immediately on arriving, the Sultan ordered the fort to be closely invested. This time, with their Sultan himself leading them in person, the forces of the Delhi Sultanate were in a completely different mood altogether. Detachments were stationed on all sides of the fort, and no quarter was given to the besieged. A ceaseless shower of projectiles was maintained, and the siege pressed on with great vigour.

A little more than two months after, the citadel capitulated to the Khilji arms. The entire garrison perished — most died fighting, while those that tried fleeing were overtaken, and then promptly put to the sword – and the fort in its entirety was given up to plunder.

Next, a search was ordered for Raja Shital Deva, and his lifeless body having been discovered, was brought before the Sultan on a certain Tuesday morning. The late Shital Deva, we are told, had been a man of garguantan size: when his severed head was paraded around the camp, the onlookers were struck with amazement at its extraordinary proportions.

Siwana was then declared annexed to the Delhi Sultanate, and the charge of looking after it was entrusted to one Kamaluddin Gurg.

Not long after, the Sultanate soldiers once again set out for Rajputana, this time to overrun and annex Jalore. Its Chauhana ruler, Kanhar Deva, had previously accepted Alauddin's suzerainty, but a very trivial incident soured the relationship between the two to such an extent that war had to be taken recourse to.

Raja Kanhar Deva used to attend Sultan Alauddin's court and there, one fine day, Ferishta tells us, the Sultan boasted that there remained not even a single raja in Hindustan, who could make a stand against his army. The Chauhana Raja, "in the plenitude of folly", countered the Sultan at once, and boldly asserted: "I will suffer death, if I do not myself raise an army that shall defeat any attempt of the King's troops to take the fort of Jalwur (sic)."[287]

---

[287] Tarikh-i Ferishta. Translated by John Briggs. Page 370

Sultan Alauddin Khilji was incensed at this display of audacity, and he immediately ordered Kanhar Deva to retire at once to his home in Jalore.

The imperial army was made ready, and then to add insult to injury, Alauddin placed the army under the command of a slave girl of his palace, named Gul Bahisht (The Rose of the Heaven).

The imperial troops moved towards Jalore, and their female commander, we are told, displayed remarkable courage on her part. But all of a sudden she was laid up by a certain illness, and she passed away not long after. Thereafter, her son, Shahin, assumed the command of the army. But, unfortunately for the imperialists, the young Shahin was nowhere near his mother as far as manfully leading the soldiers on the field of battle was concerned.

Sensing a weak leadership on the opposite side, Raja Kanhar Dev and his men sallied out of the fort, and beat the imperialists back with great slaughter. Their leader Shahin also perished in the action: he was killed, according to Ferishta, by Raja Kanhar Dev with his own hands. In fact, so vigorous had been the Rajput assault that the imperialists had to push on towards Delhi for four successive days, without being able to afford a halt anywhere on the way.

This setback irked Sultan Alauddin greatly. He now summoned Malik Kamaluddin Gurg from Siwana, put him at the head of a truly formidable army, and then sent him off to exact a terrible revenge from the Chauhana Rajputs.

Kamaluddin Gurg did exactly as he was told: he stormed into the Jalore fort, annihilated the entire garrison, and then finally put Kanhar Dev and his entire family to the sword.

With this campaign came to an end the blaze of Khilji belligerence that had raged across North India for well nigh a decade, bringing within that period the vast stretch from the marches beyond Punjab in the west to the border of Bengal in the east under the single and undisputed authority of Sultan Alauddin Khilji. The local players had been sidelined, and the foreign threat to his authority had been decimated. It was now possible for Sultan Alauddin Khilji to devote his single-minded attention to the pursuit of the single greatest desire of his life, one that would bring to him incredible repute and unthinkable wealth. This was the subjugation of the Deccan, and it is to that we turn now.

The Land Of Gold

No person wore bracelets, chains, or rings of any other metal than gold; while all the plate in the houses of the great, and in the temples, was of beaten gold.

— Tarikh-i Ferishta, by Muhammad Qasim Ferishta.

The conquest of Malwa and the obliteration of the Mongol threat were events that presaged doom for the autonomous Hindu kingdoms down south. Each of them was master of great wealth, but none of them saw eye to eye with their neighbours. Alauddin, even as a prince, had had a taste of the Deccan's fabled wealth. Why, it was the loot from Deogir that had made possible his accession to the throne of the Delhi Sultanate. And if Deogir could provide that much, how much more could be wrung from the three other autonomous kingdoms that draped the Deccan? The thought itself was enough to fire Alauddin's imagination, and now that he was relatively free from other concerns, there was no time to lose to streamroller his southern foes into submission.

Alauddin's first target in the Deccan was Deogir: not only because of its relatively northward location, but also because its king had gone back on his word. Back in 1296, Alauddin had entered into an agreement with Ram Deo, the ruler of Deogir, according to which the latter was supposed to despatch the revenues of Elichpur every year to Delhi. But over time the arrangement had fallen apart: Ferishta informs us that Ram Deo had neglected to send the stipulated amount for the three preceding years. So, in 1307, Sultan Alauddin Khilji flagged off his Deccan drive by sending a large army to Deogir to browbeat its king into submission, and to enforce him into compliance with the treaty.

Apart from these political reasons, there also was involved another, more personal vein to this entire affair. The tract of Elichpur, the revenues of which Sultan Alauddin claimed for himself, had lately been assigned by Ram Deo to Rai Karan Deo, that fugitive former king of Gujarat. Granting succour to an imperial enemy, and that too in this fashion, was construed by the Sultan as a slight to his stature.

Besides, there was another account to be settled with Rai Karan. His ex-wife, Kamala Devi, whose beauty had once fascinated Alauddin in an instant, had in the intervening years risen so much in the Sultan's estimation that there was hardly anything that he would refuse her for. So, when she asked Alauddin to reunite her with her daughter, whom Rai Karan had managed to carry away with himself into the safety of the Deccan, the Sultan didn't think twice before consenting to her request. Thus, Rai Karan was not only to be driven out of Elichpure, but his daughter too was to be snatched away from him. This was the Sultan's desire, and he briefed it up before his favourite slave Malik Kafur, who was nominated to lead the attack on Deccan.

The whole situation was not bereft of a certain peculiarity: one captive from Gujarat being ordered at the behest of another captive of Gujarat, to take on the ex-king of Gujarat and wrest from him the princess of Gujarat. Gujarat, the readers must remember, did have something to do with the Khilji dynasty.

A huge force then set out southward from Delhi: Amir Khusrau puts the strength of the Delhi army at 30,000 cavalrymen, while Ferishta claims it was composed of no less than one lakh troopers. This mega expedition was put under the charge of Malik Kafur, who was also allowed to use the Red Canopy, a prerogative that was otherwise strictly reserved for the princes of royal blood.

Veterans of many a battle were placed under Malik Kafur, and they were strictly ordered, tells Ferishta, to pay their daily respects to Kafur in the same manner as they would do to their sovereign. Staying subordinate to an eunuch, and in so abject a fashion, must have created much disgust among the premier nobles, but all of them being familiar with their Sultan's temperament, not even a murmur of complaint was heard.

As the Delhi army progressed towards the Deccan, it was joined on its way by the contingents of Alp Khan and Ain ul Mulk, the governors of Gujarat and Malwa respectively. Before long, the Sultanate army was thundering at the gates of the Deccan: Malik Kafur, as his king's deputy, "sent the king's order to Karan Rai, to deliver up his daughter Dewal Devi."[288] But Karan was in

[288] Tarikh-i Ferishta. Translated by John Briggs. Page 366

no mood to budge: his kingdom and his wife, he had lost to the Khiljis, and now he wouldn't lose his daughter to them, come what may.

Negotiation having failed, the sword was taken up to arbitrate. Surprisingly however, this time Rai Karan had the upper hand in the contest: for two months full, Ferishta writes, Karan foiled all attempts of the Delhi army to force their way through the mountainous passes of Baglana.

Even as bloody actions continued between Rai Karan and the imperialists, a strange decree of fate caused a rather peculiar situation to emerge. It so happened that Shankar Deva, that valiant crown prince of Deogir who had a decade earlier given battle to Alauddin Khilji and had almost defeated him, developed amorous feelings for Dewal Devi, the Gujarati princess who, at that point, was on the cusp of her youth. But the age-old caste system reared its ugly head once again: "she (Dewal Devi) being of the tribe of Rajput, and Shankar Deo a Maratha, her father (Rai Karan) withheld his consent to her union," reports Ferishta.[289]

This time however, realising that it was Dewal Devi who was the crux of all hostilities between Karan Rai and Alauddin, Shankar Deva played his cards right: he sent his brother Bhim Dev to persuade Karan Rai to deliver her to him, because if he did so, "the troops of the Mahomedans, in despair of obtaining their end, would return to their own country."[290]

---

[289] Tarikh-i Ferishta. Translated by John Briggs. Page 367

[290] ibid

Karan Rai, evidently, had not forgotten how roughly he had been handled by the Khiljis earlier: so after some deliberation, he consented to Bhim Dev's proposal.

Alp Khan, however, on learning about this development, plunged into a deep despair. Malik Kafur might have been the head of this camapaign, but it was he who had been singled out to get hold of Dewal Devi. Thinking about the horrible fate that awaited him if he failed in his mission scared him to the bone. "He was apprehensive that his own life depended on success."[291] He therefore decided to make a last-ditch attempt.

Summoning all his subordinates to his side, "he (Alp Khan) acquainted his officers with the peculiarity of this situation, and they unanimously promised him their support." Battle commenced soon, and this time the tables were turned on the Rajput Raja — "They entered the mountains in all directions, and engaging the Raja, gave him a total defeat."[292]

Karan Rai fled straightaway to his patron Ram Deo, leaving his bag and baggage behind for the Khiljis to capture once again. Alp Khan gave him a hot chase, but the Raja, being better aware of the local topography, took a meandering route. Soon, the imperialists lost sight of him, and Alp Khan saw that for all his efforts, he had only managed to draw his doom near.

---

[291] Tarikh-i Ferishta. Translated by John Briggs. Page 367

[292] ibid

Just at that very moment, "an accident threw the object of his desire in his way."[293]

It so happened that when Alp Khan had ordered his army to halt, so that he could get some time to think a way of getting out of his predicament, a party of his soldiers, numbering around 300, went without permission to the Ellora caves nearby, evidently to enjoy sightseeing.

"During this excursion, they perceived a body of horsemen approaching, whom they apprehended to belong to Shankar Dev."[294] The Delhi soldiers realised that there was no safety in flight: the main army under Alp Khan was quite far away, and by the time they could reach their general, the Marathas would surely overtake them. They therefore, in spite of their numerical inferiority, decided to hold their ground and give battle to the Maratha prince. Little did the Muslims realise however that the cavalcade approaching them wasn't the vanguard of Shankar Dev's army, but the retinue of Bhim Dev, "who was conveying the young bride (Dewal Devi) to his brother."[295] Totally oblivious to the truth, the Delhi soldiers straightaway swung into action: they engaged the Marathas vigorously, and before long emerged victorious in the engagement that only recently had appeared suicidal.

Amidst this mayhem, a chance arrow struck the horse of Dewal Devi — she fell down, and was left behind by her

---

[293] Tarikh-i Ferishta. Translated by John Briggs. Page 367

[294] ibid. Page 368

[295] ibid

guards, who were too busy in saving their own lives to take any notice of her.

Before long, the prying eyes of the imperial troops fell on the lithe figure of Dewal Devi: their lust was inflamed, and they brawled among themselves for the possession of this coveted prize. In all probability, Dewal Devi would have been violated and killed at that very spot, had not one of her female attendants given out her true identity just in the nick of time. "On hearing this the soldiers knew the peril of treating her with indignity, and while an express was despatched with the news to Alp Khan, they conducted her with great care and respect to his camp."[296] From almost getting killed at the hands of the Khiljis to being regally treated by the same bunch of men, the tables had been turned rather quickly for Dewal Devi.

Alp Khan, says Ferishta, erupted with happiness on hearing this news, "knowing how acceptable it would be to his sovereign, over whom the lady's mother exercised so great an influence."[297] He bid adieu to Malik Kafur, and right away made for Delhi with the Gujarati princess.

As was only to be expected, Kamala Devi was moved with joy on being reunited with her daughter after so long. There, in the royal palace of Delhi, with time a romantic affair took shape between Dewal Devi and Alauddin's eldest son, Khizr Khan. Culminating in a great tragedy, this dalliance between the two royals has been immortalised in history by the literary genius of Amir

---

[296] Tarikh-i Ferishta. Translated by John Briggs. Page 368

[297] ibid

Khusrau. But more on that later, it's now time we turn once again to the affairs of Malik Kafur.

Rai Karan's resistanace having been broken down by Alp Khan, Malik Kafur straightaway proceeded to besiege Deogir. After a brief struggle, the Maratha soldiers dispersed and the Khiljis scored a complete victory. "The Muslim horsemen being victorious, the Malik-i Sahkash (Malik Kafur) ordered that such booty as was fit for the troopers should be given back to them, while things only suitable for the sublime court ... were reviewed, recorded, and then entrusted to the officers," records Amir Khusrau. [298]

Malik Kafur then dutifully despatched the news of his victory to Delhi — "A **fathnama** (letter of victory) of Deogir reached Delhi and was read from the pulpits of the mosques and drums were beaten to express joy," writes Barani.[299]

Raja Ram Deo was no longer in a position to offer any further resistance: leaving his son Shankar Dev behind in the fort, he himself advanced with such presents as he could arrange to purchase peace from the invaders from the north.

Sultan Alauddin Khilji had expressly ordered Malik Kafur not to harm Raja Ram Deo's person, therefore, "the great commander restricted his efforts to catching the

---

[298] Khazain ul Futuh. Translated by Muhammad Habib. Page 52

[299] Tarikh-i Firoz Shahi. Translated by Ishtiyaq Ahmad Zilli. Page 200

refractory Ram Deo and most of his men alive."[300] Peace could be made, Malik Kafur stated, but for that Raja Ram Deo himself would have to visit Delhi and submit personally before the Sultan.

Raja Ram Deo, at any rate, didn't have any option but to consent — he hardly had any bargaining strength left in him. Accordingly, "Malik Naib returned victorious from Deogir and arrived at Delhi with Ram Deo and his gold, treasure and elephants and presented before the throne all that he had brought."[301]

In Delhi, to the surprise of everyone, not to mention Raja Ram Deo who must have had his heart in his mouth, Sultan Alauddin Khilji actually treated the King of Deogir exceedingly well. Ram Deo and his family were kept in Delhi for no less than six months, and in this long period, they were simply blown away by the Sultan's magnanimity: "For full six months the fortunate Rai remained in the rays of imperial favour ... day by day his honour and dignity increased, till in the course of time he attained to the orbit of prosperity like the full moon," narrates Amir Khusrau.[302]

Finally, before granting leave to Raja Ram Deo, "Sultan Alauddin ... bestowed **chatr** (royal canopy) upon him and gave him the title of **Ray-i Rayan** (King of Kings)."[303] Besides, one lakh golden coins were also made over to the

---

[300] Khazain ul Futuh. Translated by Muhammad Habib. Page 52

[301] Tarikh-i Firoz Shahi. Translated by Ishtiyaq Ahmad Zilli. Page 200

[302] Khazain ul Futuh. Translated by Muhammad Habib. Page 53

[303] Tarikh-i Firoz Shahi. Translated by Ishtiyaq Ahmad Zilli. Page 200

Raja... as a parting gift, "and he was not only restored to his government, but other districts were [also] added to his dominions." [304]

So smitten was Ram Deo by Alauddin's largesses that he willingly requested the Sultan on his own to accept his daughter's hand in marriage. Alauddin obliged, and thus began an extraordinary alliance between the Yadavas and the Khiljis, the benefits of which accrued to both the houses. The Khilji dynasty might not have been fated to survive for long, but this act on the part of Alauddin Khilji was undoubtedly a political masterstroke, and could rightly be considered as the precursor to Akbar's strong marital ties with the Rajput ruling houses of Rajputana.

"From that date until the end of his life," says Barani, "Ram Deo continued to be loyal to Sultan Alauddin and never looked beyond his command."[305] In the subsequent campaigns that Sultan Alauddin launched in the Deccan, the Yadava King of Deogir wholeheartedly cooperated with the imperialists in every way possible, earning in the process rich praises for himself from every other Muslim chronicler.

Confidant about Malik Kafur's consummate capacity in the southern world, "the next year, 707 A.H., Sultan Alauddin again sent Malik Naib to Warangal along with great maliks and amirs accompanied with the Red Canopy **(Sayaban-i Lal)**."[306] This was actually the second army

---

[304] Tarikh-i Ferishta. Translated by John Briggs. Page 369

[305] Tarikh-i Firoz Shahi. Translated by Ishtiyaq Ahmad Zilli. Page 200

[306] ibid

that Sultan Alauddin Khilji was sending to Warangal. The first expedition to Warangal, some six years earlier, had been led by Fakhruddin Jauna, the future Muhammad bin Tughluq. For reasons better known to him, Jauna had led the army under his command to Telangana through the unfamiliar routes that passed through the unsubdued states of Bengal and Orissa. Quite predictably, as in almost everything that Muhammad bin Tughluq would later undertake as the Sultan, the campaign failed disastrously. It was beset by difficuties right from the very outset. And then the hostile roads coupled with the incessant downpour made life utterly difficult for the Delhi soldiers. Finally, a humiliating defeat at the hands of the Kakatiyas of Warangal brought the camapaign to its end, and the Sultanate army, or whatever was left of it, headed by Jauna Khan, returned to Delhi in complete disarray.

The Kakatiya King of Warangal, Raja Prataprudra Deva II, was by far the most powerful potentate in the whole of Deccan, and this realisation was not lost on the cautious Alauddin either. He therefore warned his lieutenant Malik Kafur not to let his guard down even for one moment. Alauddin's motive behind this expedition was simply to secure plunder, and when that had been done, Malik Kafur was to return right away to Delhi. "Do not expect that he (the Kakatiya King) would come to you and do not make an attempt to bring the Rai along with you to Delhi seeking name and fame," Alauddin expressly instructed Malik Kafur.[307]

---

[307] Tarikh-i Firoz Shahi. Translated by Ishtiyaq Ahmad Zilli. Page 200

All said and done, on the 1st of November, 1309, Malik Kafur set out with Delhi along with his deputy, Khwaja Haji. At Chanderi, as per imperial orders, "the maliks and amirs of Hindustan joined Malik Naib with their infantry and cavalry. A muster of troops was held there."[308] From Chanderi, Malik Kafur moved southward with great speed and managed to reach Deogir in a short time.

Before crossing over into the Yadava Kingdom, the Sultan's order was proclaimed before the Sultanate soldiers. Alauddin had sternly warned his men against disturbing Ram Deo and his subjects. The imperial command was so vigorously enforced that "no one dared to touch the door or the wall of a building or take anything from the barns or fields of the peasant."[309]

Raja Ram Deo, on the other hand, hastened to reciprocate the kind gesture of the Sultan, now his son-in-law. "Rai-i Rayan Ram Deo welcomed the armies of Islam and offered many presents to Malik Naib and offered gifts to the nobles," informs Barani.[310]

The entire responsibility of looking after the commissariat requirements of the Delhi army was willingly taken up by Ram Deo who, according to Ferishta, regularly sent merchants to the imperial camp "with strict orders to sell

---

[308] ibid. Page 201

[309] Khazain ul Futuh. Translated by Muhammad Habib. Page 58-59

[310] Tarikh-i Firoz Shahi. Translated by Ishtiyaq Ahmad Zilli. Page 201

everything according to the King's (Alauddin's) established prices in his own dominions."[311]

The King of Deogir's conduct as a subordinate ally of the Sultan of Delhi left absolutely nothing to be desired: he not only looked after the multifarious requirements of the Delhi army, but as a gesture of loyal submission, he also made it a point to arrive regularly before the Red Canopy and then kiss the ground in full public view.

After resting for a few days in Deogir, the Delhi army got refreshed and became ready to once again swing into action. Before the Sultanate soldiers left Deogir, according to Barani, "Raja Ram Deo sent his men to all the towns on the way to the borders of Warangal to keep ready necessary provisions, grains and other necessities."[312] So scrupulous was the King of Deogir about the norms of hospitality that he even went to the extent of warning his own men of dire consequences "if even a rope belonging to the [Delhi] army was lost."[313] They were to obey Malik Kafur in the same way the people of Delhi obeyed Sultan Alauddin, Raja Ram Deo told his Maratha captains, as they set off to guide the Delhi army on its way to Warangal.

Still, it took the imperialists no less than sixteen days to reach the frontiers of the Kakatiya kingdom. The road to Telanagana was indeed a challenging one — "the road went up and down like the subtle wit of a clever cheat and

[311] Tarikh-i Ferishta. Translated by John Briggs. Page 371

[312] Tarikh-i Firoz Shahi. Translated by Ishtiyaq Ahmad Zilli. Page 201

[313] ibid

was at the same time as long as a miser's greed," Amir Khusrau describes the route in his characteristic style — and if not for the Yadava King's assistance, the jouney would have turned out to be extremely difficult for the Khiljis.[314]

On reaching the frontiers of Telangana, "[Malik Kafur] issued orders to lay waste the country with fire and sword." This savage brutality of the invaders ... perplexed the local inhabitants greatly, Ferishta continues, "[for they] had never injured their wanton enemies."[315]

Faced with such savagery most of the nobles and chieftains of the Kakatiya Kingdom rushed for protection towards the fortress of Warangal.

Now, the fort of Warangal was incredibly big in size, so big that even after refuge had been granted to so many people, there still remained in it enough room for military maneuvering. This colossal citadel had two layers of fortification: there was a monstrous wall made of mud on the outside, while on the inside, a wall of stone separately guarded the royal apartments. Commenting on the fort's uncommon strength, Amir Khusrau says that "its wall, though made of mud, was so hard that a spear of steel could make no impression upon it; if a stone were to strike it, it would rebound like a nut thrown by a child."[316] Besides, to take its security a step further, the fort was provided with two moats: one outside beyond the mud

---

[314] Khazain ul Futuh. Translated by Muhammad Habib. Page 59

[315] Tarikh-i Ferishta. Translated by John Briggs. Page 372

[316] Khazain ul Futuh. Translated by Muhammad Habib. Page 62

wall, the other one inside between the mud wall and the stone wall.

To properly assess the seemingly endless citadel of Warangal, Malik Kafur himself ascended the nearby Hanamkonda hill. After surveying the landscape to his satisfaction, he ordered his men to straightaway commence the siege operations.

The entire circumference of the fort — measuring 12, 546 yards, according to Amir Khusrau — was completely surrounded by the Delhi army who formed themselves into a full circle round the citadel. So closely were the tents pitched that, in the picturesque words of Khusrau, "the head of a needle could not go between them."[317]

A close siege was about to commence, but Malik Kafur's political instincts were yet to be satisfied. There still remained at large some subordinate commanders of the Kakatiya King, the Malik was aware, and therefore he felt the need to secure the rear of his camp from any surprise attack.

"Every soldier was ordered to erect a **Kath-garh** (wooden defense) behind his tent." One lakh souls straightaway sprang into action — "Immediately all hatchets became busy and every soldier was transformed into Ishaq, the wood-cutter," informs Amir Khusrau. Before long, a sturdy wooden fence came up behind the imperialists' encampment. "It was so strong," Khusrau claims, "that if

[317] Khazain ul Futuh. Translated by Muhammad Habib. Page 63.

fire had rained from the sky, the wooden fort would have been as safe from fire as Noah's arc was from water."[318]

Hostilities now began in the true earnest. "Every day intense fighting took place between the insiders and the outsiders," Barani tells us. "Both sides sent **sang-i maghribi** (stones hurled from catapults) against each other and inflicted injuries."[319] The resistance put up by the garrison was stiff, and the Khilji army had to fight every inch of their way.

Meanwhile, not long after, Malik Kafur's apprehensions came true, and the uncommon military genius that he was possessed of became manifest to one and all in the imperial camp. It so happened that one midnight, Banik Deo, one of the chieftains attached to the Kakatiya court, launched a surprise attack on the Khilji encampment. But, unknown to Banik Deo, the Delhi army's rear had already been secured. So, when the watchmen, "with their shields on their back and drawn swords in their hands," spotted the party of Banik Deo, they immediately raised a cry which aroused the entire imperial army from slumber.[320]

Banik Deo was taken completely by surprise at this strange turn of events. The imperial soldiers would be caught unaware and a great deal of damage could be inflicted on them, Banik Deo had thought, but Malik Kafur's intelligence turned the tables on him.

---

[318] Khazain ul Futuh. Translated by Muhammad Habib. Pages 63-64

[319] Tarikh-i Firoz Shahi. Translated by Ishtiyaq Ahmad Zilli. Pages 201-202

[320] Khazain ul Futuh. Translated by Muhammad Habib. Page 64

A terrible carnage now began. The Khiljis fiercely fell upon their nemesis, and destruction stared the Hindus in the face. "Those wounded by spears and arrows cried as frogs cry when caught by snakes," writes Amir Khusrau. "Others who tried to run away received wounds on their backs, which like cancer-sores opened a door for the entry of death. Finally, most of the Hindus were either killed, overpowered or driven away."[321]

Hostilities now greatly intensified. The bloody annihilation of Banik Deo and his men was a great setback for the Kakatiyas. The Khiljis, however, were greatly encouraged by this success and they doubled their efforts to capture the fortress of Warangal. Great exertions were now made by the imperial army to fill up the outside ditch (of ditches, the Warangal fort had two), a task which they succeeded in accomplishing before long. "Ultimately, the Mussalmans threw mud into its mouth," records Amir Khusrau, "and filled it in so completely that its two lips were joined together."[322]

The ditch having been filled up, the turn of the mud fort came next. In spite of the volley of arrows that the besieged garrison continued shooting, the Khilji army didn't retreat even by an inch. "The intrepid and brave soldiers of the army of Islam threw in lassos and ladders,"

---

[321] Khazain ul Futuh. Translated by Muhammad Habib. Page 64

[322] ibid. Page 66

writes Barani.[323] On the other hand, diggers and miners attached to the imperial army got busy in weakening the foundation of the fortification.

“Though the [mud] fort had been so excellently constructed, that there was nothing on its walls that one could catch hold of or lay one’s finger,” narrates Amir Khusrau, “the besiegers clung to it with the edges of their nails.”[324]

The desperate bravery paid dividends rather quickly, and before long, “[the imperial army] with the strike of sword, lance, and axe wrought havoc on the insiders and captured the mud fort.”[325]

The capture of the outlying mud fort totally broke the back of Kakatiya resistance, because, as Ferishta puts it, “the inner fort to which Luddur Dew (Raja Prataparudra) had retired, was insufficient to contain the whole [garrison].”[326] Defeat now stared the Kakatiya king in the face. He had relied heavily on the defence system of his fort, which no doubt was impregnable — “He had fastened his hopes on being able to place before the invaders an obstacle, which would cause them to stumble and retrace their steps,” Amir Khusrau notes — but when the Delhi army pulled off this herculean task and achieved

---

323 Tarikh-i Firoz Shahi. Translated by Ishtiyaq Ahmad Zilli. Page 202

324 Khazain ul Futuh. Translated by Muhammad Habib. Page 68

325 Tarikh-i Firoz Shahi. Translated by Ishtiyaq Ahmad Zilli. Page 202

326 Tarikh-i Ferishta. Translated by John Briggs. Page 372

the impossible, Raja Prataparudra realised that further resistance was futile.[327]

So long so belligerent, the Kakatiya king now decided to sue for peace. "He sent eminent Brahmins and renowned Bhats with many gifts to Malik Naib," records Ziauddin Barani. "He offered to surrender all the treasures, gems, elephants, horses, and other precious materials that he possessed. Moreover, he undertook to send a specified amount of money to the royal treasury and a number of elephants to the royal stables in Delhi every year in future."[328] This proposal suited Malik Kafur's plans perfectly — the Kakatiya king laying down arms and giving up his treasures — after all, this was what his master Sultan Alauddin Khilji had wanted while despatching his army to the faraway land of Deccan.

Raja Prataparudra, however, had not been an inconsequential man: therefore, even in his surrender, he chose grandeur. He had a golden image of himself constructed, "and in acknowledgement of having become a tribute-payer, he placed a golden chain round its neck." He then forwarded this gold figurine of himself to Malik Kafur through his ambassadors, the eminent Brahmins and renowned Bhats, "whose honest word was more unchanging than the purest gold."[329]

"If the good-will of the officers of the world-protecting court is to be won by treasures and valuables," ran the

---

[327] Khazain ul Futuh. Translated by Muhammad Habib. Page 70

[328] Tarikh-i Firoz Shahi. Translated by Ishtiyaq Ahmad Zilli. Page 202

[329] Khazain ul Futuh. Translated by Muhammad Habib. Page 70

Kakatiya King's flattering letter, "[then] I have as much gold with me as will suffice to gild all the mountains of Hind ... If precious stones, gems and pearls are demanded, [then] I have a stock of them such as the eyes of the mountains have not seen and the ears of the fish have not heard of. All these will be scattered on the path of the imperial officers."[330]

Malik Kafur, although inwardly very happy at the turn the events had taken, took care to maintain his hauteur before the Kakatiya ambassadors. "He would not even look at the golden statue (of the Kakatiya King)," writes Amir Khusrau.[331] With great poise, he only repeated the command of his Sultan, who had ordered not to cause any harm to the Rai's life.

After the Kakatiya King's prayer had been granted and peace agreed upon, "[Malik Kafur] stretched forth his right hand, placed his sword in its scabbard, and struck his open hand by way of admonition, so forcibly on the backs of the ambassadors that they bent under the blow."[332] Evidently, an act of condescension!

The next day, the Kakatiya ambassadors arrived in the imperial camp with the promised tribute. The bearers placed before Malik Kafur innumerable boxes – each box being filled with such gems, "the excellence of which drove the onlookers mad."[333] Emeralds, rubies, diamonds,

---

[330] Khazain ul Futuh. Translated by Muhammad Habib. Page 71

[331] ibid. Page 73

[332] ibid. Page 74

[333] ibid. Page 76

pearls and gold — the Kakatiya King had virtually given his entire treasury away to propitiate his Khilji overlord.

"The rubies dazzled the eye of the Sun," writes Amir Khusrau. "[And] The lustre of the rubies illuminated the darkness of the night ... The emeralds had a fineness of water that could eclipse the lawn of paradise. The diamonds would have penetrated into an iron heart like an arrow of steel, and yet owing to their delicate nature, would have been shattered by the stroke of a hammer. The other stones were such that the sun blushed to look at them. As for the pearls, you would not find the like of them, even if you kept diving into the sea through all eternity."[334]

Among the valuables that Malik Kafur received was one incredibly fabulous diamond: "unparalleled in the whole world," according to Amir Khusrau.[335] It probably was the famous Kohinoor diamond, which Mughal Emperor Babur would obtain in Agra when he went on to capture that city in 1526, and which eventually, after changing many a hand, would become a part of the British crown jewels in the nineteenth century. "Its reputation is that every appraiser has estimated its value at two and a half days' food for the whole world," Babur had remarked about the Kohinoor in his memoirs.[336]

---

[334]Khazain ul Futuh. Translated by Muhammad Habib. Page 76

[335] ibid. Page 77

[336] The Baburnama. Vol II. Translated by Annette Susannah Beveridge. Page 477

Besides receiving such priceless gems and jewels by the score, Malik Kafur also managed to secure one hundred elephants — "the mad elephants of Ma'bar," by the Kakatiya King's own admission — and as many as seven thousand horses, all of them belonging to a foreign breed.[337]

Laden with such spoils as baffled imagination, Malik Kafur finally returned to Delhi on the 10th of June, 1310, after being away for a little more than six months.

The Sultan was immensely pleased with his slave's success, and decided to celebrate the occasion publicly, and in grand style. Preparations started right away. A fortnight later, a black pavilion of colossal proportions came up near the Badaun Gate. Sultan Alauddin Khilji would hold his court there.

"The Maliks, who had been sent on the expedition from the Capital, came before the Emperor, and after moistening the ground with the sweat of their brows, presented the spoils," reports Amir Khusrau.[338] "The gold, gems, elephants, horses and other precious material which were brought by Malik Naib were presented before the Sultan and the city's population witnessed this spectacle," records Ziauddin Barani, another eyewitness to that extravagant occasion.[339]

The people of Delhi were thoroughly amazed by the spectacle on offer — "The day looked like a second Id for

---

[337] Khazain ul Futuh. Translated by Muhammad Habib. Page 72

[338] ibid. Page 79

[339] Tarikh-i Firoz Shahi. Translated by Ishtiyaq Ahmad Zilli. Page 202

the people," says Amir Khusrau, without resorting to exaggeration. "The spectators went round and round the court," Khusrau continues, "[and] everyone present was allowed, without any hindrance, to see the display."[340]

In the course of this campaign in Telangana, a peculiar event took place in the capital, one that involved the greatest Sufi master of the time, Hazrat Nizamuddin Auliya. It so happened that some of the chieftains of the Kakatiya King managed to cut all communications off between Delhi and Warangal. Sultan Alauddin Khilji grew extremely anxious on not receiving any update from Malik Kafur for several days. "The dignitaries, amirs and eminent people of the city thought that perhaps some calamity or sedition had taken place in the army," reports Ziauddin Barani.[341] Such gossips and rumours only served to exacerbate the Sultan's distress all the more.

One day, finding that he could bear this anxiety no longer, Alauddin sent two of his trusted men, Qara Beg[342] and Qazi Mughisuddin, to Sheikh Nizamuddin Auliya. "He

---

[340] Khazain ul Futuh. Translated by Muhammad Habib. Page 79

[341] Tarikh-i Firoz Shahi. Translated by Ishtiyaq Ahmad Zilli. Page 203

[342] Qara Beg was an interesting personality. In the political realm, he had a brilliant career: he not only served Alauddin well, but also survived Malik Kafur's regency, and then in the volatile reign of Qutbuddin Mubarak Shah, Qara Beg was entrusted with as many as fourteen offices. Even in the spiritual sphere, his achievemnets were not inconsiderable, for he was one of those few high-ups whose residence was graced by the visit of Sheikh Nizamuddin Auliya in person.

asked them to convey his respects to the Sheikh and tell him that he was deeply concerned as there was no news about the army of Islam," narrates Barani. Because the Shiekh's concern for Islam was beyond question, therefore, "if he had come to know something about the army through divine intervention, the Sultan would be glad to know of the happy news."[343]

As ordered, Qara Beg and Qazi Mughisuddin at once made for the Sheikh's khanqah, and conveyed to him what they were supposed to. Hazrat Nizamuddin Auliya immediately assured the duo: "What to say of this victory, we expect many more victories!"[344]

The message, though short, was absolutely clear. The two messengers then took leave from the Sheikh, and lost no time in conveying the glad tidings to Alauddin. "The Sultan was overjoyed to hear the speech of the Shiekh," reports Barani, "and was convinced that Warangal had been conquered and the objective had been achieved."[345]

Needless to say, the Sheikh's prediction came true, and that too within a few hours. "By the grace of Allah the same day at the evening prayer messengers arrived from Malik Naib and brought the fathnamas of Warangal," continues Barani. "The faith of Sultan Alauddin in the

---

[343] Tarikh-i Firoz Shahi. Translated by Ishtiyaq Ahmad Zilli. Page 203

[344] ibid

[345] ibid

miraculous powers and holiness of the Sheikh increased."[346]

A hagiographical work, **Siyar ul Arifin**, tells us that as a token of his gratitude, Sultan Alauddin Khilji humbly offered the Sheikh five hundred gold coins **(surkh-i dinar)**. The Sheikh accepted it, but as was his wont, he immediately handed over the sum to a destitute dervish who had come to Delhi all the way from Khurasan.[347]

But more on Sufis and their supernatural ways later in this book. It's now time we return to the main narrative. Sure, the success achieved at Warangal had been a resounding one, but for neither Sultan Alauddin Khilji nor Malik Kafur was this the end of the road. At any rate, Malik Kafur was too restless by temperament to remain militarily inactive for long, and likewise Sultan Alauddin Khilji was too ambitious by nature to give up expansionist designs ever in his lifetime.

So in November 1310, hardly five months after he had returned to Delhi, Malik Kafur once again set out with the imperial army, this time to penetrate even deeper into South India. After coming out of Delhi, Malik Kafur stayed put on the bank of Yamuna for two weeks, using this time to meticulously review and inspect the troops that had been placed under his command. "Owing to the

---

[346] Tarikh-i Firoz Shahi. Translated by Ishtiyaq Ahmad Zilli. Page 203

[347] Siyar ul Arifin. By Hamid bin Fazlullah Jamali. Ridwi Press, Delhi. 1893. Page 78

multitude of horsemen," says Amir Khusrau, "the earth looked like the pages of the Shahnama."[348]

In February 1311, the imperial army reached Deogir. Raja Ram Deo, as usual, welcomed his guests warmly and took every care to make their stay comfortable. The city of Deogir had been brilliantly decorated to honour the guests from north — "They saw a city more beautiful than the Paradise of Shadad," writes Khusrau. "At the order of the noble Rai, who was a tree planted by the imperial court," Khusrau continues, "the markets of the city (Deogir) were decorated like the garden of Aram, and the men of the army rode up to them on their horses."[349] Money changers were kept ready; the cloth merchants laid out before the imperialists their pile of stocks, which ranged from textiles made in India to fabrics imported from Khurasan; and fruits, including even the rare and exotic ones, were put on sale.

The imperial army behaved most courteously with the locals — Ram Deo was Alauddin's father-in-law, the soldiers knew, and displeasing him would earn them their Sultan's ire. "The Turk did not oppress the Hindu and the will of the Hindu was not opposed to the will of the Turk," remarks Amir Khusrau, correctly.[350]

After resting for four days at Deogir, the imperial army once again resumed its southward march. Crossing

---

[348] Khazain ul Futuh. By Amir Khusrau. Translated by Muhammad Habib. Page 82

[349] ibid. Page 84

[350] ibid. Page 85

turbulent rivers and negotiating challenging routes, on the 25th of February, 1311, Malik Kafur and his men finally reached the town of Dwarsamudra, "[where] they saw a fort so magnificient, that after viewing it one began to despise the sky."[351]

But for all his fortifications, the Hoysala King Vira Ballala simply didn't have enough courage to resist the formidable forces of the Delhi Sultanate which, he had seen, had come rushing into the Deccan like a mighty deluge and had carried everything before it. "We have no alternative but to turn away our faces from the fiery arrows of the Turks," the Hoysala King admitted before his men, and prudently sued for peace.[352]

Malik Kafur accepted the Hoysala King's proposal for peace, but not before emphasising his position of strength: thus, if the Hoysalas wanted to pay tribute, they were welcome, but if not, then he was only too glad to "simply relieve their necks of the burden of their heads."[353]

"Dwarsamudra was conquered," records Barani, "[and] 36 elephants and the treasures of Dwarsamudra fell into their hands."[354] Amir Khusrau plays up the attributes of those elephants: "Everyone of them was valiant in slaying the brave, gigantic in stature, yet like man in intelligence," he writes.[355]

---

[351] Translated by Muhammad Habib. Page 88

[352] ibid. Page 89

[353] ibid. Page 91

[354] Tarikh-i Firoz Shahi. Translated by Ishtiyaq Ahmad Zilli. Page 204

[355] Khazain ul Futuh. Translated by Muhammad Habib. Page 93

The news of this victory duly reached Delhi, but the victor, Malik Kafur, didn't return to the capital just yet. The Sultan had allowed him vast discretion, and after settling affairs in Dwarsamudra, that general decided to penetrate even deeper into the peninsula.

While at Dwarasamudra, Malik Kafur had got winds of a fratricidal war that had broken out between Vira Pandya and Sundara Pandya, the two scions of the ruling house that ruled over the southernmost tip of the subcontinent. Maravarmana Kulasekhara, the Pandya King of Madurai, was openly partial towards his illegitimate son, Vira Pandya. This irked Sundara Pandya greatly, who thought himself to be the rightful heir to the kingdom given that he was the legitimate son of his father. The climax of this feud was reached when one day, in a fit of rage, Sundara murdered his father, the Pandyan king Kulasekhara. Vira Pandya was not slow to strike back: he dealt a crushing defeat to his brother Sundara, and hounded him out of the kingdom. In distress, Sundara Pandya appealed to Malik Kafur for succour, and his prayer was immediately granted. This was an offer that the Malik couldn't refuse — his sovereign, at any rate, wished to subjugate the whole of the peninsula, and now when a prince of the only remaining power was providing Malik Kafur an offer to accomplish just that, he wasn't going to let go of that golden opportunity at all costs.

Malik Kafur ordered the Hoysala king to accompany him on the southward march, and the latter had no choice but to agree. The imperialists, with the Hoysala guide by their side, set off for Ma'bar on the Wednesday, the 10th of March, 1311.[356] The route southward turned out to be extremely challenging for the northerners — "The sharp thorns drove their points into the feet of the camels," writes Khusrau, "[and] the pointed stones tore the horses' hoofs."[357] Still, the imperialists marched on without demur, and in only five days they managed to reach the frontier of Ma'bar.

Once inside the Pandyan territory, the Khiljis first saw action in a town which Khusrau calls as 'Mardi'. The town evidently had a fort in it, which the imperialists captured without much hassle, and then slaughtered the entire garrison without any fanfare. From Mardi, Malik Kafur and his men proceeded to Birdhul, identified by some scholars with the town of Virudhachalam in Tamil Nadu which, at that point, must have been Vira Pandya's headquarters. Vira Pandya, however, lost his courage at the approach of the imperialists: he fled pell-mell from Birdhul, leaving the town and its inhabitants to the scant mercy of the Sultanate soldiers. From Birdhul, Vira Pandya moved to Kannanur, but the fear of the invaders haunted him so much that he didn't feel secure even there, and he set out to hide himself in the thick forests.

---

[356] The Kingdom of the Pandyas was known by the name of Ma'bar. According to a rough estimate, it extended from Nellore in the north to Kollam in the south. (Reference: History of the Khaljis, by K.S. Lal. Page 207)

[357] Khazain ul Futuh. Translated by Muhammad Habib. Page 95

At this point, as many as 20,000 Muslim soldiers of the Pandyan King came over to the imperialists' side, and with their guidance, Malik Kafur decided to give the Pandya fugitive a hot chase. But unfavourable elements forced him to cut his plan short. So the Malik had no option but to return to Birdhul.

As soon as the rains abated somewhat, Malik Kafur resumed his pursuit. In vain, however. For no matter how hard the imperialists tried, they couldn't get hold of Vira Pandya, who evidently had a much better knowledge of the local geography and used that knowledge to his advantage. "The head-throwing Turks found no traces of the lost man anywhere," writes Amir Khursau, "though they cut off a number of heads under the suspicion that they were his."[358] Malik Kafur, seething with rage at having failed to capture his target, vented his wrath on all the towns and villages that fell his way, amassing a considerable plunder in the process. Still not satisfied, the Malik now turned to the magnificent temples that virtually dotted the Pandyan kingdom.

Information was brought that at Barmatpur, there was a temple that was made completely of gold, where also could be found all the elephants that belonged to the Pandya King. Malik Kafur, "who, if he heard of so much as the picture of an elephant on silk cloth, would have run his sharp scissors into it in the darkest night," would obviously not let go of this opportunity to seize so many of those prized beasts, not to mention the allure of gold

[358] Khazain ul Futuh. Translated by Muhammad Habib. Page 101

that could be had in the temple in plenty.[359] At once, Malik Kafur and his men set out to ransack the temple, and they reached their destination at midnight. "Two hundred and fifty elephants, who roared like thunder, were captured before dawn by the fleet-footed horsemen," writes Amir Khusrau.[360] Next, it was the turn of the temple.

A building more magnificent than anything they had ever seen now stood before the Sultanate soldiers. "You might say that it was the Paradise of Shaddad," says Amir Khusrau, "or that it was the golden Lanka of Ram ... It rose from the earth, a structure of gold scratching the eyes of the stars and piercing the people of the sun ... its golden foundations went deep into the earth ... Its walls and roofs were inlaid with sparkling rubies and emeralds ... The jewelled figure of the idol looked like a bubble on the surface of the sun, and gazing at it would have weakened the eye."[361]

But its brilliance was its bane — the profusion of gems on display in this temple dedicated to Lord Shiva didn't kindle in Malik Kafur's heart any poetic reverence for the structure, but only served to stoke his greed for gold all the more. And in no time did the soldiers get busy in dismantling this grand structure, brick by brick and stone by stone. "The golden bricks rolled down and brought with them the plaster of sandal-wood; the yellow gold

[359] Khazain ul Futuh. Translated by Muhammad Habib. Page 102

[360] ibid

[361] ibid. Pages 102-103

became red with blood; and the white sandal turned scarlet. The sword flashed where jewels had once been sparkling; where mire used to be created by rose-water and musk, there was now a mud of blood and dirt; the stench of blood was now emitted by ground once fragrant with musk ..."[362]

Meanwhile, Sundara Pandya, who himself had brought so great a calamity upon his land, felt his courage slipping when he saw with his own eyes the extent of savagery these northern invaders were capable of. Far from remaining by Malik Kafur's side, he took the first available opportunity to slip into the security of the thick forests, where his rival brother Vira Pandya had also taken shelter. Malik Kafur, however, didn't like this behaviour of his inviter: therefore, to teach Sundara Pandya a lesson, he decided to dash into the latter's headquarters, Madurai.

Of course, Sundara Pandya couldn't be found anywhere in Madurai, as he had escaped long back to save his back. That, however, hardly deterred Malik Kafur — at any rate, he was more interested in plunder than in the hospitality of his host, and he thought he would make the best of Sundara's absence by looting his palace to his heart's content. But this is where he went wrong — Sundara Pandya had fled, sure, but not before taking all his valuables with him into the wilderness, leaving only two elephants for his guests, the imperialists. This infuriated Malik Kafur, and he gave vent to his wrath by

[362] Khazain ul Futuh. Translated by Muhammad Habib. Page 103

stripping the magnificent temple of Madurai of all the riches that it had.

Madurai, according to some scholars, was the furthest point that Alauddin's army penetrated into the south. Others, basing themselves primarily on Ferishta's account, claim that Malik Kafur didn't stop at Madurai, but carried the Khilji flag all the way up to Rameshwaram, where the general got a mosque constructed and the khutba read therein in the name of his sovereign, Sultan Alauddin Khilji. This debate need not deter us further, and we had better shifted our focus to the spoils that Malik Kafur managed to accumulate after several months of hard campaigning.

612 elephants, 20,000 horses, 96,000 mans of gold, and innumerable boxes containing jewels and pearls — this was what, according to Ziauddin Barani, Malik Kafur had seized in this expedition.[363] Amir Khusrau compares the height of the elephants to the clouds in the sky — "But while other clouds rain water and cause vegetation to grow," he writes, "these clouds drank water and ate vegetables." And when a mahout sat on one of its neck, it appeared "like an angel directing a cloud." As to the horses, Khusrau continues, "they were swift as lightning," and, "a man could never attain to their swiftness except in imagination." The ultimate praise, however, is reserved for the peerless gems that had come into the Malik's hands. Each of the diamonds sparkled so brightly, says the poet, that "it seemed as if it was a drop fallen from the

[363] 1 man was equal to 25.44 lbs avoirudupois, or around 11.55 kgs. So, 96,000 man of gold was more than 11 lakhs kg of gold!

sky." The rubies were of so brilliant a colour that to produce their likes, "for generations the mines will have to drink blood."[364]

With such a booty as would have turned Mahmud of Ghazni in his grave with wistful eyes, Malik Kafur finally reached Delhi in October 1311, after covering the long journey that took him almost six months. That evening, as the sun sank in the horizon, setting the western sky past the towering Qutb Minar ablaze in shades of gold, Sultan Alauddin Khilji must have felt some pride in his heart. From being a nobody only some decades ago, to now being the richest and most powerful Sultan to have ever ruled from Delhi — Alauddin Khilji, for sure, had come a long way. The fading sunlight in the evening sky must have contrasted in his mind to the high noon which his life was now poised at, and the view of the distant Qutb Minar from his palace windows must have brought home to him the colossal height he had scaled in his life, that had put him head and shoulders above his contemporaries, within India as well as outside it. A public celebration to mark such a great success as had attended the Sultanate deep in the south was desirable, the Sultan must have thought, one that would also involve sharing the riches that had come his way with those who were not as fortunate.

Accordingly, on Monday, the 18th of October, a grand public durbar was held in Delhi, and Malik Kafur took this opportunity to ceremoniously present before his sovereign, the Sultan, everything that he had seized from the south. "The old men of Delhi," says Barani, "were

---

[364] Khazain ul Futuh. Translated by Muhammad Habib. Pages 105-107

unanimous in saying that so much booty, elephants and gold that was brought to Delhi in the conquest of Ma'bar and Dwarsamudra, had never been brought to Delhi before in any age and at any time. No book of history had also recorded that in any age so much gold and elephants have ever reached Delhi."[365]

It was a most grand affair, this public durbar, with the Sultan sitting under a magnificient canopy and all the spoils from the south being arrayed at his feet. All the nobles and grandees of the Delhi Sultanate stood in attendance to their Sultan — "The Maliks in innumerable rows rubbed their waists together," says Khusrau.366 They were both Muslims and Hindus — the Hindus, says Khusrau, had their sectarian mark on their forehead, and after they were done prostrating, because of the great number in which they had come, the ground below the Sultan's throne took on a saffron hue. Cries of "Bismillah!" and "Hadakallah!" reverberated far and wide as the nobles, one after the other, were ushered in to pay their respects to their Sultan.

All done, it was now time for the Sultan's largesse. It was pure gold, of all things, that was to be gifted to all the nobles that had assembled. Of the innumerable grandees that were present in the grand durbar, none received from the Sultan less than half a man of gold, while those that had distinguished themselves by their performance received as much as four mans of gold. It was an

---

[365] Tarikh-i Firoz Shahi. Translated by Ishtiyaq Ahmad Zilli. Page 204

[366] Khazain ul Futuh. Translated by Muhammad Habib. Page 108

extravaganza of everything extravagant, and a spectacle of everything spectacular.

The successful completion of these extraordinary Deccan campaigns proved to be the apogee of Sultan Alauddin Khilji's career. A historian working for the Mongols, the arch enemy of Alauddin, had no choice but to admit that the series of brilliant vitories that the Sultan achieved in the faraway land of the Deccan put him on a higher pedestal than even Mahmud of Ghazni.[367]

Overpowering the southern armies, at any rate, was not a difficult job for a force that had trounced the formidable Mongols time and again. "Where should the army that defeats the Mongol host be afraid of fighting the Hindu?" asks Isami sardonically.[368] However, the length of the distance that had to be covered, coupled with the unfamiliarity of the northeners with the land they were called upon to invade, were issues that were serious and had to be taken into consideration accordingly. But, Malik Kafur handled his charge so well, and carried out his assignment so brilliantly, that the magnitude of the perils that he had to surmount almost paled into insignifance before his stunning victories. Sultan Alauddin Khilji, too, deserves rich praises — he not only selected the right man for the right job, but also gave him enough latitude so as not to inhibit in any way the man's natural aptitude for warfare. All the same, he kept himself fully aware of all the affairs pertaining to his army, and maintained a close

---

[367] History of the Khaljis. By K.S. Lal. Page 219

[368] Quoted in the Delhi Sultanate. By Peter Jackson. Cambridge University Press. Page 216

watch on the operations of his soldiers as they took the field against their opponents. There, therefore, was no question of any subversion of authority — Malik Kafur was a slave, a very talented and successful one no doubt, but still only a slave. The master of the army remained as before Sultan Alauddin Khilji, and on that issue, the Sultan himself made sure that there remained no ambiguity whatsoever.

Be that as it may, the vast wealth sequestered out of the Deccan on the point of sword was employed to lubricate the state machinery of the Delhi Sultanate. The colossal administrative structure, the countless forts scattered throughout the empire, and a huge army that was composed of almost half a million men — all of that required money, and funds from the Deccan were channelized to that end. Besides, because of the influx of so much of wealth and the security that such wealth provided, Delhi, the capital of the Delhi Sultanate, emerged as a city with no rivals as far as the pursuit of finer elements of life was concerned. It is to that cultural efflorescence which blossomed in Delhi at the dawn of the fourteenth century, that we are now going to turn.

Delhi

Delhi is the seat of government of Hindustan, the centre of the circle of Islam, the sanctuary of the mandates and inhibitions of the law, the kernel of the Muhammadi religion, the marrow of the Ahmadi belief, and the tabernacle of the eastern parts of the universe — Guard it, O God, from calamities, and molestation!

— Tabaqat-i Nasiri, by Minhaj Siraj.

"The gathering of incomparable and distinguished persons made the capital of Delhi an object of envy to Baghdad and Egypt and an equal to Constantinople and Jerusalem," writes Ziauddin Barani, and no, he is not one bit guilty of exaggeration.[369] In the reign of Sultan Alauddin Khilji, there was such a glorious outburst of art, culture and all such finer pursuits in the city of Delhi as had never been witnessed before, and would remain equally unparalleled at least for three hundred years after that Sultan's death.

Alauddin himself might not have been a very erudite man, having had to wield his sword for far too long in his life to forge any intimacy with the pen. Nevertheless, his was

369 The Reign of Alauddin Khilji. Translated from Ziauddin Barani's Tarikh-i Firoz Shahi. By A.R. Fuller AND A. Khallaque. Page 149

the court that had the distinction of counting among its members such prodigal poets as Amir Khusrau and Amir Sijzi. And if these two giants were not enough, the Sultan had on his payroll at least another half a dozen other poets of comparable calibre. "Every one of them," opines Barani, "had a particular style of his own in poetry and his own anthology of poetry."[370]

And not just poets, there were historians too, and at least two of them were distinguished enough to merit a mention in Barani's work which, according to the author's own admission, otherwise stands out for its concise nature. Amir Arsalan and Kabiruddin were the two great historians in Alauddin's Delhi — the former had so prodigal a memory that whenever he was asked anything pertaining to history, "he would narrate it from memory and was never obliged to consult books of history"; the latter was adept at writing history down given his expertise in Persian as well as Arabic.[371] Though neither of them was of a stature equal to Ziauddin Barani, who was hands down the finest historian in the entire period that covered the rule of the Delhi Sultanate, yet they definitely had considerable expertise in the field of history, not least because they received rich accolades from Barani himself.

Then there were the musicians: for all the rhetoric of Delhi being the bastion of Islamic orthodoxy a generation or two earlier, under Alauddin Khilji music reached new heights in the city of Delhi. The foremost among them, of

---

[370] Tarikh-i Firoz Shahi. Translated by Ishtiyaq Ahmad Zilli. Page 222

[371] ibid

course, was once again Amir Khusrau who, Barani tells us, "was deeply given to Sufi music **(sama)** and was a man of ecstasy."[372] As is well known, along with singing he composed songs too, and if later traditions are to be believed, then he also had to his credit the invention of multiple musical instruments. Amir Hasan, that matchless poet and peer to Amir Khusrau, was adept at composing ghazals.

At any rate, it was ghazal, of all forms of music, that was chiefly cultivated in Delhi: much of what we enjoy today in the voice of Jagjit Singh and Ghulam Ali Khan, then, had its genesis in the reign of Sultan Alauddin Khilji. Among the chief exponents of ghazal were men like Mahmud bin Sikka, Isu Nishyan, Muhammad Muqri, and Isa Khudadi, and we are told, anybody fortunate enough to witness the performance of any one of them treasured the experience for their lifetime. "The city of Delhi could not remember such skilled artisans and master professionals in any other age. Happy was their gathering and happy was the perfection of their skill that could become the subject matter of the writing of history."[373]

A city can't do without doctors, and neither could Alauddin's Delhi. The most eminent physician of the city, we are told, was a certain Maulana Badruddin Dimashqi, who had such an expertise in his field that he regularly conducted classes which were attended by other physicians of the city. "Almighty God had endowed him

---

[372] Tarikh-i Firoz Shahi. Translated by Ishtiyaq Ahmad Zilli. Pages 221-222

[373] ibid. Page 225

with such expertise in the art of medicine," Barani tells us, "that merely by putting his finger on the pulse of the patient he would know the source of the ailment and with what medicines he could be cured."[374]

Once, it is said, the people of Delhi tried to test the depth of his knowledge in a rather bizarre way. Urine of different animals, we are told, was mixed with the urine of a man in the same jar, and the container was then handed to the Maulana and he was asked to name all the animals whose urine had went into the jar. This task, to everyone's surprise, the Maulana accomplished easily, and that too by merely casting a glance at the jar.

So much for the chief physician of Delhi. There were in the city other men of medicine too, of course, and among them the Hindus featured prominently. Brahmins, we are told, were highly skilled as physicians, so much so that some of them diagnosed the ailment at the very first glance, and then proceeded to cure it with medicines which, more often than not, turned out to be effective.

The practises of chiromancy and fortune telling, in spite of Quranic prohibitions and arguments against it by theologians as eminent as al-Ghazzali, bloomed in Alauddin's Delhi. In his reign, the chroniclers say, there was virtually no locality in Delhi where astrologers could not be found. For every correct prediction that they made, they were rewarded lavishly by the city's elites, so that most of the fortune-tellers led a very prosperous life.

---

[374] Tarikh-i Firoz Shahi. Translated by Ishtiyaq Ahmad Zilli. Page 223

"Thus even circumcision, marriage ceremonies, and proposals for marriage," we are told, "would not be undertaken in Delhi without consulting astrologers."[375] The wonder of wonders, however, was that even the hard-headed Sultan himself was not immune to their influence. He had in his service a host of astrologers, some of them Hindus, who tended exclusively to him and his family, and in return "got so many alms from Sultan Alauddin and his harem that they built properties."[376]

But attempts at alchemy, even though that discipline enjoyed a higher status than palm-reading in the orthodox eyes, received no where near the same encouragement. Alchemy was fundamentally about converting base metals into gold, and whenever the issue of gold/wealth came into question, the Sultan grew apprehensive. "He believed that alchemy is a means of augmenting wealth and wealth is the bane of the state" — Alauddin was absolutely clear in his mind, and he drew an equally clear line, the crossing of which, quite predictably, evoked a harsh response from the Sultan, and that could mean the offender getting incarcerated for life.[377]

But no matter which epoch in question, any discussion on Delhi, which had been described by one author as 'the kernel of the Muhammadi religion', is incomplete without a dilation on the city's men of piety. And in Alauddin's

---

[375] Tarikh-i Firoz Shahi. Translated by Ishtiyaq Ahmad Zilli. Page 224

[376] ibid

[377] ibid. Page 225

reign, on this front too, the city of Delhi bloomed like never before.

First and foremost, there was the towering presence of Sheikh Nizamuddin Auliya whose influence, it would hardly be an exaggeration to say, still runs through the length and breadth of Delhi with an intensity that isn't much less than when the Sheikh was physically around. Tall, slim and graceful in appearance, Nizamuddin Auliya exuded an other-worldly charm in his ways, and his instinctive understanding of the very many problems that plagued the human psyche turned him into one of the most charismatic spiritual figures of all times.

Sheikh Nizamuddin Auliya was a stranger to religious particularism. If one of his favourite disciples composed impassioned verses in praise of Lord Krishna, then another of his disciples was counselled by the Sheikh himself with a story that featured a pious Brahmin who had a profound respect for his sacred thread.[378] And orthodox opinion notwithstanding, neither did gender bias carry much weight with the Sheikh. "If a lion comes out of the jungle," he would say, "nobody bothers whether it's a male or female."[379] By the same token, all those who conducted themselves in a righteous manner were worthy of respect — it mattered little whether the person in question was a man or a woman.

---

[378] A Comprehensive History of India, Volume Five, Page 441; Fawaid ul Fuad, Translated by Ziyaul Hasan Faruqi, Pages 154-55

[379] Fawaid ul Fuad. By Amir Hasan Sijzi. Translated by Ziyaul Hasan Faruqi. D.K. Printworld. New Delhi, 1995. Page 101

The Sheikh, we are told, made sure that he remained accessible to all and at all times. It was his explicit mandate to the inmates of his hospice not to turn away any visitor, no matter what the circumstances.[380] No wonder therefore, a vast multitude of people — Hindus and Muslims, rich and poor, nobles and commoners — thronged his khanqah round the clock, and none returned without receiving his grace.

Such was the charm of the Chishti master's personality that it attracted people from every echelon of the contemporary society. Thus, some of the most powerful individuals of the Delhi Sultanate felt pride in calling themselves his disciples, so much so that this has led a modern scholar, Simon Digby, to claim that 'everyone who was anyone' professed allegiance to Nizamuddin Auliya.[381] In the same way, the Sheikh's compassion towards the poor was so intense that he frequently fasted in a deliberate attempt to experience the same hardship that his impoverished followers had to suffer on a daily basis. Even when he didn't fast, one or two breads and a handful of vegetable was all that he partook of in twenty-four hours. And this frugal eating habit of the Sheikh continued well into his old age. Sure, some of his disciples tried to dissuade him from this self-inflicted ordeal, but their entreaties more often than not fell on deaf ears. Tears would well up in the Sheikh's eyes, and he would say:

---

[380] As per Amir Khwurd's *Siyar ul Auliya*, Sheikh Nizamuddin Auliya once admonished his attendant for turning away a man who had come to the hospice when the Sheikh was having his siesta.

[381] The Sufi Shaikh as a Source of Authority in Medieval India, by Simon Digby.

"Think how many poor people and beggars are suffering hunger and deprivation, huddled around the mosques and sleeping in the streets of the city — how can this food go down my throat?"[382]

A substantial section of Delhi's Muslim population, the sources say, took initiation from the Sheikh. That, at any rate, wasn't a difficult task: the Sheikh didn't insist on any precondition and agreed, without demur, to accept as his disciple anyone who wanted to become one.[383] And of the Sheikh's disciples, it is said, most of them took care to cultivate a high moral character. "The thought that they were disciples of the Sheikh prevented many people from committing unlawful things both in open and in secret," writes Barani. "The masses became inclined ... towards acts of devotion and worship. Men and women, old and young, market people and common men, slaves and servants and even children of tender age would come regularly for prayers."[384]

Many of Sheikh Nizamuddin Auliya's contemporaries thought that the city of Delhi owed its prosperity to his holy presence. Barani boldly claimed that it was only due

---

[382] Sufi Martyrs of Love, by Carl W. Ernst and Bruce B. lawrence. Palgrave Macmillan. 2002. Page 74

[383] *"Ask me anything,"* the Sheikh used to say, *"but do not ask me why I give the hand of discipleship to all comers without first examining them. It is out of fear of hell that people have cast themselves on the protection of the lovers of God. Hence the Sheikhs have made disciples from both the elites and the masses."* (Reference: The Earliest Chishtiya and Shaikh Nizamuddin Awliya, by Bruce B. Lawrence; Delhi Through The Ages, Oxford University Press, Page 119)

[384] Tarikh-i Firoz Shahi. Translated by Ishtiyaq Ahmad Zilli. Pages 210-211

to the benedictions of the Sheikh that "the undertakings of both the ruler and the ruled of the reign of Sultan Alauddin were fulfilled according to their hearts' desire and the standard of Islam was raised."[385] Likewise, another contemporary, Abdul Malik Isami, asserted that it was Hazrat Nizamuddin Auliya who was responsible for the peace and security that came to pervade the length and breadth of the Delhi Sultanate.[386]

It was then a fervour of piety that came to grip Delhi. There hardly was such a locality in Delhi, where the locals would not organize sufistic musical gatherings for at least twenty days in a month. In those assemblies, qawwalis would be sung and incantations would be uttered, which would then induce among the audience a sensation of ecstasy. Indeed, matters reached such an extent that special arrangements had to be made for the travellers on the road leading to Sheikh Nizamuddin Auliya's khanqah. "Between Ghayaspur and the city (Mehrauli)," Barani informs us, "the pious and charitable people built platforms and put up thatched roofs on a number of places, and excavated wells, and jars, ewers and earthen

---

[385] Tarikh-i Firoz Shahi. Translated by Ishtiyaq Ahmad Zilli. Page 199

[386]" *He was one of the friends of God/Through whom the realm of Hindustan was maintained.*" (Reference: The Sufi Shaykh and the Sultan: A Conflict of Claims to Authority in Medieval India, by Simon Digby)

water pots were kept ready full of water, and mats were spread."[387]

Of the countless devotees that Sheikh Nizamuddin Auliya had, one individual stood out from the rest: he was Alauddin Khilji, the Sultan of the Delhi Sultanate.388 Sultan Alauddin, Barani would have us believe, had developed a very sincere faith in the Sheikh, not least beacuse of the latter's successful prediction of the outcome of the Telangana campaign. "Still they never met," laments Barani.[389] But the reason behind the two of them not meeting each other remains obscure. Tradition, of course, attributes it to the Sheikh's refusal to attend the King's court. But that argument is hardly tenable: if Alauddin so wanted, he could have met the Sheikh at his khanqah. Not that his royal prestige would have suffered any setback in that case, for his illustrious predecessor on the Delhi Throne, Sultan Balban, was in the habit of personally paying visits to holy men who resided in his capital. Sufic literature, however, has a reason to offer: it was the Second Alexander's bashful humility, they say, that prevented him from reaching out to the Sheikh. Thus, the Sultan is reported to have once admitted before one of his confidants: "I am a king in this world and I am steeped in it from head to toe. On account of this pollution, I am

[387] Tarikh-i Firoz Shahi. Translated by Ishtiyaq Ahmad Zilli. Page 211

[388] In the Sultan's family, apart from his two sons, Khizr Khan and Shadi Khan, two of his wives were also devoted followers of Sheikh Nizamuddin Auliya. (Reference: *Qiwam al-Aqaid*, by Mohammad Jamal Qiwam)

[389] Tarikh-i Firoz Shahi. Translated by Ihstiyaq Ahmad Zilli. Page 203

ashamed of myself and dare not present myself personally before such a holy man."[390]

So much for Sheikh Nizamuddin Auliya. But if in any aspect, the provinces of Alauddin's vast empire could find themselves on a similar footing with the capital, Delhi, then it was definitely in matters of piety. In the Sultanate at large, besides Sheikh Nizamuddin Auliya, there were two other great Sufi masters: one was Sheikh Alauddin, the grandson of Sheikh Fariduddin of Ajodhan (the spiritual preceptor of Nizamuddin Auliya); the other was Sheikh Ruknuddin, grandson of Bahauddin Zakariya of Multan. These three men — Sheikh Nizamuddin, Sheikh Alauddin, and Sheikh Ruknuddin — constituted what could be called as the cornerstone of Indian Sufism in the early fourteenth century.[391]

About Sheikh Alauddin, it is said that he hardly slept, and most of his nights were spent in the worship and contemplation of the Almighty. Many among those who got a chance to spend some days at his residence claimed that "they never saw Sheikh Alauddin in any other position except praying or reciting the Quran or perusing

---

[390] From the *Siyar ul Auliya*, by Amir Khurd. Quoted in The Life and Works of Sultan Alauddin Khilji, by Dr. Ghulam Sarwar Khan Niazi. Atlantic Publishers, New Delhi. Pages 78-79.

[391] Perfect cordiality existed among these three holy men. That, however, doesn't mean that in the age under question there was no acrimony between the different Sufi orders. On the contrary, even in the capital city of Delhi, the votaries of the Chishti silsilah were often at loggerheads with the adherents of the Firdausi order. (Reference: The Sufi Shaikh as a Source of Authority in Medieval India, by Simon Digby)

books of **Hadith** and mysticism."[392] He commanded an international fame, and his plaudits could be heard in mystic circles even in places as far as Alexandria in Egypt. His renown didn't diminish so long as he lived, and it was to his credit that he managed to enlist as his pupils some very distinguished personalities of the day: Muhammad bin Tughluq, a Sultan of Delhi, was one among them.[393]

Sheikh Ruknuddin inherited a vast amount of wealth, for his grandfather, Sheikh Bahauddin Zakariya, who was also called **Baz-i Sapid** (White Falcon), had been lavishly patronised by the Mamluk Sultans of Delhi. However, of Sheikh Ruknuddin, it is said that in spite of his colossal inheritence, he had to live on borrowed money: such was the scale of his generosity, that humbled many a king and prince alike. And this scale of generosity was only matched by the intensity of piety that was witnessed at his khanqah: an itinerant **qawwal** noted that at the Suhrawardi hospice in Multan, even while going about their daily chores, the inmates would continue to recite verses in praise of the Almighty.[394]

Besides, Ferishta also claims that the family of Bahauddin Zakariya exercised vast political influence, so much so that anyone guilty of almost any crime received immunity

---

[392] Tarikh-i Firoz Shahi. By Ziauddin Barani. Translated by Ishtiyaq Ahmad Zilli. Page 213

[393] Travels of Ibn Battuta. Translated by H.A.R. Gibb. Page 613

[394] Some Aspects of Religion and Politics in India during the Thirteenth Century. By K.A. Nizami. Aligarh Muslim University, 1961. Page 227

from the state if he sought asylum with them. This statement, perhaps, was not entirely devoid of truth. Bahauddin Zakariya, at any rate, had been highly influential in contemporary politics, and he had helped Sultan Iltutmish to oust his rival Nasiruddin Qubacha from Multan. As a reward for this service, the Sultan had bestowed on the Sheikh the exalted title of 'Sheikh ul Islam' besides very many gifts.

That the same state of affairs continued even afterwards is proved by an episode that played out almost a hundred years after Shiekh Bahauddin Zakariya's demise. Early in Sultan Muhammad bin Tughluq's reign, Bahram Aiba, the governor of Multan, rebelled against the Sultan. The rebellion was snuffed out in no time: Bahram Aiba was killed, his men were routed, and his severed head was brought to the Sultan. But this easy victory failed to satisfy Muhammad bin Tughluq, who wanted to slake his thirst for revenge by punishing the inhabitants of Multan for a fault in which they had no hand. At that point, Sheikh Ruknuddin interceded with the Sultan, and the otherwise implacable Muhamamd bin Tughluq at once accepted his request, and agreed to spare the people of Multan.

The efflorescence of Sufism in Alauddin's reign, however, didn't mean that theological learning was allowed to suffer any setback. As to the scholars of traditional Islamic works, our chief chronicler, Ziauddin Barani, mentions as many as forty-six of them, all residing together, at the same time, in the capital city of Delhi. Among them was also included a grandson of Bahauddin Zakariya, Maulana Alamuddin, who was a brother or a cousin of the aforementioned Sheikh Ruknuddin of

Multan. "During the entire reign of Sultan Alauddin there were **ulama** in the capital city of Delhi, every one of whom was a master in his field and the likes of which could not be found in Bukhara, Samarkand, Baghdad, Egypt, Khwarazm, Damascus, Tabriz, Isfahan, Ray, Rome and the rest of the inhabited world.

"In every branch of learning such as traditional sciences **(manqulat)**, rational sciences **(maqulat)**, exigencies of the Quran **(Tafsir)**, jurisprudence **(Fiqh)**, principles of jurisprudence **(usul-i fiqh)**, principles of religion **(usul-i din)**, grammar **(nahv)**, lexicography, knowledge of figures of speech, kalam **(scholastic theology)**, and logic **(mantiq)** could be discussed by them threadbare ... In the life of those great scholars when a new book in any new branch of knowledge was brought to Delhi from Bukhara, Samarkand, Khwarizm and Iraq, if the great scholars of our city approved it and gave credence to it, [only then] it received acceptance, otherwise it was consigned to oblivion."[395]

So much of cultural efflorescence happened in the city, but our chief chronicler, Ziauddin Barani, hesitates to give even a fraction of credit for it to the master of the city, Sultan Alauddin Khilji. "Sultan Alauddin was a ruler who had no familiarity with learning and had never been associated with the Ulema ... The learned rarely frequented his court," Barani tries to dismiss any role that

[395] Tarikh-i Firoz Shahi. Translated by Ishtiyaq Ahmad Zilli. Pages 217-218

Alauddin might have had in Delhi's cultural bloom.396 But this time he misses the mark. Entirely. Sure, when he ascended the throne of the Delhi Sultanate, Alauddin Khilji was definitely an illiterate man, but he didn't die an illiterate man. In this conncetion, a most facsinating anecdote has come down to us from the pen of an authority different from Barani.

As the Sultan, Alauddin realised how hard it was for an illiterate man like himself to look after the nuances of administration and statecraft. "He was, however, so sensible of the disadvantages under which he laboured," records Ferishta, "that he applied himself privately to study, and notwithstanding the difficulty of acquiring knowledge of Persian, after he once bent his mind to it, he soon read all addresses, and made himself acquainted with the best authors in the language."[397]

That Khilji Sultan, at any rate, had a thing for pulling off extraordinary feats, and keeping that in mind, this account doesn't appear to be impossible at all. Even if otherwise, Barani's claim that "the learned rarely frequented his court" can hardly be believed, not least because Barani himself contradicts it in other parts of the same work.

A Sultan who counted among his courtiers prodigies like Amir Khusrau could, by no means, be lacking learned men at his court. Besides, Barani himself has mentioned as many as five boon companions of Sultan Alauddin Khilji, each of whom was learned, dignified and claimed

---

[396] Tarikh-i Firoz Shahi. Translated by Ishtiyaq Ahmad Zilli. Pages 175-176

[397] Tarikh-i Ferishta. Translated by John Briggs. Page 348

universal respect for their sterling character. Readers would find it interesting to note that among these five was also included one grandson of Sultan Balban of Mamluk dynasty — his name was Khudawandzada Chashnigir, and apart from his blood relation to Balban, unfortunately we don't know much about him.

Also, there was a famous book reader **(kitabkhwan)** on Alauddin's payroll, and his task was to read out famous books to the Sultan. We are told, he was unrivalled in his profession.

Going by such unimpeachable evidence, the claim that Sultan Alauddin Khilji didn't adequately patronise learned men, falls flat to the ground.

Another charge that is levelled against the Sultan is that of parsimony: Barani criticizes Alauddin Khilji for annually paying Amir Khusrau only 1,000 tankas, a sum which, according to him, was far less than what the poet merited. Of course, to some extent we must agree with Barani: the talent of Amir Khusrau was priceless in itself, and the sum of 1,000 tankas does look rather paltry on the face.

But a closer investigation reveals a completely different picture. What must not be forgotten is how cheap the essential commodities had become in Alauddin's reign — when one remembers that an elite cavalry soldier in Alauddin's army drew no more than 250 tankas a year from the royal treasury, then Amir Khusrau's emolument, which was four times as much, no longer appears as paltry. Besides, the poet Amir Khusrau himself admitted in some of his works that over and above his officially fixed salary, he often received sumptuous presents from the Sultan, his brothers and the inmates of his harem.

Even if we choose to concur fully with Barani and agree that Alauddin wasn't as generous towards men of literary talents as other kings of Delhi had been, it still can't be denied that the cultural efflorescence that Delhi witnessed in that period wouldn't have been possible without the robust security, both external and internal, that Sultan Alauddin Khilji provided to his capital and his empire at large.

To sum it up, it wouldn't be wrong to say that while Delhi was the garden (of talents), her Sultan, even if not the gardener himself, at least ensured that the garden remained unmolested.

Alaudding Khilji & Religion

> *I am neither an infidel nor a Muslim ...*
> *Only God knows the condition of my heart and how I am.*
>
> *— Tarikh-i Firoz Shahi, by Ziauddin Barani.*

Given how much Sultan Alauddin Khilji was vilified in a film that was released not too long ago, I felt myself called upon to dilate on this topic. I would sift facts from fiction, and history from propaganda, and present as accurate a picture as possible before my readers.

"Sultan Alauddin repeatedly said," records Nizamuddin Ahmad Bakshi, "that the orders and rules of government depended solely on the judgement of the sovereign, and that the law (of the Prophet) had no concern with them ... Accordingly he carried into effect whatever he judged, in his mind, for the better government of the country; and paid no heed to the question as to whether what he did was or was not authorised by the [Islamic] law."[398]

---

[398] Tabaqat-i Akbari. By Khwaja NIzamuddin Ahmad. Translated by B. DE. Page 170

Likewise, Barani says: "When he (Sultan Alauddin) assumed kingship, he came to the conclusion that kingship is one thing, and the traditions and rules of the Shariat are altogether a different thing. The rules and regulations of kingship are concerned with kings, and the regulations of the shariat belong to the domain of **Qazis** and **Muftis**. In accordance with this belief, he would do whatever he considered to be in the interest of governance, whether it was sanctioned by the Shariat or not, and would never seek the opinion of [religious] scholars in matters related to the state."[399]

Such descriptions of Sultan Alauddin Khilji by medieval chroniclers, each of whom was an orthodox Muslim, should be enough to bust the myth of the Sultan's purported bigotry. And if perchance that is not enough, then we have even more evidences to offer.

Readers shall remember that Barani, a contemporary of the Sultan and the foremost authority on his reign, had told us about how Sultan Alauddin, early in his reign, wanted to abjure Islam, create a new creed of his own, and then rival none other than the Prophet of Islam himself. Surely, most surely, such a man couldn't be regarded, by any stretch of imagination, as an Islamic bigot who was driven solely by the zeal to proselytize his subjects and convert the whole of Hindustan into Islam. In fact, a thorough study of the Sultan's character would make it absolutely clear. A superficial study, however, could lead

---

[399] Tarikh-i Firoz Shahi. Translated by Ishtiyaq Ahmad Zilli. Pages 175-176

to erroneous conclusions: that's because Ziauddin Barani, the main authority on Alauddin's reign, had this really bad habit of dragging religion into affairs that were essentially secular in nature, and of employing sectarian jargons in places where they were not at all required.

Like, when the Sultan imposed high revenue demand on the cultivators, Barani construed it as an act against the Hindus. Then, to protect the same lot of peasants from the illegal exactions of their co-religionists, when the Sultan took away the power and privileges of the village headmen, Barani claimed even that as a punitive measure directed against the Hindus. Of course, such unwarranted usage of religious terminology can elicit nothing more than a chuckle from any serious reader of history.

If Alauddin's revenue demand was heavy, it was not demanded from the Hindus alone. If Alauddin was harsh towards the traders, it was not only the Hindu traders that were brought to the book. If Alauddin's treatment of his nobles was severe, it too was by no means directed only against the Hindu noblemen.

In fact, although we have no means to ascertain the real figures, Sultan Alauddin Khilji certainly entertained more Hindu nobles at his court than any of his Muslim predecessors on the throne of Delhi ever did. Thus, we hear of a general named Malik Naik, who was given the command over thirty thousand imperial horsemen by the Sultan, and then sent off to take the Mongols on, a task which the aforementioned Hindu carried out with consummate efficiency. Then there was one Thakkura Pheru, another Hindu, who was in charge of the Sultan's mint.[400] Likewise, Sadharana was an important Hindu officer of Sultan Alauddin Khilji whose job was to look after the imperial treasury.[401] These are only a few names that have survived from among the presumably substantial number of Hindus who were appointed to different offices of distinction in the reign of Sultan Alauddin.

As circumstances would have it, most of the battles that Sultan Alauddin Khilji had to fight were with his non-Muslim opponents, the Mongols and the Hindu Rajas. While he was exceptionally ruthless towards his Mongol foes, by contrast he was rather magnanimous in his treatment of the vanquished Hindu kings. Thus, Raja Ram Deo, the defeated Hindu king of Deogir, visited Delhi multiple times, and not once could he find anything amiss in the Sultan;s hospitality. And if Isami's account is to be believed, then the Hoysala King of Dwarsamudra also called on Sultan Alauddin Khilji — he was accorded the grandest reception imaginable which featured, among other things, the grant of a gift of one million tankas.

After Prince Khizr Khan abdicated the charge of Chittor, that fort was handed over to a certain Rajput aristocrat who enjoyed cordial relations with Sultan Alauddin. Every year, he sent large sums of money, besides "valuable presents", according to Ferishta, "and always

---

[400] Mentioned in M. Athar Ali's *Nobility under Muhammad Tughluq.*

[401] Mentioned in M. Athar Ali's *Nobility under Muhammad Tughluq.*

joined the imperial standards in the field with 5,000 horse and 10,000 foot."[402]

Sultan Alauddin Khilji, in the course of his long political career, destroyed several Hindu temples while waging war against his Hindu opponents. It served two purposes, both scrupulously worldly: first, the hoarded treasures of several generations of Hindu kings that were stored in those temples fell into the hands of the Sultan's men; second, it destroyed the political legitimacy of the temple's patron-king, who happened to be a political enemy of the Delhi Sultanate. "Since they (the temples) visually expressed a king's claims to legitimate authority," as Richard Eaton bluntly puts it, "royal temples were also highly charged political institutions, and as such were subject to attack by enemy kings who ... sought to desecrate the most visible sign of a king's sovereignty - his temple."[403]

Indeed, no different was Alauddin's acts of temple destruction from those undertaken by Rajendra Chola, some three centuries before.[404] The only difference was in

---

[402] Tarikh-i Ferishta. Translated by John Briggs. Page 363

[403] India in the Persianate Age. By Richard Eaton. Allen Lane (Penguin Books), 2019. Page 28

[404] *"Unnecessary emphasis is sometimes laid on the destruction of cities and temples by the Turks in the 12th and the 13th centuries. These acts were the necessary concomitant of medieval warfare. Every invader and conqueror delighted in presenting his exploits and achievements before the people in complimentary colours. These things were not unknown to the Hindus. One west Chalukyan inscription formally accuses the Chola king of having burnt Jain temples in the Belvola province. The Vaisnavas of the South level similar charges against the Cholas ... In the middle ages the destruction of temples and houses of worship was practised by all —*

the creed of the aggressors: while the Chola Maharaja was a Hindu, the Khilji Sultan wasn't one. And it is this difference in creed, more than anything else, that has been appropriated by the current crop of communalists, and then blown out of proportion to vilify Alauddin as an iconoclast proselytizer, which the man in question never was. That in times of peace and in the heartland of the empire, temple destruction, far from being the norm, was not even in practise, is attested to by Thakkur Pheru, the same Hindu master of mint we alluded to before, in his book named **Wastusara**. In that work, the various designs of the temples constructed in the contemporary period have been discussed, and the details of as many as twenty-five different designs of temple construction have been provided. More proofs abound, but more on that later.

In this context of temple destruction, a most interesting story has come down to us which, though not really up to the mark as far as historicity is concerned, is nonetheless too fascinating an anecdote to be skipped.

Malik Kafur, it is said, raided the Ranganatha Temple of Srirangam, and carried the sacred idol away with him. There, however, was a woman who was in the habit of

---

Indians, Turks, Mongols and others. Every invader, like the Turkish Sultans of Delhi, delighted in magnifying his achievements. In almost the same strain in which Hasan Nizami extols the achievements of the Ghurids, the Hindu kings of medieval India prided in the destruction of cities and houses of worship ... Neither the medieval Hindus nor the medieval Turks need be condemned for what they did. They simply followed an established practise of their age." (Source: Some Aspects of Religion and Politics in India during the Thirteenth Century, by Khaliq Ahmad Nizami. Department of History, Aligarh Muslim University. 1961. Page 88)

never having her food without worshipping the deity in the temple. As the imperial army embarked on its return journey to Delhi, she gave up her household and started following the northerners in the guise of a mendicant. On reaching Delhi, she came to know that the idols had been locked up in a safe chamber of the royal palace. A Khilji princess, the story continues, having been struck with the beauty of the Ranganatha idol, obtained permission from the Sultan to keep it with her. Knowing this much, the old woman then set off for down south.

Once back in Srirangam, she narrated what she had heard and learnt in Delhi. Some of the devotees believed the woman's account, and decided to travel to Delhi and try their luck there with the Sultan.

Accordingly, they travelled to Delhi, and managed to secure an audience with the Sultan, before whom they exhibited their music and dance for which they were famous in their homeland. Alauddin was extremely pleased with their performance, and quite predictably, told them to ask for a reward. The performers, in one voice, demanded the restoration of the idol of Ranganath. The Sultan consented, and although the royal princess was unwilling to part with it, the idol was still handed over to them, who then carried it back to where it belonged.[405]

Coming back to the main narrative, all in all, it can be easily inferred that the Hindus, who constituted the vast majority of Sultan Alauddin's subjects, lived by and large

---

[405] Reference: South India and her Muhammadan Invaders. By S. Krishnaswami Aiyangar. Oxford University Press, 1921. Pages 113-116

a life of peace and security. That even in the capital city, Delhi, the Hindus had the complete freedom to practise and preach their religion, is attested to in no unclear terms by the same old Barani, in another of his works, the **Fatwa-i Jahandari**.

The Sultan of Delhi, Barani says, permits in his capital and in the cities under his control, the customs of Hinduism to be openly practised and their deities to be publicly worshipped. "Openly and without fear," he continues, "the infidels continue the teaching of the principles of their false creed; they also colour their idols and celebrate their festivals with the beat of drums and dhols and with singing and dancing."[406]

The Sultan of Delhi doesn't have the desire to uproot infidelity, the orthodox Barani complains. "On the other hand, out of consideration for the fact that infidels and polytheists are payers of tribute and protected persons (zimmis), these infidels are honoured, distinguished, favoured and made eminent; the kings bestow drums, banners, ornaments, cloaks of brocade and caparisioned horses upon them. And in the capital (Delhi) ... [the] Muslim Kings not only allow but are pleased with the fact that infidels, polytheists, idol-worshippers and cow-dung worshippers build houses like palaces, wear clothes of brocade and ride Arab horses caparisoned with gold and silver ornaments.

---

[406] The Political Theory of the Delhi Sultanate. By Muhammad Habib and Dr. Afsar Umar Salim Khan. Kitab Mahal. Page 48

"They are equipped with a hundred thousand sources of strength. They live in delights and comforts. They take Mussalmans into their service, and make them run before their horses; the poor Mussalmans beg of them at their doors; and in the capital of Islam (Delhi), ... they are called **rais** (great rulers), **ranas** (minor rulers), **thakurs** (warriors), **sahas** (bankers), **mehtas** (clerks) and **pandits** (priests)."[407]

The last sentence is significant, for it makes it clear that not only the warrior class, but virtually the entire corpus of the Hindu society was deeply involved in the effective functioning of the polity that was the Delhi Sultanate.

But for all his youthful talks of outdoing the Prophet of Islam, it would be unjust on our part if we fail to mention that in the final years of his life, Sultan Alauddin Khilji's confrontational attitude towards Islam had mellowed, even if by a little. He would no longer say anything derogatory about his creed, nor would he allow anyone else to speak in that vein in his presence. "I am a Musalman and the son of a Musalman," he was wont to repeat.[408]

The medieval chroniclers, perhaps not inaccurately, attributed this change of heart to Sheikh Nizamuddin Auliya, who is supposed to have exercised a great deal of influence over the Sultan and most in his family. "During the last years of his reign," says Barani, "he (Sultan

---

[407] The Political Theory of the Delhi Sultanate. By Muhammad Habib and Dr. Afsar Umar Salim Khan. Kitab Mahal. Page 48

[408] Tabaqat-i Akbari. By Khwaja NIzamuddin Ahmad. Translated by B. DE. Page 173

Alauddin) had developed a very sincere faith in the Sheikh (Nizamuddin Auliya)."[409]

In spite of this new-found love for Islam, the Sultan still continued to abstain from participating in the congregational prayers. Perhaps he never felt the need to do so, or maybe he was apprehensive about the security of his own person in the midst of such a vast crowd. Such an apprehension, at any rate, was far from unfounded, because several murderous attacks on the persons of the former Sultans of Delhi, namely Iltutmish and his daughter Raziya, did take place in the congregational mosque of Mehrauli, and Sultan Alauddin perhaps didn't want to run a similar risk.

Also is interesting to note that it was precisely during this period that the Sultan ordered a bloody massacre of non-Sunni Muslims in his capital, Delhi. Was it because of a growing spirit of orthodoxy in him? Or, was it because he sensed political dangers from those that he massacred? Here again the latter alternative is more probable. Not only were the people in question, the Qaramatians, accused of assassinating Muhammad Ghori, but thereafter they had also attempted to violently seize control of the city of Delhi on two separate occasions. Alauddin, therefore, had reasons to be wary of them right from the very outset. Perhaps, he didn't want to experience for himself what his predecessors on the throne of Delhi had to. Nonetheless, the act was exceptionally barbaric, even by Alauddin's sanguinary standards.

---

[409] Tarikh-i Firoz Shahi. Translated by Ishtiyaq Ahmad Zilli. Page 203

At any rate, this was precisely the period in which, according to Barani, the Sultan was fast losing his discretion and his decision-making capacity was getting impaired. Also, lest we forget, shortly before he did away with the non-Sunni visitors to his capital, he also massacred a whole bunch of converted Mongols, who were all Sunni by persuasion. Both acts, therefore, should be seen in the same vein: the despotic measures of an autocrat who was fast losing his mental faculties. Nothing more, nothing less.

All in all, it could be safely assumed that Sultan Alauddin Khilji was a ruler who subordinated the dictates of religion to the needs of administration. For him, more than anything else, it was his political goal that determined his course of action: when wealth was required to sustain his vast army, he felt no hesitation in raiding temples and divesting them of their fabulous wealth; when new laws had to be enacted to tighten his control over the state machinery, the injunctions of the Shariat were flouted and the grumblings of the clerics conveniently ignored. Still, he neither died a heretic nor a bigot. Such was Alauddin Khilji, the Sultan!

The Sultan's Legacy: In Stones And Coins

> *Alauddin Khilji was one of the best of sultans, and the people of India are full of his praises.*
>
> *— Ibn Battuta.*

Architecture

One of the great wonders of Sultan Alauddin Khilji's reign, says Ziauddin Barani, "was the great activity in the field of construction and the erection of buildings such as mosques, minarets, forts and excavation of tanks. There had been no king and [there] would be no king in whose karkhanas (workshops) of imarat (building department), 70,000 artisans associated with building construction would assemble, as was the case with Sultan Alauddin. Because of this a palace could be built in two-three days and a fort would come up in two weeks time."[410]

The thirty-years-long reign of the Khilji Sultans constitutes an important watershed in the evolution of Indo-Islamic architecture. Particularly with Alauddin's accession to the throne of Delhi, the renowned art historian Percy Brown feels, a decisive advance in the

---

[410] Tarikh-i Firoz Shahi. Translated by Ishtiyaq Ahmad Zilli. Page 209

field of architecture took place. And there is no better illustration of that Sultan's taste for architecture than the fabulous Alai Darwaza in the Qutb Complex.

Erected in 1305, the Alai Darwaza was meant to serve as only one of the total four entrances to the Quwwat ul Islam mosque. Two gateways were supposed to be on the long eastern side, and one each on the northern and the southern side. Today, only the one on the south, the Alai Darwaza, survives. There, however, is also another theory, according to which, out of the four gateways originally planned, Sultan Alauddin Khilji could finish in his lifetime only the Alai Darwaza.

Be that as it may, the Alai Darwaza, resting on a high plinth, beautified by unique horse-shoe arches, and decorated with bold calligraphy, offers for a most captivating sight. And the history behind its construction is no less captivating either, for it connects Delhi with a city at least a thousand miles to its west, and with an exotic culture that had propelled the production of some of the finest works of art in the Islamic world.

In the construction of Alai Darwaza, Percy Brown notes, there was some fresh influence that was at work. The shape of its arches, the method of its walling, the conception of its dome and then the support provided for that dome — all of that give away a distinctly Seljukid influence.

The Seljuks had once been mighty Turkish Sultans who, at the height of their power, ruled over a vast empire that stretched all the way from the shores of the Meditteranean Sea to the mountains of the Hindu Kush. But for all their might, when the Mongol deluge came, they were annihilated and their magnificent empire came crumbling down.

The Muslim artists who had hitherto worked for their Seljuk masters were now forced to seek new avenues of employment. Little wonder therefore, it was to Delhi that they now turned, for they knew that in the whole Islamic world, it was the master of Delhi, Sultan Alauddin Khilji, who alone could successfully hold out against the formidable Mongols.

The Alai Darwaza then, according to Percy Brown, occupies an unique significance as an Indianized version of Seljuk architecture. And also because many of its salient features were reproduced in the Indo-Islamic works that followed.

The unusual method of stone masonry employed in that building could serve as an example. It consisted of laying the masonry in two different courses, a narrow course of headers alternating with a wider course of stretchers. Long after the Khiljis were gone, this method of masonry would be employed to perfection by the Great Mughals in the sixteenth-seventeenth centuries.

Also, the style of putting up buildings in red sandstone and then embellishing them with decorative elements in marble, which was first seen in the tomb of Sultan Iltutmish and then repeated in a finer, grander way in the Alai Darwaza, would persist in the subcontinent for several centuries more. It would be adopted by such giants among men as Sher Shah Suri and Jalaluddin Muhammad Akbar in the grand architectural projects of their own.

However, one thing that must be remembered about the Alai Darwaza is that it was not created in any fixed style. "For its chief characteristics, and one on which much of its beauty depends," thinks Percy Brown, "is that in spite of its essential nature being exotic, it embodies many purely indigenous features ... It is the skilful fusion of the best of the two modes that has produced in this building such an outstanding work of art."[411]

The beautiful and bold calligraphy, the aesthetic horseshoe arches, the delicate lotus-bud fringes on the underside of the arches, and the wonderful manner in which red sandstone and marble have been used alternatively — all of that come together to produce a most pleasant effect on the mind of the beholder, and serve to justify Percy Brown's claim of Alai Darwaza being the demonstration of Islamic architecture at its very best.

"Nothing so complete had been done before," the highest tribute comes from another authority, Fergusson, "[and] nothing so complete was attempted by them (the Sultans of Delhi) afterwards."[412]

Another building in the city of Delhi, belonging to the same era and put up by the same patron, was the Jamaat Khana masjid at the Dargah of Sheikh Nizamuddin

---

411 Indian Architecture (Islamic Period), by Percy Brown. D.B. Taraporevala Sons & Co. Private Limited. 1981. Page 17

412 History of Indian and Eastern Architecture. By James Fergusson. London, 1910. Page 210

Auliya. In beauty and grace, however, this Masjid is nowhere near the Alai Darwaza.

The Jamaat Khana Masjid is a stocky building of red sandstone, and consists of three chambers: a square one in the centre, and two oblong ones on both sides of it. The facade consists of three archways, with each archway having a wide band of Quranic inscription above, and the lotus-bud fringes on their interior attesting to the structure's similarity with the Alai Darwaza.

Once inside the Masjid, the similarities with the Alai Darwaza are even more striking. Like the interior of the Alai Darwaza, here too could be seen several squint arches, introduced at very specific angles, to support the weight of the not-so-conspicious dome topping the whole structure.

But for all its similarities with the Alai Darwaza, the differences are only too glaring to be ignored. "That in a very short time the style as expressed in the Alai Darwaza was losing its initial forcefulness, is shown by the treatment of this mosque," Percy Brown notes accurately.[413]

The distinction between the two structures is best reflected in the archways of the Jamaat Khana Masjid: though still of the horse-shoe type, as seen in the Alai Darwaza, there is nonetheless a good deal of difference in finesse and execution. The arches of the Jamaat Khana Masjid have their horse-shoe character much less pronounced than the ones employed in the Alai Darwaza:

---

[413] Indian Architecture (Islamic Period), by Percy Brown. Page 18

instead of having smooth crowns, the ogee tends to reappear in these arches.

The architectural difference between the two edifices, Percy Brown surmises, was due to the time interval of around a decade in their constructions. "It seems not improbable that the accomplished workmen who carried out the design and execution of the [Alai] Darwaza were no longer available and the [Jamaat Khana] Mosque was produced by others less familiar with the essentials of the style."[414]

Sure enough, the gateway called Alai Darwaza was gorgeous, but Alauddin Khilji had absolutely no desire to stop at just that. The Sultan had grand architectural aspirations, and felt he needed a bigger arena to bring his visions to fruition. And so came into being Siri: the second of the seven cities of Delhi, and the capital of the Second Alexander himself.

Siri, according to Professor M.Athar Ali, was a plain waste ground adjoining Mehruali to its north-west.[415] It was here that Sultan Alauddin Khilji had pitched his camp, when his capital was under siege by the Mongol commander Targhi. After Targhi returned, we are told by Barani, "he (Sultan Alauddin) built a palace in Siri and settled there. He made it his capital and got it to be built and populated."[416]

---

[414] Indian Architecture (Islamic Period), by Percy Brown. Page 18

[415] Capital of the Sultans: Delhi during the Thirteenth and Fourteenth Centuries, by M. Athar Ali

[416] Tarikh-i Firoz Shahi. Translated by Ishtiyaq Ahmad Zilli. Page 184

The fortress that came up in Siri, we are told by Sir Syed Ahmed Khan, was circular in shape, with strongly built walls of stones and bricks, and had as many as seven gates. Indeed, even before the fort could be completed, he adds, another battle with the Mongols took place in which the Sultan achieved a complete victory, and the heads of as many as 8,000 Mongol prisoners were substituted for stones in the construction of the citadel.

The contemporary Amir Khusrau's account too insinuates in the same direction: "many thousand goat-bearded Mongols have been sacrificed," the relevant passage in his work reads, "[because] it is a necessary condition that blood be given to a new building."[417]

Khusrau had high hopes of Divine mercy granting perpetuity to his master's creation, but unfortunately such was not to be. Because three centuries down the line, such a man came to power in Delhi who, though he looked up to Alauddin Khilji, still felt no hesitation in pulling down his idol's composition. This was Sher Shah Suri, the famous Pashtun Sultan of the sixteenth century, who used the dismantled bastions and ramparts of the Siri fort to support his own architectural projects at Shergarh.

Walls and ramparts defend a city, palaces and minars embellish it, but nothing is so important to the sustenance of a city as the continuous supply of water is. "There can be no doubt," says Amir Khusrau, "that Delhi is a city which even the Nile and the Euphrates cannot provide

[417] Khazain ul Futuh. Translated by Muhammad Habib. Page 18

with sufficient drinking water."[418] Khusrau exaggerates greatly, no doubt, but the water problem in Delhi was indeed a pressing one. It becomes apparent from one incidental remark of another contemporary, Ziauddin Barani, when he says that on special occasions, no less than half a tanka had to be paid for procuring only one small earthen cup of water.

When Alauddin Khilji ascended the throne of Delhi, he found out that the Hauz-i Shamsi, the tank excavated by Sultan Shamsuddin Iltutmish where, according to the **malfuzat** of Khwaja Qutbuddin Bakhtiyar Kaki, that Sultan had seen the Prophet of Islam in his dream, had completely dried up.

Large amounts of mud and slit were removed from it, and the tank was thoroughly repaired by Sultan Alauddin. Therafter, he proceeded to erect a platform in the middle of the tank, and then crown it with a beautiful dome. Amir Khusrau, in his characteristics style, compared this new structure with an ostrich's egg, that was half inside water and half outside it. Ibn Battuta, visiting Delhi several decades later, said that the Hauz-i Shamsi, after it had been renovated by Sultan Alauddin Khilji, was two miles by one miles in size, and had pavilions on its four sides for for sightseers and excursionists.

But for all the efforts of Sultan Alauddin Khilji to revamp it, the Hauz-i Shamsi proved insufficient for the sprawling urban landscape of Delhi. At any rate, the Hauz-i Shamsi

---

[418] Khazain ul Futuh. Translated by Muhammad Habib. Page 20

would have proved too far for the new settlements like Siri, that had come up to the north of the Qutb Complex.

Sultan Alauddin Khilji, therefore, excavated a new tank several miles north to the Hauz-i Shamsi, and bestowed upon it his own name, calling it the 'Hauz-i Alai'. It was square in shape, each side of it measuring some 600 metres in length, and the total space enclosed by it was somewhere around 70 acres.

Ibn Battuta remarked that the Hauz-i Alai/Hauz-i Khas was larger in size than the Hauz-i Shamsi. Around its sides, he said, there were as many as forty pavilions, where musicians would assemble and play their instruments.[419] Yazdi, in his work the **Zafarnama**, described it as a "small sea", and said that it was filled during the rainy season and served to supply the inhabitants of Delhi the whole year round with fresh water.[420]

Strange as it may seem, the other extant edifice of Sultan Alauddin's reign is not in Delhi, or even anywhere near it: instead, it lies deep inside Rajputana, in the historic Rajput stronghold of Chittor.

After the Sultan's conquest of Chittor in 1303, he constructed a bridge over the Gambhiri river, just below the famous fortress. Perhaps, anxious to retain control over this turbulent territory, the Sultan had the bridge

---

[419] The Travels of Ibn Battuta. Translated by H.A.R. Gibb. Pages 624-625

[420] Mentioned in M. Athar Ali's *Capital of the Sultans: Delhi during the Thirteenth and Fourteenth Centuries*

constructed to facilitate the rapid movement of his troops, if in case such a situation arose.

"Unfortunately its chief architectural features," notes Percy Brown, "the gateways and towers raised over the abutments at each end have disappeared."[421] Nonetheless, ten massive arches of grey limestone still exist, and they serve to show that competent engineers and accomplished architects were engaged in carrying this project out.

Coinage

Unlike Muhammad bin Tughluq, Alauddin Khilji didn't initiate any new fanciful numismatic innovations, but of all the Sultans of Delhi, it was his coins that were the most celebrated. Nearly a hundred years after Alauddin's death, when that ferocious warlord Amir Timur raided Delhi, of his entire loot, what he valued the most was those gold and silver coins that bore Alauddin's name.422 And that's not all. More than two and a half centuries after Alauddin's death, a descendant of Timur, Akbar by name, would also value Alauddin's coins most highly, anytime he could get hold of them.[423]

Sultan Alauddin Khilji struck tankas of both gold and silver. Each tanka, whether of gold or silver, weighed a tola (a little less than 12 grams). A jital was a small copper coin, the exact weight of it is not kniwn, but 50 jitals

---

[421] Indian Architecture (Islamic Period), by Percy Brown. Page 19

[422] The History of India, as told by its own historians. The Muhammadan Period. By Sir H.M. Elliot. Vol III. London, 1871. Page 446

[423] Akbarnama, Volume 4. Translated by Wheeler M. Thackston. Murty Classical Library of India. London, 2018. Page 39

together equalled one silver tanka in value. It however has been argued by some scholars that this exchange rate, which Ferishta provides, prevailed only in the Deccan, not in Delhi, where 48 copper jitals equalled one silver tanka in value.

The exchange value between the two tankas was the same as it had been under the earlier Sultans of Delhi: 10 silver tankas for one gold tanka. Though perhaps in the second half of his reign, due to the relative paucity of silver, this ratio might have gone down. The colossal amount of gold that was brought to Delhi from the lands beyond the Vindhyas seems to have reduced its value relative to silver. Precisely for the same reason, Alauddin contemplated a reduction in the weight of his silver tanka by around 15%, but didn't execute it. At any rate, this scarcity of silver didn't have any remarkable ramifications in the reign of Sultan Alauddin, and it was left to Muhammad bin Tughluq to bear the brunt of it: according to multiple sources, his introduction of token currency was dictated more by compulsion than by choice.

Alauddin's coins bear the names of mints of **Hazrat Delhi, Dar-ul-Islam**, and **Qila-i-Deogir**. From the last named mint, coins came to be struck only in the later years of the Sultan, when his favorite general Malik Kafur had made Deogir his capital after snuffing out a local rebellion there. **Hazrat Delhi** could mean Siri, and **Dar-ul-Islam** could stand for Old Delhi (Mehrauli): the vice versa, however, is also equally probable.[424]

In one respect, however, Sultan Alauddin Khilji set a precedent in Indian numismatic history. Of all the Sultans of Delhi, he was the first to experiment with square shaped coins. The design stayed put in the subcontinent, and was later put to better, finer use by men like Akbar and Jahangir.

Besides, like many of his predecessors on the throne of Delhi, Alauddin Khilji also issued bilingual coins, on which appeared the Sultan's name in Devanagri script, prefaced with a Sanskrit honorific title: 'Srih Sultan Alavadin', the inscription on the coin read.[425]

[424] The Coinage and Metrology of the Sultans of Delhi. By H. Nelson Wright. Delhi, 1936. Page 106

[425] The Chronicles of the Pathan Kings of Delhi. By Edward Thomas. London, 1871. Page 172

An Estimate

> *Ascending the throne at the age of thirty Alauddin had reached the apogee of power at forty-five through unrivalled skill, studied tact, and phenomenal energy. From nothingness he rose to be one of the greatest rulers of medieval times.*
>
> — *History of the Khaljis, by K.S. Lal.*

There is scarcely scope for any doubt that Sultan Alauddin Khilji was one of the most fascinating personalities of medieval India. Wading through a pool of blood to the throne, he vindicated his rise to power through a series of successes that catapulted the Delhi Sultanate to the apogee of its glory, and transformed it into the most dominant political force in the entire Indian subcontinent. Delhi's polity he transformed, Delhi's people he protected — both from the ravages of the Mongols, and the vagaries of nature. Little wonder therefore, long after he was gone, his memory was cherished a great deal by the people of Delhi.

As a man, Alauddin was incredibly hardworking. Actually, that was inevitable, given the man's obsession with perfection. Everything had to work out exactly as per his plan for the Sultan to feel satisfied. Thus, about the affairs of the market, he received reports daily from as many as three sources, but he was still not satisfied — as we have seen, he would still send his secret agents in the market to make sure nothing was amiss there. No wonder, a man with such a penchant for perfection had to toil extremely hard.

Such a busy lifestyle, of course, was compatible neither with licentiousness nor with inebriation. Sure, Alauddin in his youth had been infatuated with those things, but it had been only that: an infatuation, and that too a rather ephemeral one. Later in his life, the Sultan sought respite from his busy life in music and sports. Among musicians, apart from Amir Khsusrau and Amir Hasan Sijzi, the Khilji king's court was also graced by one Gopal Naik, a Hindu maestro from South India. And the Sultan's passion for outdoor sports remained unabated even after his nephew's murderous assault on him in the midst of a hunt. In fact, even in his final years, when his health had started deteriorating, Alauddin still didn't stop indulging in this particular hobby — a fact that is proved by the conspiracy of the neo-Muslim Mongols to do away with him when the Sultan would go hawking.

As a soldier, Alauddin hardly had any equal. In the field of battle, his exploits were legendary. Whether as a prince or a king, he emerged victorious in every assault that he led. His attack on Deogir in 1296 with a paltry force stands out in the annals of medieval India: an incredible blitzkrieg, Ferishta is right in terming it an unparalleled feat in the military history of India.

Personally, he was brave to an uncommon degree. Courage carried a high premium with him, and of all things, he despised cowardice the most. Thus, in the face of a terrible Mongol onslaught, when a certain officer of his asked him to temporise with the enemy, Alauddin rebuffed that advice outright. "How would I go to my harem and where will I stand in the estimate of the people of my kingdom and what courage and intrepidity of mine would force the rebels and recalcitrants to obey me?"[426]

Alauddin's bravery, however, was not rash. He was also endowed with a cool, calculating mind that guided his courage in the right direction. Thus, along with the machismo that he displayed in his Deogir expedition, he also made it sure that not even an inkling of his movement could reach the royal court in Delhi. Again, even when the odds were stacked against him, as it was when Targhi, the Mongol chief, had attacked Delhi in 1303, Sultan Alauddin Khilji persisted in his defence down to the very end, not for once dropping his own guard or allowing anyone to drop theirs. Undoubtedly, it was this uncommon combination of brain and bravado that turned Alauddin into such a lethal force.

Alauddin's resolve was legendary. When he had set his heart on something, not even the devil himself could budge him. Thus, when he was besieging the fortress of Ranthambore, all at once he came to be beset by a number of problems, each of which was grave enough in itself to dissaude a lesser man than Alauddin. But, Alauddin was Alauddin: neither would he allow anyone, nor would he

---

[426] Tarikh-i Firoz Shahi. Translated by Ishtiyaq Ahmad Zilli. Page 158

himself move even an inch without accomplishing his objective.

But before he had decided on something, Sultan Alauddin Khilji was absolutely amenable to suggestions. This trait, in fact, set him apart from Muhammad bin Tughluq who, though much more educated than Alauddin, was too headstrong by nature to listen to anybody's advice. Thus, an officer could dare to upbraid Alauddin for entertaining chimeric dreams, and far from being punished for the same, he went on to receive handsome rewards from the Sultan for his boldness. Likewise, when Alauddin engaged in arguments, he did so sportingly: his rival could come up with the most caustic remark, and still stay sure that no harm would come his way.

The Sultan's willpower was amazing. He ascended the throne an illiterate man. But he soon realised how big an impediment illiteracy was for a man who wished to rule as a totalitarian king. He then applied himself to learning diligently: squeezing time out of his busy routine, he made it a point to sit down with his books everyday, and devote at least a few hours to learning. In a short time, we are told, the Sultan made such progress that he was soon seen reading Persian classics. Again, in spite of being such a heavy drinker, the Sultan's giving up of wine all at once was a feat that was nothing short of wonderful.

One trait which the Sultan hated with every ounce of his being was treachery. Sure, the Sultan himself often offered encouragement to the traitors in the enemy ranks to serve his own ends. But once his purpose was over, he then felt no compunction whatsoever in doing away with them. "Those who have betrayed their natural sovereign will never be true to another," the Sultan would say, and in accordance with this maxim would punish any and every turncoat that came his way.[427] Thus, he could ascend the throne of Delhi only because the nobles of his uncle, Jalaluddin Khilji, forsook their master's cause and hurriedly joined standards. But once he felt safe on his throne, Alauddin turned on the same bunch of people and awarded each one of them the most sanguinary punishment imaginable. Likewise, his conquest of Ranthambore was facilitated by the defection of Ranmal, a minister of the Chauhana Raja. But once the fort had been taken, Ranmal was promptly executed, while Muhammad Shah, the gallant Mongol who died fighting for his Rajput overlord, was granted an honorable burial.

Alauddin Khilji's man management skills were remarkable. Gifted with an uncommon tact, he had that uncanny ability to turn foes into friends. Thus, the Hindu kings of Deogir and Dwarsamudra were struck by the Sultan's magnanimity, and returned from his capital staunch supporters of the Sultanate. The awesome authority that the Sultan wielded over his men is exhibited in the way he kept his commanders firmly under his thumb. In an age when strife and disaffection were rife, such brilliant generals as Zafar Khan, Alp Khan and Ghazi Malik remained utterly obedient to their Sultan and carried his commands out to the letter. It was only because of his incredible leadership that "Sultan Alauddin sat within the four walls of his own palace and a mad, deficient and crop-eared slave, who had been paraded in

[427] Tarikh-i Ferishta. Translated by John Briggs. Page 344

the market, would go on conquering territories and countries for him."[428]

Another remarkable aspect of Alauddin's character was his genuine concern for the welfare of the people he ruled. It behoved him, he would say, "that I should do something the benefit of which may be enjoyed by everybody."429 Accordingly, prices of foodstuffs were slashed at one stroke. The rationing system, which was introduced as an adjunct to the price control measures, was also geared in such a way that it benefited the poor the most. Besides, his strong sense of justice — on account of which "from the banks of the river Sind (Indus) to the seacoast no one has heard the name of robber, thief or pickpocket" — also evinces his strong solicitude for the welfare of the masses.[430]

But for all that, Alauddin Khilji was not a benign man. Not by any means. Rather, he was singularly brutal in wiping out all who stood in his way. Even in that sanguinary age, his reign stood out for its excesses. The punishments that Alauddin was wont to inflict horrified even a medieval chronicler like Barani. "The people of Delhi expressed their astonishment and surprise and trembled among themselves."[431] And 'pardon' was a word that was alien to him: he was vindictive by nature,

---

[428] Tarikh-i Firoz Shahi. Translated by Ishtiyaq Ahmad Zilli. Page 226

[429] History of the Khaljis. By K.S. Lal. Page 267

[430] Khazain ul Futuh. Translated by Muhammad Habib. Page 11

[431] Tarikh-i Firoz Shahi. Translated by Ishtiyaq Ahmad Zilli. Page 155

and never forgave anyone in his life.[432] His grudges, he held on to them tight, and carried them with him to the grave.

That, however, doesn't mean that Alauddin was a man bereft of emotions. Men cry, they do, and Alauddin Khilji was not an exception either. Thus, when he witnessed the macabre sight of his nephew's severed head, the Sultan is reported to have burst into tears.[433] Again, while banishing his favorite son Khizr Khan to the fortress-prison of Gwalior, Alauddin wept profusely and in public.434 Statecraft demanded violence of him, and he almost always complied with that demand, but there were times, even if few and far between, when he simply couldn't rise to the challenge: on those occasions, in spite of his best efforts, his choked emotions came to the forefront, and the onlookers got a chance to peep into the person behind the persona.

All in all, it is safe to assert that Alauddin's shortcomings were fewer than his successes, and the latter easily overshadowed the former. Ambition being his ruling passion, the Sultan thirsted for immortality, and in the relatively short span of twenty years, he made sure that he

---

432 *"If he (Sultan Alauddin Khilji) got angry with anyone,"* writes Barani, *"he would cause him injury and pain and due to the excessive harshness of his nature he would never reconcile with him and would never make an effort to heal his wound."* (Reference: Tarikh-i Firoz Shahi, translated by Ishtiyaq Ahmad Zilli. Page 207)

433 The Life and Works of Sultan Alauddin Khilji. By Dr. Ghulam Sarwar Khan Niazi. Atlantic Publishers. Page 167

434 History of the Khaljis. By K.S. Lal. Page 303

achieved enough to merit a place among the immortals of history.

Whether in affairs civil or military, Alauddin Khilji was a pioneer: he broke new grounds, and others either followed in his footsteps or rode on his success. It was Sultan Alauddin Khilji who, for the first time in almost thousand years, dismantled the political divide between North and South India. It was only on account of Alauddin's military success down south that Muhammad bin Tughluq could encompass virtually the whole of India in his megalithic empire. Again, the Khilji Sultan's method of recruiting the soldiers directly and paying them cash salary, his system of maintaining a descriptive roll of his soldiers and branding their horses — all of these were adopted in toto by Sher Shah Suri, that successful Pashtun Sultan of the sixteenth century. Then, the measurement of land that Alauddin insisted upon, would go on to become the bedrock of Todarmal's legendary revenue system.

The best tribute to Sultan Alauddin Khilji, ultimately, comes from the pen of Ziauddin Barani who, it must be remembered, was a staunch critic of the Sultan's brash manners and harsh ways. The first wonder of Alauddin's reign, he says, was the cheapness of the necessities of life. The second wonder was the multitudinous military victories that the Sultan achieved, so much so that "any direction and fort that his armies headed on, one could say that it was already conquered even before they could reach there."[435] The third wonder was the total elimination of the Mongol threat, "the likes of which could not be

---

[435] Tarikh-i Firoz Shahi. Translated by Ishtiyaq Ahmad Zilli. Page 208

achieved by any king in any age."[436] The fourth wonder was the maintenance of a huge army — readers shall remember that the strength of Alauddin's army came at around half a million men — on remarkably low emoluments. The fifth wonder was the complete suppression of the refractory elements, so much so that "with lamps in their hands they guarded travellers."[437] The sixth wonder was the complete safety on the roads and highways across the empire, so that "even a traveller and stranger would not lose a thread of rope."[438] The seventh wonder, "that was in fact the most wondrous of all wonders", was the honest and upright behaviour that was witnessed among traders and merchants.[439] The eighth wonder was the vigorous activity in the construction sector that was observed in his reign, because of which "a palace could be built in two-three days and a fort would come up in two week's time."[440] The ninth wonder was the rectitude and obedience that appeared to have taken hold of the Sultan's millions of subjects. The tenth wonder, which Barani claims had come into being without any effort on the Sultan's part, was the assemblage of experts of every branch of learning in his capital, Delhi.

[436] Tarikh-i Firoz Shahi. Translated by Ishtiyaq Ahmad Zilli. Page 208

[437] ibid

[438] ibid

[439] ibid

[440] ibid. Page 209

The Dreary End

> *Come, and take a lesson from the dust,*
> *It is the place of repose of honourable kings!*
>
> — *Tarikh-i Mubarakshahi, by Yahya bin Ahmad Sirhindi.*

As the years rolled on, the intelligent, pragmatic and sagacious Alauddin gave way, slowly but surely, to a much inferior version of himself that was as terrible as it was thoughtless. And this deterioration first manifested itself in the wholesale massacre of all the neo-Muslims of Delhi, which he ordered sometime in 1312. But to make sense of this bloody episode, it is necessary that we digress a little.

In 1292, Abdullah, one of the grandsons of Hulagu Khan, invaded India with a huge Mongol army. Jalauddin Khilji, who was the Sultan then, advanced with his own army to meet this threat. As the two armies came face to face, Jalaluddin Khilji, by dint of a masterstroke, scored a brillant political victory over his rival. The Sultan won over Abdullah with his kind words: an armistice was agreed upon, and Abdullah soon retraced his steps from India, not before, however, leaving behind to serve the Sultan thousands of Mongol warriors, that even included a certain Alghu, reputed to be a direct descendant of Chengiz Khan himself.

Jalaluddin Khilji welcomed all of them warmly — all the Mongols embraced Islam — and to Alghu, the Sultan even went to the extent of offering the hand of his own daughter in marriage.

After doing away with Jalaluddin Khilji, along with all his surviving sons, his son-in-law Alghu was also blinded by Alauddin Khilji.

So much for Alghu. As to the rest of the neo-Muslims (newly converted Muslims), perhaps sometime in 1312, Ferishta tells us, "although no particular cause is assigned for it, the King (Alauddin Khilji) suddenly took it into his head to discharge all the soldiers of this class (neo-Muslims), desiring them to look out for other services."441 Some authorities believe that this decision on the part of the Sultan was prompted by the attempt towards rebellion that a Mongol general of note had made in far away Ma'bar. Still, as Ferishta's account shows, there was absolutely no lack of ambiguity as to why all the Mongol soldiers in the service of Sultan Alauddin Khilji were disbanded at one stroke.

The men who had come to Delhi in Abdullah's train were, of course, soldiers, and now that their martial service was no longer required by the state, they were at once thrown into the deepest of distress. A few of them managed to get into the service of some noblemen, but the vast majority of them continued to remain unemployed and utterly distressed. They hoped that the Sultan would be moved

---

[441] Tarikh-i Ferishta. Translated by John Briggs. Page 375

seeing them in such a state of penury. Alauddin Khilji, however, was the last man to entertain sentimental considerations, and therefore the hopes of the unemployed Mongols came to nothing.

Not surprisingly, therefore, "some daring fellows among them, forced by their misfortunes, entered into a conspiracy to murder him."[442] However, of all the Sultans of Delhi, Alauddin Khilji had the finest espionage network, and in no time he got wind of all that was brewing in his backyard.

The Sultan's wrath was aroused, and this time to an extreme degree. "He issued orders that the [entire] race of neo-Muslims were to be massacred," informs Barani. "They were to be killed in the span of one day and in such a way that not a single neo-Muslim was to be left on the face of the earth."[443]

The order was dutifully carried out, and no less than 20,000 Mongol converts to Islam were slaughtered in one day: most of those slaughtered, however, were such men who had absolutely no knowledge about the conspiracy. The families of those killed were not spared either: their wives had their modesty publicly outraged, and their children forced into slavery.

Barani justifiably condemns this bloody act of the Sultan in the most forceful terms: he likens Alauddin to the tyrannical Pharaohs, and says that the king couldn't have

---

[442] Tarikh-i Ferishta. Translated by John Briggs. Page 375

[442] ibid. Page 376

[443] Tarikh-i Firoz Shahi. Translated by Ishtiyaq Ahmad Zilli. Page 205

come up with such a brutal punishment if not for "his harshness of temper, brutality of disposition, [and] cruelty of heart."[444]

The nobles as well as the commoners must have been appalled by this bloodshed, but none could muster enough courage and ask the Sultan to rescind the orders. "The King was so inexorable and vindictive," writes Ferishta, "that no one durst attempt to conceal (however nearly connected) one of this unfortunate race [of Mongols], and not one of them is supposed to have escaped."[445]

In fact, this whole episode of bloodbath seems to have been a forerunner to Amir Timur's sack of Delhi almost a century later, when the Chaghtai warlord had ordered his men on the pain of death to slaughter one lakh native captives, so that even Maulana Nasiruddin Umar, otherwise a man given to much piety, in fear of the Amir's rage had to do away with as many as 15 captives singlehandedly.

Sultan Alauddin Khilji, who is often credited with bringing about the seperation of the church and the state in the Delhi Sultanate, committed another act in the same year that was equally unjustifiable and equally out of keeping with his original, pragmatic character.

It so happened that a group of non-Sunni Muslims arrived in Delhi, perhaps for no other reason than excursion. But their arrival somehow attracted the attention of the city-dwellers, and as was only to be expected, news of their

---

[444] Tarikh-i Firoz Shahi. Translated by Ishtiyaq Ahmad Zilli. Page 205

[445] Tarikh-i Ferishta. Translated by John Briggs. Page 376

presence soon made its way to the Sultan's ears. "Sultan Alauddin ordered that thorough investigation were to be carried," records Barani.[446] Who conducted those investigations, and how they were conducted, we know not, but we are certain that the results of the investigation didn't please the Sultan..

The visitors were dubbed as 'the fraternity of incest', and an order was issued to bring all of them before the Sultan. "It was discovered that among those shameless wretches," writes Amir Khusrau, perhaps more as a court chronicler than a man of integrity, "mothers had cohabited with their own son and aunts (mother's sisters) with their nephews; that the father has taken his daughter for his bride and there had been connections between brothers and sisters."[447]

No matter how true those allegations were, but the Sultan didn't waste much time in issuing a sanguinary and summary order. "They were sawed from the head into two," writes Barani.[448] And this time no distinction of gender was maintained either, with the women suffering the same fate as did their menfolk: "Over the head of all of them, men as well as women, the saw of punishment was drawn."[449]

Hand in hand with his mental faculties, the Sultan's physical condition also started deteriorating: while it is difficult to say whether the latter was the cause of the

---

446 Tarikh-i Firoz Shahi. Translated by Ishtiyaq Ahmad Zilli. Page 205

447 Khazain ul Futuh. Translated by Muhammad Habib. Page 12

448 Tarikh-i Firoz Shahi. Translated by Ishtiyaq Ahmad Zilli. Page 205

449 Khazain ul Futuh. Translated by Muhammad Habib. Page 12

former, the possibility of it certainly can't be ruled out. He was laid up by oedema, and day by day his constitution deteriorated. Perhaps, sensing his health decline rapidly, Alauddin hastened to settle the succession issue: he appointed his eldest son, Khizr Khan, as his heir apparent. To that end, he also had an undertaking (of allegiance towards Khizr Khan) prepared, and then duly signed by all the nobles attached to his court.

Khizr Khan, in any case, was his father's favourite son: apart from the ostentatious paraphernalia he received from the Sultan at Chittor, his marriage too was celebrated by his father with such pomp and gaiety as warranted a detailed description in a Persian work of history that was composed a century after.

But for all his father's love, Khizr Khan hadn't turned out to be even as half as competent as his father, and none but Sultan Alauddin is to be blamed for that. He took Khizr Khan out of his harem, Barani tells us, even before the prince "could develop proper reasoning faculties and a sense of discretion."[450] When he was hardly a teenager, Khizr Khan was allotted a seperate establishment of his own, and the charge of administering the newly-conquered territory of Chittor was also made over to him. The result of these measures, of course, was obvious: "he (Khizr Khan) busied himself with personal gratification, indulgence and seeking pleasure," reports Barani.[451] But, to Khizr Khan, we shall turn later, for now the pressing problem before the Sultan wasn't his son's character, but

[450] Tarikh-i Firoz Shahi. Translated by Ishtiyaq Ahmad Zili. Page 227

[451] ibid

the conduct of his family: more specifically, the female members of his family.

Here too Alauddin himself had set the precedent: in keeping with his kingly grandeur, "in organising his (Khizr Khan's) marriage and those of his (Alauddin's) other sons he went to excesses and his harem in fact commenced entertaining guests and celebrating without any end."[452] Even as Alauddin got increasingly confined to bed, his wives, the chroniclers say, continued making merry as before. This irritated the Sultan. Greatly. Feeling friendless in his own palace, Alauddin then turned to his favorite slave, Malik Kafur, who had gone to Deogir to tackle certain disturbances that had surfaced after the death of Ram Deo, Delhi's loyal vassal.

And now it's time for a word or two about the relationship that existed between Sultan Alauddin Khilji and Malik Kafur. That the relationship was curious is absolutely beyond doubt. Every single source of the medieval era attests to it — from Barani's **Tarikh-i Firoz Shahi,** through Yahya's **Tarikh-i Mubarakshahi,** Nizamuddin Ahmad Bakshi's **Tabaqat-i Akbari,** Badayuni's **Muntakhab ut Tawarikh**, all the way to Muahmmad Qasim Ferishta's **Tarikh-i Ferishta.**

Among them, Ziauddin Barani, who is the biggest authority on Alauddin's reign, is also the most explicit: he talks about 'that evil deed' which Alauddin performed with Malik Kafur, in the context of one of the Sultan's sons who inherited his father's bisexual traits, as we shall

---

[452] Tarikh-i Firoz Shahi. Translated by Ishtiyaq Ahmad Zili. Page 227

see later on . Such being the case, it is hardly surprising that the Sultan, at his hour of distress, should summon to his presence Malik Kafur, who also happened to be perhaps the only great noble of the empire whose rise to a high office and sustenance at that high station depended solely on the king himself (that is, he had no relatives and hardly any friend at the court).

Be that as it may, along with Malik Kafur, the Sultan also summoned from Gujarat his brother-in-law, Alp Khan. Both the nobles, on receiving the imperial summon, made post-haste for Delhi.

Now, coming back to Khizr Khan. That prince, we are told, relinquished the charge of Chittor after a few years. Thereafter, he remained in Delhi, where he fell violently in love with Dewal Rani, the daughter of Kamala Devi and her first husband, the ex-King of Gujarat. The two got married after some time, and the occassion entailed such a humongous expenditure as warranted a detailed description in the fifteenth-century account of Yahya Sirhindi. Even as his father's health deteoriated, Khizr Khan kept himself busy in making love and making merry. As Khizr followed in his mother's footsteps in neglecting his father, the Sultan therefore had legitimate reasons to be upset about this mother-son duo, not to mention the other, less significant female characters in the imperial harem.

Immediately on arriving in Delhi, Malik Kafur could sense the winds of change that were blustering in the capital. The Sultan, on the other hand, gave free vent to his pain before his two trusted nobles, Malik Kafur and Alp Khan, "complaining to them in private of the undutiful and cruel behaviour of his wife and his son during his illness."[453]

Alp Khan, because he was the brother-in-law to the Sultan, tried his best to calm him down. The other man, however, had no such intentions: "Malik Kafur, who had long aspired to the throne, now began seriously to form schemes for the extirpation of the royal line," says Ferishta.[454]

"The ungrateful Malik Naib saw that the Sultan was unhappy with his harem and Khizr Khan, and he seized this oppurtunity to create problems."[455] First, he tried to convince the Sultan that Khizr Khan was after his life: attributing Khizr Khan's carelessness to his lust for power, Malik Kafur argued that the prince didn't tend to his ailing father only because he wanted to get rid of him as quickly as possible. Persuading Alauddin, at any rate, didn't turn out to be too difficult a task: an usurper, after all, always stays wary of his crown being usurped by somebody else. The Sultan soon grew suspicious about Khizr Khan's designs, and as a precautionary measure, sent the prince to Amroha, and told him to remain there until he received orders to return.

---

[453] Tarikh-i Ferishta. Translated by John Briggs. Page 379

[454] ibid

[455] Tarikh-i Firoz Shahi. Translated by Ishtiyaq Ahmad Zili. Page 227

This punishment from his father, we are told, moved the prince greatly, and he was filled with deep remorse for having hitherto neglected his duties as a son. “At his departure, he therefore took an oath privately, that if God should spare the life of his father, he would return all the way on foot to the capital (to circumambulate the tombs of the saints of Delhi),” Ferishta informs us.[456]

Not long after, the Sultan’s health showed signs of improvement, and the happy tidings didn’t fail to reach Khizr Khan in Amroha. “When he (Khizr Khan) heard a report of the Sultan’s recovery,” the author of the **Tabaqat-i Akbari** tells us, “before the command for his return could issue, he came on foot and bare-footed to Delhi on the [promised] pilgrimage.”[457]

The unsuspecting and guileless prince, after completing the ardous journey of travelling almost a hundred miles on naked feet, must have thought that his overjoyed father would embrace him in love and gratitude. But, nothing of that sort was destined to happen, because, “the traitor, Malik Kafoor, [had already] turned this act of filial piety entirely against Khizr Khan. He [had] insinuated that this behaviour, by such a sudden change, could be imputed to nothing but hypocrisy, and ascribed his disobedience of coming without his father’s leave, to an intention, on his

---

[456] Tarikh-i Ferishta. Translated by John Briggs. Page 380

[457] Tabaqat-i Akbari. By Khwaja NIzamuddin Ahmad. Translated by B. DE. Page 189

part, of intriguing with the nobles, in order to excite a revolution."[458]

The Sultan was now fully convinced that a sinister plot against his life was indeed underway. Quite predictably, Alauddin's ruthless spirit immediately sprung into action. An order was issued forthwith to arrest Khizr Khan, and then send him off with his wife, Dewal Devi, to the fortress-prison of Gwalior. His mother, the Malika-i Jahan, unfortunately fared no better. She was chained up, and then dumped in the fabled Red Palace of Balban which, at that point, served as a prison of sorts for high profile offenders.

But the worst fate was reserved for Alp Khan. His only crime was that he had spoken in favour of Khizr Khan. Malik Kafur, says Barani, because of the "deep animosity" that existed between him and Alp Khan, was quick to construe Alp Khan's support to the prince as an evidence of his involvement in the so-called conspiracy. Besides being his brother-in-law, Alp Khan had also been the Sultan's friend for more than two decades — and now that old friend was brought before the Sultan, and beheaded right under his nose.[459] "The house of Alauddin

---

[458] Tarikh-i Ferishta. Translated by John Briggs. Page 380

[459] Ibn Battuta offers a graphic description of the execution of Alp Khan. Alauddin, the Moroccan traveller says, had ordered his assassins: "*When Sanjar (Alp Khan's former name) comes before me I shall* give *him a robe, and when he puts it on seize him by the sleeves, pull him to the ground and cut his throat.*" The servants, the author continues, did exactly as they were told. (Source: The Rehla, translated by H.A.R. Gibb, Page 642)

was in fact ruined the day Alp Khan was killed," observes Barani, poignantly.[460]

But for all that he did at his beloved Malik Kafur's instigation, Alauddin's condition, however, only kept deteriorating from that point onwards: the Sultan's end, evidently, had drawn nigh. Day by day his oedema worsened, and even as he groaned and moaned in pain, a flurry of ominous news reached his ears which only made his condition even worse.

First, a rebellion broke out in Gujarat: Alp Khan's men there, unable to bear their master's unfair execution, took to arms against Delhi.[461] "To suppress this rebellion, Kamal Khan was sent thither, but the adherents of the late Alp Khan defeated him with great slaughter," informs Ferishta. "Kamal Khan was taken prisoner, and suffered a cruel death (at the hands of the rebels)."[462]

After Gujarat, came the turn of Chittor, 'that paradise of Hindus', by Amir Khusrau's own admission. The Rajputs of Mewar, we are told, launched a vigorous assault on the imperial contingent that was posted there. Slaying a number of Muslim officers, the Rajputs made Mewar independent of Delhi's control.

Down south, Harpal Deo, the son-in-law of the late Raja Ram Deo, "stirred up the Deccan to arms, and expelled a

---

460 Tarikh-i Firoz Shahi. By Ziauddin Barani. Translated by Ishtiyaq Ahmad Zili. Page 227

461 *Haider* and *Zirak*, we are told, were the two leaders of this formidable uprising.

462 Tarikh-i Ferishta. Translated by John Briggs. Page 381

number of the Mahomedan garrisons."[463] The entire empire was clearly aflame, and the gravity of the situation was not lost on the bedridden emperor either.

"On receiving these accounts, the King bit his own flesh with fury. His grief and rage only tended to increase his disorder, which seemed to resist the power of medicine," Ferishta informs us.[464] And in such a pitiful state, with no one in his family by his side, one day in the winter of 1316, Sultan Alauddin Khilji finally gave up the deposit of his life and returned his soul to its Creator. "Some say," Barani records, "that this eunuch (Malik Kafur) had in fact killed the Sultan in his extreme suffering."[465] Nizamuddin Ahmad Bakshi agrees with Barani — "some say Malik Naib poisoned him," he writes[466] — and after him, Ferishta also repeats the same story.

"Towards the later part of the night of six Shawwal (Januray 4, 1316)," informs Barani, "they brought the body of Sultan Alauddin from the Kauhsak-i Siri, and took it to his mausoleum situated in front of the Masjid-i Juma (Quwwatul Islam Mosque) and buried him there."[467]

Barani, as expected, sees an element of poetic justice in the conditions that Sultan Alauddin died under: because

---

[463] Tarikh-i Ferishta. Translated by John Briggs. Page 381

[464] ibid

[465] Tarikh-i Firoz Shahi. Translated by Ishtiyaq Ahmad Zilli. Page 228

[466] Tabaqat-i Akbari. By Khwaja NIzamuddin Ahmad. Translated by B. DE. Page 190

[467] Tarikh-i Firoz Shahi. Translated by Ishtiyaq Ahmad Zilli. Page 228

"Sultan Alauddin had killed his uncle, father-in-law, patron and benefactor and took over his kingdom," therefore, he was bound to perish in so unbecoming a manner.[468] Nizamuddin's remark, by contrast, is a succinct one: "It is said that no other Emperor of Hindustan gained so many victories as Sultan Alauddin," he says only so much.[469] Ferishta's obituary is by far the best: "His (Sultan Alauddin's) wealth and power were never equalled by any prince who sat before him on the throne of Hindustan, and they surpassed by far the riches accumulated in the ten campaigns of Mahmud Ghaznavi, all of which were left for others to enjoy."[470]

Be that as it may, it is now time for us to turn to the affairs of the capital immediately after the death of Sultan Alauddin. "On the second day after the death of Sultan Alauddin," Barani tells us, "Malik Naib summoned the maliks, amirs, dignitaries and eminent people in the palace and showed them the Ahdnama (undertaking) that Sultan Alauddin had got prepared for his younger son, Malik Shihabuddin, removing Khizr Khan from the position of heir apparent."[471] Even if the ahdnama was not forged, it is quite clear that it had been prepared under the influence of Malik Kafur, when Sultan Alauddin was on

---

468 Tarikh-i Firoz Shahi. Translated by Ishtiyaq Ahmad Zilli. Page 233.

469 Tabaqat-i Akbari. By Khwaja NIzamuddin Ahmad. Translated by B. DE. Page 185

470 Tarikh-i Ferishta. Translated by John Briggs. Page 382

471 Tarikh-i Firoz Shahi. Translated by Ishtiyaq Ahamd Zilli. Page 229

his death bed. In fact, Ferishta is unequivocal in dismissing the ahdnama as downright spurious.

"With the approval of the maliks and the amirs, he (Malik Kafur) [then] placed Malik Shihabuddin, who was almost six years old, on the throne."[472] It goes without saying that Malik Kafur was to act as the regent to this boy-sultan, and it was the regent who would henceforth exercise de-facto authority over the entire empire. "On the very day of his assumption of authority," Barani tells us, "he (Malik Kafur) sent the wretch Malik Sunbul to Gwalior to blind Khizr Khan." The regent also took steps to blind Shadi Khan, "who was the brother and companion of Khzir Khan." In the palace of Siri, Shadi Khan was blinded by the regent's henchman, who extricated "the eyeballs with the help of a razor from their sockets like the slice of a melon."[473]

Even as Malik Kafur continued his spree of destruction, he remained scrupulous in maintaining the facade of decorum. "Meanwhile, Malik Kafur, as a cloak to his design," writes Ferishta, "placed the young King every day upon the throne and ordered the nobles to pay their respects to him."[474]

Ferishta also makes another interesting claim: "However ridiculous it may appear," he says, "Malik Kafur, though an eunuch, married the mother of the Prince

[472] Tarikh-i Firoz Shahi. Translated by Ishtiyaq Ahamd Zilli. Page 229

[473] ibid. Page 230

[474] Tarikh-i Ferishta. Translated by John Briggs. Page 384

[Shihabuddin] Umar, the late Emperor's third wife (the daughter of Ram Deo)."[475] Even if this claim is true, we will never know with what motive did Malik Kafur marry Alauddin's widow: was it to strengthen his position at the court as the regent of the Sultanate, or was it the stirring of a sadistic impulse that spurred him to share the bed of his late master's wife even though he was impotent? We can only speculate.

Malik Kafur's supremacy however, says Barani, "did not have any base or foundation." And he further weakened his position by his acts of high-handedness: simply placing the boy-king on the throne daily, and getting everyone to pay their respects to him were not enough; people could still get wind of what he was up to. "In fact, time laughed on him and death sharpened its teeth for him. The wise men could visualise his head hanging from the head of a lance and his blood and the blood of his collaborators spilled on the ground."[476]

Khizr Khan and Shadi Khan had been blinded; the child Shihabuddin was Malik Kafur's puppet; but there still remained another son of Sultan Alauddin Khilji: not at large, but not blinded either. His name was Mubarak Khan, and he was about the same age as Khizr Khan.

It so happened that one night Malik Kafur, realising that to procastinate Mubarak Khan's blinding was tantamount to inviting trouble for himself, sent some of his men off to carry that act out. But when the assassins entered

---

[475] Tarikh-i Ferishta. Translated by John Briggs. Page 384

[476] Tarikh-i Firoz Shahi. Translated by Ishtiyaq Ahmad Zilli. Page 231

Mubarak Khan's apartment, the prince earnestly pleaded with them to remember his late father, whose servants they had once been. "He then untied a string of rich jewels from his neck, which probably had more influence than his entreaties, and gave it [to] them."[477]

Whatever might have been the reason, Mubarak Khan's appeal worked: Malik Kafur's men now turned on him.[478] "They accordingly entered his (Malik Kafur's) apartment a few hours after," Ferishta narrates in detail, "and assasinated him, with some of the principal eunuchs, who were attached to his interest. This event happened 35 days after Alauddin's death."[479]

Malik Kafur, finally, was over and done with: his "evil head" was severed from his impure body, says Barani. "When the night in which Malik Naib was killed passed and the morning dawned, and the maliks, amirs, dignitaries and holders of various offices arrived at the palace and found that ignoble wretch killed and thrown into dust, they offered thanksgiving to Almighty and congratulated each other."[480]

Next, Mubarak Khan was released from the prison, and installed, in Malik Kafur's stead, as the new regent of his half-brother, the boy-sultan Shihabuddin Umar. This new duty Mubarak executed for two months, "till he had

---

477 Tarikh-i Ferishta. Translated by John Briggs. Page 384

478 Malik Kafur's assasination, according to Abdul Malik Isami's *Futuh us Salatin*, was carried out by four men: *Mubshar*, *Bashir*, *Saleh* and *Munir*.

479 Tarikh-i Ferishta. Translated by John Briggs. Pages 384-385

480 Tarikh-i Firoz Shahi. Translated by Ishtiyaq Ahmad Zilli. Page 232

brought over the nobles to his interest. He then claimed his birthright, deposed his brother, and succeeded to the regal dignity. But, according to the barbarous custom and policy of those days, he deprived the Prince Umar Khan of his eyesight, and confined him for life in the fort of Gwalior."[481]

Delhi Sultanate now had a new sovereign, Sultan Qutbuddin Mubarak Shah, the third Sultan in less than as many months, an apt indication of the murky waters of imperial politics at that point.

One of the first acts of the new Sultan was to rid himself of those men who had made his accesssion to the throne possible. It was the payaks — who had done away with Malik Kafur, and freed Mubrak Khan from his fetters — who now topped the hitlist of the same Mubarak Khan, now styled as Qutbuddin Mubarak Shah. Barani offers some justification for this singularly ungrateful act. "The payaks who had killed Malik Naib," he says, "started behaving insolently. They openly said in the palace that it was they who had killed Malik Naib and put Sultan Qutbuddin on the throne. Out of their extreme insolence and baseness they desired to be at a position above the maliks and amirs, get robes before them and white waistbands (a mark of honour)." Not surprisingly therefore, the same author continues, "Sultan Qutbuddin was obliged to take action against them. He issued orders for these payaks to be seperated from each other. They were [then] taken to the towns around the capital and

[481] Tarikh-i Ferishta. Translated by John Briggs. Page 385

beheaded there. In this way their nuisance in the palace was brought to an end."[482]

After doing away with the payaks, the new Sultan then set about elevating his favorites to high positions. He rewarded one of his relatives with the exalted title of Sher Khan. Likewise, Maulana Ziauddin, who had once taught the Sultan calligraphy, was made the Sadr-i Jahan of the empire and invested with the title of Qazi Khan. A lance made of pure gold was also handed over to him as a part of his paraphernalia.

But none gained so much as a young man named Hasan did. Hasan was a Hindu convert to Islam and had been in the retinue of Malik Shadi, an important officer of Sultan Alauddin Khilji. Of Hasan's background, we are told that he hailed from Gujarat, and that he originally belonged to a caste called Parwari: "Parwari is the name of a caste of the menial class, who are found in large numbers in Gujarat," notes Nizamuddin Ahmad Bakshi.[483]

It is clear that Sultan Qutbudddin, right from his early days, had set his sights on Hasan, because "in the very first year of his accession, he took him (Hasan) out [of Malik Shadi's service] and bestowed great distinctions upon him and gave him the title of Khusrau Khan."[484] Also was made over to Hasan, now titled Khusrau Khan, all the troops and estates that had once belonged to Malik Kafur.

[482] Tarikh-i Firoz Shahi. Translated by Ishtiyaq Ahmad Zilli. Page 232

[483] Tabaqat-i Akbari. Translated by B. DE. Page 192

[484] Tarikh-i Firoz Shahi. Translated by Ishtiyaq Ahmad Zilli.. Page 234

While Sultan Qutbuddin took Sultan Alauddin's position, Khusrau Khan took Malik Naib's: history was taking an uneasy turn! It didn't take much time, says Ferishta, to become clear to one and all that Khusrau Khan was now the "greatest man in the realm", courtesy his sovereign's extraordinary attachment towards him.[485] So infatuated was the Sultan with Khusrau Khan, Barani tells us, that he couldn't brook even a moment of separation from him.

Qutbuddin Mubarak Shah might not have inherited his father's aptitude for statecraft and flare for warfare, but two qualities he did inherit to the full: one was the sanguinary nature, and the second was the bisexual habits, which the son took to a far greater extent than the father had ever done. But, more about that later on.

On the flip side, Sultan Qutbuddin Mubarak Shah, early in his reign, undertook some populist measures. On the very first day of his accession, we are told, he ordered all the prisoners — who numbered no less than 17,000, as per Ferishta — to be set free at once. Likewise, all those who had been exiled by his father were permitted by him to return to the capital city. Barani attributes these acts to Qutbuddin's good character. Ferishta, however, is a lot more sceptical: he thinks that the main reason behind such show of benevolence was "to affect popularity."[486]

At any rate, more popularity was on its way to the Sultan, for "he then commanded a present of six months' pay to be made to the whole of the trrops, and conferred upon

---

[485] Tarikh-i Ferishta. By Muhammad Qasim Ferishta. Translated by John Briggs. Page 387

[486]ibid

them many other advantages. He at the same time issued orders to give free access to all petitioners. He restored the lands and villages to those persons from whom they had been forcibly wrested in the late reign (that is, in Alauddin's reign); and by degrees removed all the obnoxiois restrictions on commerce, and the heavy tributes and taxes which had been exacted by his father."[487]

Not surprisingly therefore, as Barani would have us believe, the 'bazaar people' invoked blessings for Sultan Qutbuddin, and cursed Sultan Alauddin to their heart's content.[488]

After settling the affairs at the centre to the best of his abilities, the Sultan turned towards the provinces: the rich province of Gujarat had been lost to the Sultanate, and it was now time to recover it. Mailk Ain ul Mulk Multani, a veteran of Alauddin's reign, was despatched with a strong army to Gujarat. The rebels were soon overpowered, and Gujarat brought afresh under the control of Delhi.

In spite of his military success, Ain ul Mulk Multani wasn't appointed as the new governor of Gujarat: that distinction went to Zafar Khan, whose daughter the Sultan had lately married. That, at any rate, wasn't a bad decision, because Zafar Khan, according to Barani, "was very wise and experienced ... and within a period of about

---

[487]Tarikh-i Ferishta. Translated by John Briggs. Pages 387-388.

[488] Tarikh-i Firoz Shahi. Translated by Ishtiyaq Ahmad Zilli. Page 236

four months brought Gujarat under better control than [even] Alp Khan."[489]

After Gujarat, came the turn of Deogir: the reconquest of Mewar evidently had been struck off the list of priorities by the new Sultan for some reason or the other. And to Deogir, the Sultan himself decided to march in person "to chastise Harpal Deo, the son-in-law of Ram Deo, who, by the assistance of the other princes of the Deccan, had recovered the country of the Marathas."[490] Delhi was left in charge of a certain Shahin, whom Barani calls a 'slave lad', and before departing the Sultan gave Shahin the new title of Wafa Malik.[491]

Down south, the affairs didn't turn out to be challenging: the army hastily assembled by Harpal Deo proved no match to the Sultanate army, and was routed in the very first encounter. Harpal himself was soon captured and then brought before the Sultan, whose sanguinary nature then manifested itself in its full fury. Sultan Qutbuddin ordered Harpal to be flayed alive, then beheaded, and finally his severed head to be fixed above the gate of his own capital, Deogir.

The insurrection in Deogir being snuffed out, Sultan Qutbuddin Mubarak Shah, "in imitation of Alauddin, gave to his favorite, Malik Khusrau, the ensigns of

---

[489] Tarikh-i Firoz Shahi. Translated by Ishtiyaq Ahmad Zilli. Pages 238-239

[490] Tarikh-i Ferishta. Translated by John Briggs. Pages 388-389

[491] Tarikh-i Firoz Shahi. Translated by Ishtiyaq Ahmad Zilli. Page 239

royalty. He [then] sent the latter towards Ma'bar, with part of his army, and returned to Delhi."[492]

Qutbuddin was thus consciously emulating his father's example. "It did not occur to him," writes Barani, "as to what good it did in the end and what that infamous one brought upon the household and sons of Alauddin when Sultan Alauddin got infatuated with him (Malik Kafur) and openly did with Malik Naib that evil deed."[493]

On the flip side, immediately after leaving Deogir, Khusrau Khan, now invested with the paraphernalia of royalty, started hatching plans to do away with his master, the Sultan. Why was it so? Was it only because of political ambitions on Khusrau's part? Perhaps, no. Khusrau Khan, for all the royal favours bestowed upon him, still had very legitimate reasons to hate his Sultan. And besides being legitimate, those reasons were also very personal.[494]

Sultan Qutbuddin Mubarak Shah, as we would see more of it later, was a monster in the shape of a man: a horrific combination of wild debauchery and bestial violence. And the monster in him, more often than not, came to the

---

[492] Tarikh-i Ferishta. Translated by John Briggs. Page 389

[493] Tarikh-i Firoz Shahi. Translated by Ishtiyaq Ahmad Zilli. Page 240

[494] In this connection, the confession of Khusrau Khan before Ghiyasuddin Tughluq at the fag end of the former's life provides for a most instructive reading: "*The facts are known to everyone. If that which should not be done, had not been done to me, then I too would not have done what I ought not to have done*." (Source: The Tughluq Nama, by Amir Khusrau; Reference: A Comprehensive History of India, Volume V. People's Publishing House, 1970. Page 459

forefront when he was in his bed, which Khusrau Khan was forced to share, night after night. Indeed, Khusrau had "often wanted to strike the Sultan with a hatchet and kill him while he was in that particular act with him or kissed him in the open ... and though apparently he gave up his body to him like shameless whores yet in his inner life he was extremely resentful of the Sultan's ravages with his person and choked with suppressed anger."[495]

Be that as it may, after despatching Khusrau to Ma'bar, the Sultan himself started for Delhi. On the way, however, an attempt was made on his life.

There was a cousin of Sultan Alauddin, Malik Asaduddin by name who, Barani tells us, "was a young man of much cunning, intrepid and very renowned."[496] He had evidently come with the Sultan to Deogir, and now on the return journey he observed that the Sultan was most of the time engaged either in drinking or in debauchery. Indeed, even on the move, the Sultan used to be invariably surrounded by his ladies, whom he would fondle, caress, crack jokes and laugh with. "They had often observed," Barani writes, "that Sultan Qutbuddin used to march with his harem, drinking and making merry, fondling the women and taking part in amorous activities with them."[497]

---

[495] Tarikh-i Firoz Shahi. Translated by Ishtiyaq Ahmad Zilli. Page 240

[496] Ibid

[497] Tarikh-i Firoz Shahi. Translated by Ishtiyaq Ahmad Zilli. Page 241

Observing such a state of affairs, Malik Asaduddin thought that it wouldn't be too difficult to do away with the Sultan under the cover of night, and then claim the throne for himself. But at the last moment one of his accomplices chickened out, and divulged the whole plot to the Sultan.[498]

The beast in Sultan Qutbuddin was aroused. Malik Asaduddin and those of his brothers who were with him were beheaded on the spot.[499] A farman was then forwarded post-haste to Delhi, in pursuance of which as many as 29 relatives of Malik Asaduddin were executed. According to Barani, "they did not have any inkling about the rebellion, but were still massacred like goats and sheep."[500] Next, Asaduddin's ancestral property was confiscated; his women and daughters were turned out of their house, publicly violated, and then made common strumpets of.

But for all that bloodbath, the Sultan's murderous rage still showed no sign of abating. Thus, when the Sultan reached Jhain, though none of his brothers had absolutely

---

498 The turncoat's name was Aram Shah, and his act vindicated his moniker.

499 The *Tarikh-i Mubarak Shahi* tells that along with Malik Asaduddin, Malik Kahjuri and Malik Masri were also beheaded. The last two appears to have been Asaduddin's brothers

500 Tarikh-i Firoz Shahi. Translated by Ishtiyaq Ahmad Zilli. Page 241

anything to do with the late conspiracy, "he sent Shadi Kita ... to Gwalior and commanded him to kill Khizr Khan, Shadi Khan and Malik Shihabuddin, sons of Sultan Alauddin, who were earlier blinded and were [thereafter only] provided with bread and cloth. Their mothers and wives were to be brought to Delhi. This Shadi Kita went to Gwalior, killed those hapless blind men and brought their mothers and wives to Delhi."[501]

The purpose behind bringing the ladies to Delhi wasn't, of course, benevolent. Thus, according to Ferishta, the beautiful Dewal Devi (the widow of Khizr Khan) was forcibly taken into the royal harem, and then dragged to the Sultan's bed.

There is every possibility that at this point Sultan Qutbuddin Mubarak Shah actually became insane. He started to see a traitor in every man, and a conspiracy in every corner. "He grew more perverse, proud, vindictive and tyrannical than ever," writes Ferishta.[502] And among the first victims of the Sultan's uncontrolled wrath was his own father-in-law, the governor of Gujarat Zafar Khan. He was killed on the Sultan's orders, in spite of "no crime

---

[501]Tarikh-i Firoz Shahi. Translated by Ishtiyaq Ahmad Zilli. Page 241. Ten assassins, we are told, were sent to do a short work of those hapless royals. Nine out of the ten found their hands trembling and their resolve faltering when the time to carry out the horrendous act actually arrived. Finally, the one executioner. who was made of a tougher stuff than his comrades, mustered all the savagery that he had, and then beheaded Khizr Khan with one slah of his sharp sword."

[502] Tarikh-i Ferishta. Translated by John Briggs. Page 390

or dishonesty on his part", and perhaps without even an accusation against him.[503]

History was now coming to a full circle — Alauddin had his governor of Gujarat, Alp Khan, unjustly killed when his own end had drawn near, and now his son Qutbuddin had his governor of Gujarat, Zafar Khan, killed without any reason whatsoever.

Next came the turn of Wafa Malik, whom the Sultan himself had only recently entrusted with the all-important task of looking after the capital, Delhi, in his absence. He too was executed for reasons that were obscure to say the least.

The height, however, was reached when the Sultan himself assumed the Caliphal title, and then turned against the most venerable Muslim divine of the day, Sheikh Nizamuddin Auliya.[504] The two — the Sultan and the Sheikh — came across each other on the **siyyum** (the ceremony of reading the Quran on the third day after the burial) of Ziauddin Rumi, a saint of the Suhrawardi order. While the Sheikh was quick to offer his greetings to the

[503] Tarikh-i Firoz Shahi. Translated by Ishtiyaq Ahmad Zilli. Page 242

[504] While the Four Pious Caliphs of Islam had only called themselves Khalifas (representatives) of the Prophet, Sultan Qutbuddin Mubarak Shah went on to claim for himself the title of Khalifatullah (representative of God Himself). Only if self-delusion came with a limit!

Sultan, the latter was too proud to even acknowledge it, let alone reciprocate it.[505]

Barani says that thereon Qutbuddin Mubarak Shah "began to openly abuse him (Sheikh Nizamuddin Auliya) and tried to do harm to him simply because he thought that Khizr Khan was his disciple."[506] In his cups, the Sultan even went to the extent of promising handsome monetary rewards to anyone who could bring to him the severed head of the Auliya.

To undermine Nizamuddin Auliya's position, the Sultan tried to use Sheikh Ruknuddin's influence, but that Suhrawardy saint of Multan straightaway rejected this unholy offer.[507] Then, the Sultan tried to set up one Sheikhzada Shihabuddin Jami as the new spiritual head of Delhi's Muslim community. To that end, even a new khanqah was set up at royal expense. But, even that move failed to cut any ice with the people.

---

[505] This, incidentally, was the first of the two times that the Sheikh had to come face to face with a sovereign. The second occasion came several years later, when Ghiyasuddin Tughluq was the Sultan of Delhi, and a bunch of covetous clerics coaxed that Sultan to ask Nizamuddin Auliya to turn up at the royal court for a public trial — the Sheikh did as he was asked, and ultimately the trial turned out in his favour.

[506] Tarikh-i Firoz Shahi. Translated by Ishtiyaq Ahmad Zilli. Page 241

[507] On Qutbuddin Mubarak Shah's invitation, Sheikh Ruknuddin did come to Delhi, but much to the Sultan's chagrin, the Suhrawardi saint behaved with the Chishti master in a most respectful manner. In fact, the relations between the two Sufis remained so cordial throughout that when Sheikh Nizamuddin Auliya passed away, it was Sheikh Ruknuddin who himself led the funeral prayers.

Finally, the Sultan ordered the Auliya to come to his court and render him his personal homage.[508] He would wait for only a month, the Sultan gave out, and if by that time Nizamuddin didn't comply with the royal order, then the saint would find himself in all sorts of troubles. But destiny — or Almighty — had decreed differently!

The die had been cast: a downward spiral had set in, and there was now no going back.

"He (the Sultan) lost all sense of modesty," narrates Barani, "and came out in gatherings in women's clothes ... He gave up prayers and openly broke fasting during the month of Ramzan."[509] It was utter obscenity that now ran riot in the capital. The Sultan, tells Ferishta, "would lead a gang of abominable prostitutes, half naked, along the terraces of the royal palaces, and oblige them to exhibit themselves before the nobles as they entered the court."[510]

Then there was that buffon from Gujarat, a short-heighted man named Buta. "This base buffon **(bhand)**," writes Barani, "would abuse the **maliks**. He used to come in the

---

[508] In those days, a custom was in vogue in Delhi, according to which all the notables of the city, whether in government service or not, had to visit the Sultan and pay him their homage on the beginning of every new lunar month. Sheikh Nizamuddin Auliya had never abided by this norm. Instead of personally attending the imperial court, the Sheikh would send on his behalf one of his disciples, Iqbal, to do the needful. But such was the reverence that Hazrat Nizamuddin commanded that prior to Qutbuddin Mubarak Shah Khilji, no other Sultan of Delhi took offense at this purported slight to royal dignity.

[509] Tarikh-i Firoz Shahi. Translated by Ishtiyaq Ahmad Zilli. Page 242

[510] Tarikh-i Ferishta. Translated by John Briggs. Page 390

assembly touting his man's organ, urinated in the clothes of the maliks, and used to release wind. Sometimes he even came among the poeple totally naked, and uttered obscenity."[511]

Even as the Sultan was busy degrading his and his throne's stature in the capital, his beloved Khusrau Khan was assiduously hatching murderous schemes against him in Ma'bar. After faring fairly well in the military expedition that he was assigned with — he had managed to capture 120 elephants besides sizeable amounts of jewels, Ferishta tells us — Khusrau stayed back in the south where, according to Barani, he did nothing save holding consultations with his confidants as to how to do away with his master, the Sultan.

It so happened that some of the veteran nobles who had accompanied him to Ma'bar got wind of his rebellious designs. They at once sent a remonstrance to the court, and also warned Khusrau of the dire punishment that was in store for him.

But, irony of ironies, the Sultan dismissed all the reports — he instead got worried if any harm should come to Khusrau from those nobles who had complained against him. In fact, so blinded was the Sultan with lust for the "delicately built body" of Khusrau Khan that, Barani tells us, "he ordered him to be put in a palanquin **(palki)** and brought to Delhi in a week. In fact at every stage a number

---

[511] Tarikh-i Firoz Shahi. Translated by Ishtiyaq Ahmad Zilli. Page 243

of palanquin carriers **(kahars)** were kept ready so that there would be no delay in the way."[512]

Khurau Khan was now unassailable. Absolutely unassailable.

"When Khusrau came before the King," reports Ferishta, "he pleaded his own cause so successfully, and retorted on his own accusers with such plausibility, that the King believed the whole accusation originated in envy."[513] Barani continues the narrative: "The Sultan had become so enamoured and infatuated with him that he believed the lies and calumnies of that ingrate about these loyal people and got incensed with them even before those loyal officers could reach the capital with their armies."[514]

And when they did arrive — Malik Tamar and Malik Telegha, two premier nobles who had been in service since Alauddin's time — Sultan Qutbuddin at once proceeded to inflict punishments on them. The Sultan, Barani says, "demoted Malik Tamar from his position and ordered that he should not be allowed to come to the court." His fief was also confiscated, and to add insult to injury, the estates were then made over to Khusrau Khan. As to Malik Telegha, "who had been more openly critical of the machinations of Khusrau Khan", he was slapped by the Sultan right across his face, chained up, and then thrown into the dungeons. "Now all the attendants of the court ... came to know for sure that anybody who would

---

[512] Tarikh-i Firozshahi. Translated by Ishtiyaq Ahmad Zilli. Page 245

[513] Tarikh-i Ferishta. Translated by John Briggs. Page 392

[514] Tarikh-i Firoz Shahi. Translated by Ishtiyaq Ahmad Zilli. Page 245

say anything [against Khusrau Khan] before Sultan Qutbuddin out of the sense of loyalty, would be punished in the same way as Malik Telegha, Malik Tamar and others who have been punished. The wise men ... felt that the time of death of Sultan Qutbuddin had drawn very near."[515]

Khusrau Khan, unlike Malik Kafur, seems to have had a strong clique in the capital. He had his relatives around, and his connection to his place of origin was strong. Thus, we find in the chronicles the account of Husamuddin, the brother of Khusrau Khan who, after the unfair execution of Zafar Khan, was made the governor of Gujarat. In Gujarat, we are told by Barani, "he turned apostate (that is, he renounced his Islamic faith), collected all his relatives there and rallied renowned Parwars around him and revolted and instigated a big sedition. [But] The nobles posted in Gujarat were quite powerful and had enough troops and retainers with them. They caught him, imprisoned him and sent him to the Sultan."[516]

But to little avail! Because, this man Husamuddin was also another homosexual partner of the Sultan: "Occasionally Sultan Qutbuddin also used him for that particular purpose as well," Barani leaves virtually nothing to imagination.[517] Therefore, for all his seditious activities, what Husamuddin ultimately received from the

---

[515]Tarikh-i Firozshahi. Translated by Ishtiyaq Ahmad Zilli. Pages 245-246

[516] ibid. Page 243

[517] ibid

Sultan was only a slap: it must have been a coquettish one, no doubt.

It now became as clear as daylight to everybody, except the man himself, that Sultan Qutbuddin Mubarak Shah's end was at hand.

Khusrau Khan too thought that the time was ripe to bring his heart's desire to culmination. "To accomplish this purpose," Ferishta tells us, "he (Khusrau Khan) told the King, that as his fidelity had been so generously rewarded, and as the King might still have occasion for his services in the conduct of military affairs, he begged that he might be permitted to send for some of his relatives from Gujarat, on whom he could more certainly depend than officers now in the King's service, who were jealous of his elevation. The King acceded to his request; and Malik Khusrau remitted a large sum of money, by some of his agents, to Gujarat, who collected about 20,000 [men] of his own caste ... and brought them to Delhi."[518]

Emboldened by the presence of so many men around who were totally dependent on him, Khusrau Khan then proceeded to take the next step towards his goal. And the final scenes of this unfolding drama are described in absorbing detail by Barani.

"Khusrau Khan," records Barani, "during the times in the night with the Sultan, made the submission that: 'Every night it is not before morning that I return from the Sultan's presence ... [Therefore] Relatives who have left their hearts and home and have come over for the sake of

518 Tarikh-i Ferishta. Translated by John Briggs. Pages 392-393

my service can not meet me ... if the keys of the gate (of the palace) were given to my men, it would be possible for me to summon them every night in the residence and see them and meet them.'"[519]

The Sultan, predictably, at once consented: his wits, at any rate, had deserted him long back. Thereafter, every night, as many as four hundred Gujaratis would come inside the royal residence with long swords in their hands, ostensibly to pay a visit to Khusrau Khan.

"The plot for the King's assassination was not even kept secret," writes Ferishta, "many people in the city heard of it from the incautious and profligate band employed by Malik Khusrau; but such was his influence over the King's mind, that none dared to mention it."[520] The whole affair was now obvious to everybody. That the Sultan would be murdered soon was known to all, save the Sultan, who remained blissfully unaware of all that was brewing around him.

At length, it was Qazi Khan, the Sultan's childhood tutor, who mustered his courage and told the Sultan how exactly things stood. The words, however, fell on deaf ears: "the Sultan," according to Barani, "was incensed at Qazi Ziauddin (Qazi Khan) and said very harsh words to him.'[521] Soon, Khusrau Khan himself entered the scene, and the Sultan at once told him all that the Qazi had been alleging against him.

---

[519] Tarikh-i Firoz Shahi. Translated by Ishtiyaq Ahmad Zilli. Page 247

[520] Tarikh-i Ferishta. Translated by John Briggs. Page 393

[521] Tarikh-i Firoz Shahi. Translated by Ishtiyaq Ahmad Zilli. Page 248

"On hearing this," continues Barani, "he (Khusrau Khan) began to cry and feigned to weep ... The amorous weeping and the sobbing mixed with blandishment of that one of delicate cheeks, stirred fresh lust in him. He (the Sultan) took him in his embrace, [and] kissed his lips several times."[522] All these happened while the old Qazi was still standing!

The Qazi however, in spite of the vile abuses he had received from his protege, couldn't forsake his sense of duty. He remained alert; he had a foreboding that something sinister would take place that very night. He therefore didn't retire to his home: instead, he took his seat in the ground floor of the royal palace and, as Barani tells us, "busied himself making enquiries about doors, night watchmen and officers of the different watches."[523]

As the night progressed, a band of armed men entered the **Hazar Sutun** (thousand-pillared palace). Randhol, the Hindu uncle of Khsurau Khan, went up to Qazi Khan and offered him a **paan**. From behind, Jaharia, another of Khsurau's men, "came close to Qazi Ziauddin (Qazi Khan) and took out the sword from beneath the clothes and struck him."[524] The loyal teacher was thus taken down, and before he passed away, he cried out for one last

[522] Tarikh-i Firozshahi. Translated by Ishtiyaq Ahmad Zilli. Page 248

[523] ibid. Page 249

[524] ibid

time: “Treason! treason! Murder and treason are on foot.”[525]

The royal palace was now full of Parwars, and there was a terrible tumult all round.

The uproar roused the Sultan from his slumber and he asked Khusrau, who was sharing the same bed with him, to go and find out what had happened. “The villain arose as if to enquire,” we are told, “and going out on the terrace, stood for some time, and returning, told the King, that some of the horses belonging to the guards had broken loose and were fighting, while the people were endeavouring to secure them.”[526]

“While the Sultan and Khusrau Khan were still talking among themselves about the matter,” tells Barani, “Jaharia had already reached the upper part of the **Hazar Sutun** with some other Parwars.”[527] Ibrahim and Ishaq, who were guarding the Sultan’s bed-chamber, were killed on the spot by Jaharia.

“The Sultan became cognisant of the state of things at last,” writes Nizamuddin Ahamd Bakshi, “[and he] jumped up and ran towards the harem. Khusrau Khan ran after him and caught him by the hair, and the two

[525] Tarikh-i Ferishta. Translated by John Briggs. Page 394

[526] ibid

[527] Tarikh-i Firoz Shahi. Translated by Ishtiyaq Ahmad Zilli. Page 249

struggled with each other, and the Sultan threw him down, and sat on his chest."[528]

Right at that very moment, Jaharia reached there. "Khusrau Khan shouted from below the Sultan," tells Barani, "and asked Jaharia to help. Jaharia struck the Sultan with the sword on the chest, got hold of his locks and took him off the chest of Khusrau Khan, and threw him on the ground. He [then] severed the head of Sultan Qutbuddin."[529]

Next, the headless trunk of Sultan Qutbuddin Mubarak Shah was flung down into the courtyard of the **Hazar Sutun** palace.

After the Khilji Sultan had been done away with, came the turn of the female inmates of the harem. One widow of Sultan Alauddin they killed, along with at least five young children of that Sultan: Farid Khan, Abu Bakr Khan, Bahauddin Khan, Ali Khan and Usman Khan. None of them was greater than fifteen years in age, while the youngest one among them was only five-years-old. Thereafter, the Parwars, in the words of Barani, "perpetrated such atrocities which had never been committed [even] by heretics and pagans in their own lands."[530] An orgy of rape is what he means, in which hardly any lady of the Khilji regime could save herself.

---

[528] Tabaqat-i Akbari. By Khwaja NIzamuddin Ahmad. Translated by B. DE. Page 203

[529] Tarikh-i Firoz Shahi. Translated by Ishtiyaq Ahmad Zilli. Page 250

[530] ibid

Khusrau Khan, however, had chosen his pick right from the outset: he would have for himself Dewal Rani, that unfortunate princess whose beauty was her bane. This was the second time that this lady was being dragged to someone's bed: first it had been Sultan Qutbuddin's, and now it was his slave Khusrau's.

"Thus," Ferishta wraps up, "the venegeance of God overtook Alauddin for his ingratitude to his uncle Firoz (Sultan Jalaluddin Khilji), and for the streams of innocent blood that flowed from his hand. Heaven also punished Mubarak (Sultan Qutbuddin Mubarak Shah), whose name and reign would be too infamous to have a place in the records of literature, did not our duty, as a historian, oblige us to this disagreeable task. Notwithstanding which, we have in some places been obliged to draw a veil over circumstances too horrid and indecent to relate."[531]

The Khilji dynasty was thus done and over with. Not at the hands of a rival Turkish or Afghan warlord, but at the hands of a band of Hindus and Hindu converts to Islam from Gujarat. The Khilji dynasty had ruled the Delhi Sultanate for 30 years: there were four kings, and out of them, it was due to the exploits of the second one, Sultan Alauddin Khilji, that the legacy of this lineage survived in the annals of history.

Be that as it may, after ousting the Khiljis, it was the turn of Khusrau Khan to rule, who ascended the throne of Delhi Sultanate as Sultan Nasiruddin. The medieval

---

[531] Tarikh-i Ferishta. Translated by John Briggs. Pages 395-396

chroniclers were quick to dub his rise to power as a sort of 'Hindu interregnum'. Barani, the foremost of them all, is also the most detailed in description: "Five-six days after the accession of that base and mean fellow (Khusrau Khan), idol worship began in the palace. The Parwars whose mouths and armpits emitted an offensive stink ran riot in the harem of Sultan Qutbuddin. Khusrau Khan took the wife of Sultan Qutbuddin (Dewal Rani) for himself. The Parwars achieved ascendency and having got control of the well-established households of the main Qutbi and Alai amirs violated Muslim women and maids and the flames of tyranny and oppression burnt high.

"Having achieved supremacy, the Parwars and Hindus used the copies of the Holy Quran as chairs and placed idols in the mihrabs (of the mosques) and worshipped them. Since the accession of that wicked person ..., the practises and customs of infidelity and infidels increased everyday ... During those days of misfortune and disaster when due to the dominance of the Hindus, customs of infidelity were gaining new heights and power and the authority of the Parwars was increasing, Hindus living in the dominions of Islam rejoiced and began to nurse the hope that Delhi would once again revert to its old Hindu past, the Muslims would be repulsed, and Islam would wither away."[532]

Barani exaggerates, no doubt. Khusrau Khan — or Sultan Nasiruddin — ruled the Delhi Sultanate not as a Hindu

---

[532] Tarikh-i Firoz Shahi. Translated by Ishtiyaq Ahmad Zilli. Pages 251-253

king, but as a Muslim sovereign.[533] Thus he had the khutba pronounced in his name from the pulpits of the mosques, besides taking care of various other requirements of Islamic kingship. In any case, dynastic toppling and palace revolutions were hardly out of the ordinary in the Delhi Sultanate. Why, the Khiljis themselves had come to power by such means. Amir Khusrau's comments, at any rate, make the non-communal nature of this upheaval absolutely clear. "All the military commanders in the east and the west (of the empire) decided to obey instead of fighting," says Khusrau. "The Turks did not raise their Turkish spears; the Hindu officers did not attack the Hindus."[534]

Be that as it may, the new Sultan wasn't destined to rule long. Because, a certain warden of the marches couldn't put up with the misfortunes that befell the dynasty of his Khilji masters, and in rage he "writhed within himself like a serpent."[535] And in less than two months, his serpentine rage would explode in the battlefield of Lahrawat: Khusrau Khan would be defeated and killed, and the

---

[533] *"Barani is conceivably right when he alleges that idolatry was practised within the royal palace, presumably by those of Khusrau Shah's adherents who were not converts. But his story, on the other hand, that Khusrau Shah and his lieutenants treated Qurans with blatant disrespect and set up idols in mosques is hardly worthy of credence; it is noteworthy that the Tughluq-Nama talks of idolatry in less specific terms and that the version of events heard by Ibn Battuta, who singles out for mention only a prohibition on slaughtering cows, is rather less extreme."* — Peter Jackson, The Delhi Sultanate. Page 158

[534] Source: The Tughluq Nama. Quoted in The Comprehensive History of India, Volume 5. Page 450

[535] Tarikh-i Firoz Shahi. Translated by Ishtiyaq Ahmad Zilli. Page 252

victor would go on to claim the throne of Delhi for himself. He would also assume the pompous title of the 'Defender of the Faith', although the force that he headed had more Hindus than Muslims in its ranks. Interesting, no doubt, but that's another story for another day.

CPSIA information can be obtained
at www.ICGtesting.com
Printed in the USA
LVHW012118280522
719996LV00005B/145

9 789392 878725